Routledge Revivals

The Passive

First published in 1984, *The Passive* surveys a wide range of different constructions, which have all been termed 'passives' by linguists, using data from a large number of genetically and typologically diverse languages. Chapter 1 raises questions about the nature of passives and exposes some of the difficulties inherent in the traditional assumptions. Chapter 2 examines the 'personal passive' and includes a discussion on the relationship between the passive and transitivity. Chapter 3 to 5 deal with impersonal, periphrastic and reflexive passives, exploring the varied problems raised by each construction and focusing particularly on English and Southeast Asian languages. The two final chapters look at various attempts to explain exceptions to the passive in both semantic and syntactic terms, with an additional section on pragmatics. This book will appeal to all of those involved in the field of comparative linguistics.

The Passive
A Comparative Linguistic Analysis

Anna Siewierska

First published in 1984
By Croom Helm Ltd

This edition first published in 2024 by Routledge
4 Park Square, Milton Park, Abingdon, Oxon, OX14 4RN
and by Routledge
605 Third Avenue, New York, NY 10017

Routledge is an imprint of the Taylor & Francis Group, an informa business

© 1984 Anna Siewierska

All rights reserved. No part of this book may be reprinted or reproduced or utilised in any form or by any electronic, mechanical, or other means, now known or hereafter invented, including photocopying and recording, or in any information storage or retrieval system, without permission in writing from the publishers.

Publisher's Note
The publisher has gone to great lengths to ensure the quality of this reprint but points out that some imperfections in the original copies may be apparent.

Disclaimer
The publisher has made every effort to trace copyright holders and welcomes correspondence from those they have been unable to contact.

A Library of Congress record exists under ISBN: 0709933185

ISBN: 978-1-032-76786-4 (hbk)
ISBN: 978-1-003-48010-5 (ebk)
ISBN: 978-1-032-76793-2 (pbk)

Book DOI 10.4324/9781003480105

The Passive
A Comparative Linguistic Analysis
Anna Siewierska

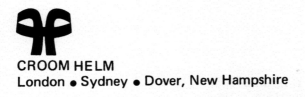

CROOM HELM
London • Sydney • Dover, New Hampshire

©1984 Anna Siewierska
Croom Helm Ltd, Provident House, Burrell Row,
Beckenham, Kent BR3 1AT
Croom Helm Australia Pty Ltd, First Floor, 139 King Street,
Sydney, NSW 2001, Australia

British Library Cataloguing in Publication Data

Siewierska, Anna
    The passive.
    1. Grammar, Comparative and general—Voice
    I. Title
    415   P281
      ISBN 0-7099-3318-5

Croom Helm, 51 Washington Street, Dover,
New Hampshire 03820, USA

Library of Congress Cataloging in Publication Data

Siewierska, Anna.
    The passive.
    Revision of the author's thesis (M.A.)—Monash
University, 1979.
    Bibliography: p.
    Includes indexes.
    1. Grammar, Comparative and general—Passive voice.
I. Title.
P281.S5 1984   415   84-15606
ISBN 0-7099-3318-5

Printed and bound in Great Britain by
Biddles Ltd, Guildford and King's Lynn

CONTENTS

Editorial Statement
Preface
List of Abbreviations and Symbols

1.	**INTRODUCTION**		**1**
	1.0	General Aims	1
	1.1	The Passive	2
		1.1.1 Different Types of Passive Constructions	2
		1.1.2 The Passive and Models of Grammar	4
	1.2	Transitivity and the Passive	8
		1.2.1 Transitivity and Morpho-syntax	9
		1.2.2 Transitivity and Discourse	15
	1.3	Language Universals	19
		1.3.1 Subject/Object vs S,A,P	19
		1.3.2 Transitivity and Ergativity	20
		1.3.3 The Passive	23
	Footnotes		23
2.	**THE PERSONAL PASSIVE**		**28**
	2.0	Introduction	28
	2.1	Properties of the Personal Passive	28
		2.1.1 The Active Counterpart	30
		2.1.2 The Passive as an Agentless Construction	35
		2.1.3 Word Order and Morphological Marking	39
	2.2	Transitivity and the Personal Passive	44
		2.2.1 Transitive or Intransitive	47
		2.2.2 The Personal Passive and Intransitive Clauses	64
	2.3	Some Tentative Conclusions	75
	2.4	The Passive in Philippine Languages	79

CONTENTS

2.4.1	The Structure of the Philippine Clause	79
2.4.2	Passive or Active	82
Footnotes		86

3. IMPERSONAL PASSIVES — 93

3.0	General Remarks	93
3.1	Characteristics of Impersonal Passives	96
3.1.1	Impersonal Passives and Transitivity	96
3.1.2	The Agent of Impersonal Passives	100
3.2	The Subject of Impersonal Passives	101
3.2.1	The Subjectless Analysis	102
3.2.2	Dummy Subjects	108
3.2.3	Indefinite Active Subjects	112
3.3	The Impersonal Passive: Promotion vs Demotion	117
Footnotes		124

4. THE PERIPHRASTIC PASSIVE — 126

4.0	Introduction	126
4.1	The Passive Auxiliary	128
4.1.1	Different Auxiliary Verbs	129
4.2	The Be-Passive as a Stative Construction	139
4.2.1	The Complex Sentence Analysis	140
4.2.2	The Adjectival Analysis	145
4.3	The Passive in South-East Asian Languages	149
4.3.1	The Direct Passive	149
4.3.2	The Indirect Passive	154
Footnotes		159

5. THE REFLEXIVE PASSIVE — 162

5.0	General Comments	162
5.1	Reflexive Passives and Other Constructions	164
5.1.1	Personal Reflexive Passives	165
5.1.2	Impersonal Reflexive Passives	173
5.2	Reflexive vs Plain Passives	180
Footnotes		184

6. EXCEPTIONS TO THE PASSIVE — 186

6.0	Introduction	186
6.1	Exceptions to the Passive and Pragmatics	187

CONTENTS

	6.1.1 The Personal Passive	188
	6.1.2 The Impersonal Passive	197
	6.1.3 Coreferentiality	205
6.2	Exceptions to the Passive in Relational Grammar	209
	Footnotes	216

7.	THE PRAGMATICS OF THE PASSIVE	217
7.0	Introduction	217
7.1	Topicalization	218
	7.1.1 The Passive and Given/New Order	223
	7.1.2 Topicalization and Initial Position	231
7.2	The Passive and Impersonalization	237
	7.2.1 Indefinite Human Agents and the Passive	238
	Footnotes	251

8.	SUMMARY	255
	BIBLIOGRAPHY	263
	INDEX OF LANGUAGES	288
	INDEX OF NAMES	292
	INDEX OF TERMS	297

EDITORIAL STATEMENT

CROOM HELM LTD are publishing a Linguistics Series under the joint editorship of James Hurford (University of Edinburgh) and John Hawkins (Max-Planck-Institut für Psycholinguistik). These editors wish to draw this series to the attention of scholars, who are invited to submit manuscripts to Jim Hurford or to John Hawkins. Following is a statement of editorial intent.

The series will not specialise in any one area of language study, nor will it limit itself to any one theoretical approach. Synchronic and diachronic descriptive studies, either syntactic, semantic, phonological or morphological, will be welcomed, as will more theoretical 'model-building' studies, and studies in sociolinguistics or psycholinguistics. The criterion for acceptance will be quality and potential contribution to the relevant field. All monographs published must advance our understanding of the nature of language in areas of substantial interest to major sectors of the linguistic research community. Traditional scholarly standards, such as clarity of presentation, factual and logical soundness of argumentation and a thorough and reasoned orientation to other relevant work, must also be adhered to. Within these indispensable limitations we welcome the submission of creative and original contributions to the study of language.

James R. Hurford, Department of Linguistics, University of Edinburgh, Adam Ferguson Building, George Square, Edinburgh EH8 9LL. John A. Hawkins, Max-Planck-Institut für Psycholinguistik, Berg en Dalseweg 79, NL-6522 BC, Nijmegen, The Netherlands.

I would like to dedicate this book to
my parents, Jadwiga and Henryk Siewierscy.

PREFACE

This book is a revised version of my Monash University
M.A. thesis written in 1979. The work was motivated
by the general interest in typological studies pre-
valent at that time. It does not therefore purport
to illustrate the problems relating to passive
occurrence in any individual language or suggest how
the passive should be handled within particular grammatical frameworks. Rather it sets out to exemplify
the range of structures which have been called
passive and the problems which these structures pose
for a unified definition of the passive.
    I have not altered the basic structure of the
original thesis, although I have included in the
discussion the more recent works on the passive.
The only major revision is the addition of chapter
seven on the pragmatics of the passive where the
discussion is mostly confined to European languages.
    There are a number of people who have been of
great assistance to me in the writing of the original
thesis and the preparation of this book. I am particularly indebted to Barry Blake for his constant
help and guidance over a long period. It will be
obvious from what follows how much I have benefited
from his expertise in the field of typological
studies. Special thanks are also due to Bernard
Comrie for commenting on earlier drafts and suggesting that I prepare a revised verion of the
thesis and to my friend and collegue Keith Allan for
his continual help and encouragement. I would also
like to express my gratitude to all the members of
the Linguistic Department at Monash University past
and present who provided me with helpful comments
and moral support, namely Göran Hammarström, John
Platt, Peter Paul, Graham Mallinson, Ian R. Smith,
Stephen R. Johnson, Stephen Paterson, Christopher

PREFACE

Bauer, Carol Budge and Edina Eisikovits. Finally I would like to thank Carleen Marshall and Daniela Antas for typing the camera-ready manuscript and June Roder for secretarial assistance.

Anna Siewierska

LIST OF ABBREVIATIONS AND SYMBOLS

A	transitive subject
abl	ablative
abs	absolutive
acc	accusative
act	active/actor
al	allative
an	animate
ant	anterior
a/p	antipassive
aor	aorist
apl	applicative
appl	applied
art	article
asp	aspect
aux	auxiliary
ben	benefactive
cau	causative
cho	chômeur
cl	class
cl. int	clause introducer
clf	classifier
comp	complementizer
compl	completive
D	dummy/determiner
dat	dative
dec	declarative
det	determiner
erg	ergative
excl	exclusive
f	feminine
foc	focus
fut	future
gen	genitive
gl	goal
hyp	hypothetical
imp	impersonal/imperative

LIST OF ABBREVIATIONS AND SYMBOLS

inan	inanimate
ind	indicative
inf	infinitive
inst	instrumental
intr	intransitive
loc	locative
m	masculine
man	manner
n	neuter
N	noun
nom	nominative
NP	noun phrase
obl	oblique
P	direct object/preposition/predicate
part	participle
partit	partitive
p. part	past participle
pass	passive
pass. part	passive participle
perf	perfective
pl	plural
poss	possessive
PP	prepositional phrase
pres	present
prog	progressive
prop	proper
purp	purposive
refl	reflexive
RG	relational grammar
S	intransitive subject
s	singular
t	tense
t/asp	tense/aspect
top	topic
tr	transitive
V	verb
vb.m	verb marker
VP	verb phrase
1	first person / subject
2	second person / direct object
3	third person / indirect object
*	ungrammatical
!	ungrammatical in the relevant sense
?	of doubtful grammaticality or acceptability
>	takes precedence over
$\emptyset$	zero (form)
–	morpheme boundary, boundary between glosses
:	joins elements of a gloss

Chapter One

INTRODUCTION

1.0 General Aims

Within the last ten years a significant amount of work has been carried out on cross-language morpho-syntactic variation, particularly case marking, word order, relativization, causativization and topicalization strategies. Studies in this area have revealed that well documented language phenomena have not, in fact, been sufficiently researched and many of the properties traditionally associated with these phenomena may not hold cross-linguistically. The passive is a case in point.

The analysis of the various constructions referred to in the literature as *passive* leads to the conclusion that there is not even one single property which all these constructions have in common. In order to determine the cross-language characteristic of passive clauses and examine the relationship between the passive and other related structures, we will survey a wide variety of constructions called passive from many different languages.

The passive constructions discussed will be classified along three parameters: personal/impersonal, periphrastic/synthetic and plain/reflexive. This classification of passive clauses is based on their morpho-syntactic properties i.e. verbal marking, case marking and presence or absence of an overt subject. Various other classifications based on different properties of passive clauses have been used in the literature. For instance, passives have been grouped into stative and nonstative on the basis of whether they involve a state or an action. This is primarily a semantic division. However, it may be also reflected in the syntax. In addition, passives have been classified into agentive, quasi-agentive and agentless in terms of whether they can

1

INTRODUCTION

or cannot occur with an agent.

The discussion of the passive will be aimed at determining what, in fact, constitutes a passive. We hope to demonstrate that the existing definitions are too broad, in the sense that they encompass too diverse a range of structures or conversely too narrow a range and thus exclude constructions of a similar type. Therefore, a compromise solution will be attempted which entails restricting the term *passive* in a way that enables a definition to be made.

In view of the fact that the term *passive* is primarily associated with the personal passive, chapter two will be devoted to a survey of the properties of the personal passive. Chapter three will deal with the more controversial impersonal passive. In chapter four the periphrastic passive will be discussed in the context of the status of the passive auxiliary and past participle. Chapter five will be devoted to the reflexive passive with special emphasis on the problem of distinguishing reflexive passives from other constructions containing a reflexive morpheme. In chapter six attempts at handling exceptions to the passive in terms of the notions *activity*, *result*, and *volition* will be evaluated. The final chapter will centre on the two main pragmatic functions of the passive, namely topicalization and impersonalization.

The remainder of this chapter will be concerned with presenting the different types of passive clauses to be discussed, briefly outlining the controversy over how passive clauses should be treated in a grammar, introducing the problem of the relation between the passive and transitivity, and finally evaluating the status of the passive and transitivity as language universals.

1.1. The Passive

1.1.1 Different Type of Passive Constructions

The term *passive* has been used to cover a wide variety of constructions in many different languages. Under the most widely accepted definition of the passive, passive constructions have the following characteristics:

a) the subject of the passive clause is a direct object in the corresponding active
b) the subject of the active clause is expressed in the passive in the form of an agentive

INTRODUCTION

adjunct or is left unexpressed
c) the verb is marked passive.

As the above characteristics commonly attributed
to passive constructions show, passive constructions
have been defined *vis-à-vis* active constructions and
thus regarded as a deviation from the syntactic norm.
Syntactically they may differ from actives in word
order, case marking, verbal morphology and in the
appearance of some additional word or particle.
Active and passive clauses also typically differ in
the pragmatic function of the agent and patient.
The agent in the most basic type of active declarative clause is usually the topic i.e. the constituent which states what the clause is primarily about
and sets the individual framework within which the
sentence holds.[1] In the overwhelming majority of
languages it appears in initial position in the
clause and in most cases conveys *given* or *old* information. In a typical passive clause on the other
hand the patient is the topic while the agent, if
present, represents *new* information and bears the
main information focus indicated by tonic stress.
Despite the overt differences between actives
and passives, both constructions in the majority of
instances express the same propositional content.
The NPs in the two constructions are generally
viewed as having the same semantic roles. Both in
(1a) and (1b) below <u>John</u> is the agent and <u>book</u> the
patient.

(1) a. John bought the book.
     b. The book was bought by John.

The term *passive* is not only used for clauses
such as (1b) where the subject corresponds to a
patient in the active, but also for clauses with
subjects corresponding to: recipient, benefactive,
source, instrumental, locative, temporal, manner and
causal NPs.
Clauses which lack an overt subject, such as the
following from Dutch (2a) (Kirsner 1976) and Ute
(3a) (Givón 1981), are called passive too.

(2) a. Er   werd   door de   vrouw gegild
         there become by   the woman scream:p.part
         'There was screaming by the woman'.

3) a. Tayúci   - gyay 'apága - ta - x̂a
         eloquence - have speak - pass - ant
         'There was eloquent speaking'.

INTRODUCTION

In the Dutch clause the subject position is occupied
by what is commonly known as a dummy pronoun. This
dummy pronoun is not present in the corresponding
active (2b).

(2) b. De   vrouw   glide
       the   woman   scream:past
       'The woman screamed'.

The Ute clause consists of a verb in the third
person singular with an incorporated manner adverb.
The closest corresponding active, as in the Dutch
example, is an intransitive clause.

(3) b. Ta' wa' - c̱i tayuci   - gyạy 'apaǧa qa
       man   - S̱/A eloquence - have speak ant
       'The man spoke eloquently'.

In addition, clauses which have no corresponding
actives, such as the German (4a) and English (5), are
also referred to by some as passive.

(4) a. Der   Tisch   ist   gedeckt
       the   table   is   lay:p.part
       'The table is laid'.

(5)   John grew more and more frightened.

The German clause (4a) denotes a state, not an action.
The English translation does not show this well, for
in English a clause similar to (4a) can be interpreted both statively and dynamically. This is not
the case in German. (4b) is not the active counterpart of (4a) in German.

(4) b. Jemand   deckte   den   Tisch
       someone   lay:past:3s   the   table
       'Someone laid the table'.

The above examples of passive clause clearly
indicate that there is a significant amount of dis-
agreement over what constitutes a passive. It is
thus not surprising that there is a similar dis-
agreement over how passives should be treated in
a grammar.

1.1.2 The Passive and Different Models of Grammar

Although passive clauses differ from actives both
syntactically and pragmatically, the common semantic
properties which they display have led linguists

INTRODUCTION

to claim that there is a strong relationship between the two constructions.

The relationship between actives and passives has been widely discussed both in traditional grammar and modern linguistics. However, it was only when language began to be generally viewed in terms of a multi-level theory of clause structure that the expression of the relationship between actives and passives became a major theoretical issue. In fact, the theories of grammar which have dominated linguistics in the last twenty odd years: Transformational Grammar (TG) in its various guises including Relational Grammar (RG) (Perlmutter and Postal 1977, 1978, 1983a,b) and Lexical Functional Grammar (Bresnan 1978, 1982a,b), as well as the particular models of Case Grammar (Fillmore 1968, 1977; J. Anderson 1977; Starosta 1976, 1978) and Functional Grammar, (Dik 1978, 1980) have evolved out of different approaches to passive constructions.

Broadly speaking, it is possible to distinguish between structurally based and relationally based approaches to the passive. Linguists such as Chomsky (1957, 1965, 1973), Jacobs and Rosenbaum (1968), Emonds (1972, 1976), Langacker and Munro (1975) and Hoard (1979) who advocate the first approach, maintain that it is possible to relate active and passive clauses in terms of changes induced in their constituent structure i.e. linear order and dominance relations[2]. Under the first version of TG, for example, active and passive clauses such as (1a,b) were assigned distinct structures, namely (1c,d).

(1) c.

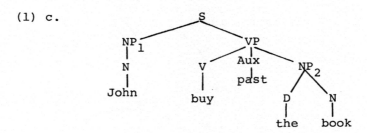

INTRODUCTION

d.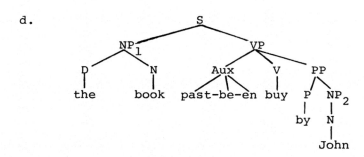

The two constructions were said to be related by a passive transformation which:

a) permutes NP_1 and NP_2
b) inserts the discontinuous auxiliary element be+en
c) inserts the element <u>by</u> to the left of the permuted NP_1

Advocates of Case Grammar and RG hold that the relationship between actives and passives is best "explained" with reference not to constituent structure, but changes in the grammatical relations between NPs and their verbs. Thus in RG (Perlmutter and Postal 1977), for instance, the passive is said to be a relational changing rule which promotes a direct object to subject and simultaneously demotes the former subject to an oblique position in the clause or deletes it. Clauses in RG are represented by a network of stratified, labeled arcs. The simplified relational representation of (1a,b) is shown in (1e,f)(Perlmutter 1980).[3]

(1) e.

f.

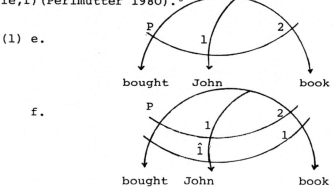

The numerals 1 and 2 stand for subject and direct

6

INTRODUCTION

object respectively which together with the indirect
object are regarded as linguistic primitives in RG
and are referred to as *terms*. NPs other than the
terms such as locatives, instrumentals, benefactives
etc. are referred to as *non-terms* or obliques. The
symbol ^ over a term indicates that the particular
NP has been demoted by the operation of syntactic
rules and is called a *chômeur*.[4] In the active (1e)
<u>John</u> is a "1" and the book a "2". As a result of
the passive, the NP which was a "2" in the first
stratum (level) is promoted to "1" in the second
stratum, while the original "1" becomes a chomêur Î.
   Among both groups of linguists opinions are
again divided on whether the relationship between
actives and passives, be it structural or in terms
of grammatical relations, should be expressed in the
syntactic component of a grammar or in the lexicon.
The main problem thus centres on the question of
whether actives and passives should be related by
means of syntactic or lexical rules. Linguists who
hold the former view propose to derive passives
from:

a) structures identical or similar to actives
   (Chomsky 1965, 1973; Burt 1971; Jacobs and
   Rosenbaum 1968)
b) structures containing actives (Bouton 1973;
   Fiengo 1974; Hasagawa 1968; Hoard 1979;
   Lakoff 1971; Langacker and Munro 1975)
c) both from some other abstract source (Emonds
   1972, 1976; Fillmore 1968, 1971).

Proponents of the other position such as Brame (1976)
Bresnan (1978), Friedin (1975a), Horn (1981), Mchombo
(1980), Shopen (1972) and Starosta (1978) claim that
passive constructions should be generated directly.
They contend that the regularities between the two
constructions can best be expressed in terms of
lexical entries for the verbs and the synonymy between actives and passives by means of lexical rules
not syntactic transformations. Yet other linguists
such as Wasow (1977), Lightfoot (1979) and Bennett
(1980) maintain that some passive clauses should be
derived transformationally and other passive clauses
lexically.
   All the turbulent discussions on the passive
have been carried out primarily in the context of
arguments for or against different models of grammar
and consequently no conclusions on the best way of
treating the passive have been reached. The focus

7

INTRODUCTION

of attention has been on the model of grammar not on
the construction itself. The very opposite approach
will be adopted here, the chief concern being not the
actual way that passive clauses should be handled in
a grammar, but determining what a passive construction is.

1.2 Transitivity and the Passive

Even a superficial look at the linguistic literature
reveals that the term *passive* is frequently coupled
with another linguistic notion, namely *transitivity*.
In fact the two notions are so closely intertwined
that it is impossible to speak about one without
mentioning the other.

The passive and transitivity have been discussed
in relation to two main problems. The first is
connected with establishing which active clauses may
have passive counterparts or to use transformational
terminology the structural conditions under which
passivization may take place. For the majority of
linguists the determining factor is transitivity.
In other words it is claimed that if a clause is
transitive it can be passivized. The second problem
concerns the recent controversy on the transitive/
intransitive status of passive clauses (Givón 1981;
Hopper and Thompson 1980; Perlmutter and Postal 1978,
1983b). Generally speaking it has not been the
custom to comment on the transitivity or intransitivity of the passive. The intransitivity of this
construction has simply been taken for granted.
Recent work on linguistic typology has brought into
question this assumption with respect to passive
clauses in some languages.

As both of the above mentioned problems have a
direct bearing on the definition of the passive, in
order to appreciate the issues involved, it is first
necessary to discuss what is meant by the term
transitive.

We will begin with the traditional morpho-
syntactic approaches to transitivity and show how the
very definition of transitivity is indirectly dependent on the passive. Next we will deal with Hopper
and Thompson's (1980) recent discourse-orientated
treatment of transitivity which in contrast to the
former approaches does not rely on the passive. The
discussion in later chapters will reveal that this
definition of transitivity entails abandoning the
claim that all passive clauses are intransitive.

INTRODUCTION

1.2.1 Transitivity and Morpho-syntax

Since the notion of transitivity is universally
recognized it seems that a good definition should
be readily available. Ironically enough the terms
transitive/intransitive have not as yet been
satisfactorily defined.

In most cases the notion of transitivity is
simply taken for granted. Those who do attempt to
present a definition usually provide something along
the following lines. A transitive verb is a verb
which takes a direct object and an intransitive verb
a verb which does not. When asked what is a direct
object they most probably will say that it is an
object of a transitive verb (Brown and Miller 1980;
Jespersen 1926; Poutsma 1926). Linguists who use
some form of this definition sometimes supplement it
with semantic criteria, for instance that the verb
must express a genuine action that passes over from
the subject to the direct object. In addition the
direct object may be said to be the NP the referent
of which is somehow affected (often physically) as
a consequence of the action expressed by the verb.
Despite the obvious circularity of all of these
arguments, this is the most widely accepted definition of transitivity.

In practice of course linguists have found it
possible to identify a subject and a direct object
and thus classify a verb as transitive on the basis
of word order and/or surface morphology.

It is generally recognized that languages tend
to place subjects and direct objects in distinct
clausal positions and/or mark either one or the
other (or occasionally both) by distinct affixes or
adpositions. For example in Polish, it is possible
to identify the verb <u>zabić</u> in (6) as transitive, because it has the semantic properties of a transitive
verb and the preverbal nominal - <u>myśliwy</u> - is in the
nominative case, while the postverbal nominal - <u>nie-
dźwiedzia</u> - is in the accusative case.

> (6) Myśliwy   zabił   niedźwiedzia
>   gamekeeper:nom kill:past bear:acc
>   'The gamekeeper killed the bear'.

The verb <u>widzieć</u> 'to see' in (7) can similarly be
identified as a transitive verb (and the clause as
transitive). Although it does not fulfil the semantic criteria of transitivity (the verb does not

9

INTRODUCTION

express an action in the traditional sense and the object is therefore unlikely to be affected), the NPs which accompany it are in the nominative and accusative cases.

(7) Myśliwy   widział niedźwiedzia
    gamekeeper:nom see:past bear:acc
    'The gamekeeper saw the bear'.

In the majority of languages, as in Polish, morphological marking, word order and semantic properties may be used as tests for transitivity.

However, the morphological marking of NPs does not always correlate with their syntactic behaviour, more specifically, with their behaviour under passivization. Passivization is the second most widely accepted test for transitivity and direct objects. Under this analysis a NP is regarded as a direct object and a clause as transitive if the NP can appear as the subject of a canonical passive construction. Consequently, the Polish (8a) is viewed as transitive although the postverbal NP is in the instrumental case and not the accusative case, because it has a corresponding passive (8b). The clause (9a) conversely is intransitive, despite the accusative case marking, due to the ungrammaticality of the corresponding passive.

(8) a. Pan   Tadeusz   administrował
       Mr:nom   Tadeusz:nom administer:past:3s
       majątkiem
       estate:instr
       'Mr Tadeusz administered the estate'.

    b. Majątek   był administrowany   przez
       estate:nom was administer:p.part by
       Pana   Tadeusza
       Mr   T
       'The estate was administered by Mr.
       Tadeusz'.

(9) a. Beczka   waży   dziesięć kg.
       Barrel:nom weigh:pres:3s ten:acc   kg.
       'The barrel weighs ten kilograms'

    b. *Dziesięć kilogramów jest ważonych
       ten:nom   kg:nom   are   weigh:p.part
       przez   beczkę
       by   barrel:acc
       (*Ten kg. are weighed by the barrel).

10

INTRODUCTION

This so called transitivity test quite evidently is no less circular than the definitions of transitivity given earlier. Linguists who use passivization as a test for transitivity in fact find themselves in the paradoxical situation of defining passivization in terms of transitivity and transitivity in terms of passivization.

Unfortunately, most of the exponents of the dominant linguistic theories have adopted either the first or second "definition" of transitivity in one form or another. Linguists who adhere to a multi-level theory of clause structure usually manage to "disguise" their definition of transitivity in such a way that its resemblance to the above is obscured. Once they begin to deal with actual language data their true position is revealed. Consider, for instance, the definition of transitivity proposed by transformational grammarians and relational grammarians.

Proponents of TG have attempted to define subjects and direct objects and transitive and intransitive clauses on the basis of order and hierarchical dominance. They claim that a subject is 'the NP immediately dominated by S' (John in (1c)) and a direct object 'the NP immediately dominated by VP' (book in (1d)) (Chomsky 1965:71). Transitive clauses are those which have a subject and a direct object. This definition of transitivity and subjects and objects is carried out at the level of underlying structure, not surface structure. Consequently, it does not always identify as subject or object constituents which we would regard as such on the basis of morphological or syntactic criteria in other grammatical models. Moreover, the configurations postulated by Chomsky are not reflected in the surface structure of some languages. For instance, in VSO languages such as Polynesian languages like Tongan, Samoan, Maori or Pukapukan or the Celtic languages, the verb and its object are non-contiguous. Therefore, it is difficult to argue that the subject and object can be distinguished in terms of the dominance relations which Chomsky suggests. According to Chomsky's theory in languages like these both the subject and direct object have to be seen as being immediately dominated by "S". There is no structural difference between these NPs apart from their relative order with respect to the verb. Positioning relative to the verb cannot, however, be taken as the basis for defining subjects and direct objects, since the direct object of VOS and SOV languages would be grouped with the S of VSO.

11

INTRODUCTION

Furthermore, this criterion would be inapplicable to SVO languages. The problem posed by VSO languages and the difficulties encountered in establishing a definite order of dominance between all the constituents of a sentence (especially in the case of subordinate clauses) have severely undermined Chomsky's definition of transitivity.

Relational Grammarians, as mentioned above, avoid the problem of defining subjects and direct objects by taking these relations to be linguistic primitives. A direct object or "2" in the RG of Perlmutter and Postal (1977, 1978, 1983,a,b) is not viewed as the same kind of entity as in traditional grammar or TG. For most linguists a direct object is a NP which occurs with a transitive verb (whatever that may be), but only together with another NP - the subject. Direct objects may be unaccompanied by overt subjects in certain derived structures e.g. imperatives or impersonal passives (cf. discussion in ch.3), but never in basic clauses. In the RG of Perlmutter and Postal a "2" can occur with an intransitive verb. For instance, the English clause (10a) is regarded as derivative of (10b) where Martians is an underlying "2".

(10) a. Martians exist.

b.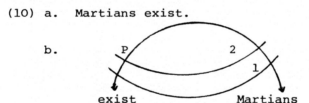

In both the underlying (10b) and surface (10a) the verb is intransitive, but in (10a) Martians is a subject while in (10b) it is a *direct object*. According to Perlumtter and Postal (1978:33), 'a stratum (level) is *transitive* if it contains both a "1"-arc and a "2"-arc as in (1e). A stratum is *intransitive* if and only if it contains either a "1"-arc or a "2"-arc (not both) as in (10b)'. Perlmutter and Postal (1978:31) claim that they have overcome the unclarity of former definitions of transitivity by introducing notions like 'head of "1"-arc' and 'head of "2"-arc' which are 'perfectly formal and precise'. Obviously they are not, for the arcs are only a means of representation of previously established relations between NPs and their verbs. Postal and Perlmutter like Chomsky have to rely on word order, morphological marking, syntactic

INTRODUCTION

properties and semantic characteristics to determine which NPs are "1s", "2s" and "3s".

In the above mentioned approaches to transitivity, the term has been defined with reference to NPs and VPs or subjects and objects. Attempts have also been made in the literature to describe clauses first of all in terms of the number of participants which obligatorily appear with a verb. The term *valency* introduced by Tesnière (1959) and developed by Kholodović (1969, 1974), Apresjan (1974), Lyons (1977), Comrie (1977b) and others has been used in this context. A verb which takes one obligatory participant or argument is said to have a valency of one; a verb which takes two obligatory participants has a valency of two; and a verb which takes three obligatory participants has a valency of three. Owing to the necessity of distinguishing between the different types of participants which can occur with a given verb in a well formed clause (compare for instance give and put), reference is made to the notions of transitivity and subject/object as well. Lyons (1977:486), for instance, states that a transitive verb is a verb that has a valency of two and governs a direct object. What constitutes a direct object again poses a problem.

Although the notion of valency does not overcome any of the problems concerned with defining transitivity and subject/object, it provides a more consistent treatment of some classes of verbs. For instance, in some languages verbs corresponding to believe, trust, help and serve as in Classical Latin (credō, fīdō, auxilior, serviō), German (glauben, vertrauen, helfen, dienen) or Polish (wierzyć, ufać, pomagać, służyć) are taken as intransitive for they govern a NP in the dative case and cannot occur in a canonical passive construction. These verbs differ from typical intransitive verbs such as go, stand, laugh, speak, sit, in that they occur with two obligatory participants. The terms *middle* or *semi-transitive* are sometimes used with reference to these verbs. In our opinion it is necessary to have a term for the grouping of trust and believe-type verbs and typical transitive verbs such as hit, cut, throw. A system of verbal classification based exclusively on the transitive/intransitive dichotomy obscures the fact that verbs like trust and believe etc. in Latin, German or Polish display the same property as the corresponding verbs in a language like English i.e. take two obligatory participants.

The notion of valency is also the basis of Dixon's (1979) definition of transitivity. Dixon

INTRODUCTION

(ibid.) regards transitivity as a linguistic universal at the level of deep structure. He claims that every language distinguishes between verbs which take one obligatory participant - intransitive verbs - and verbs which take two obligatory participants - transitive verbs. Furthermore, each language has a means of identifying these participants. The identification of the participants is made qua a number of universally occurring verbs such as hit, throw, cut, carry etc. All of these verbs involve one participant who could potentially be viewed as the controller or instigator of an event, which Dixon denotes by the symbol A, and another participant which is referred to as O. (We will use the symbol P instead). The only obligatory participant which occurs with intransitive verbs such as go, smile, dance is denoted by the symbol S. Dixon claims that languages tend to extend this identification of participants to all other type of verbs. He argues that although languages may vary in the type of extensions made, the majority of verbs pattern in the way he describes. The idea of liking, for example, may be expressed by a transitive verb, intransitive verb or even an adjectival construction in different languages. Certain verbs like endure in English and in Tagalog may be perceived as transitive although the referent of the A NP cannot be considered to be a controller in the same sense as the A of the verbs: cut, throw, carry etc. Even verbs like hit may be interpreted as intransitive verbs as for example in Turkish (Mulder 1976:299). Dixon (1979 fn. 59) suggests that:

> idiosyncratic verbs (like the above) in any language can be dealt with as institutionalised extensions to the universal definition, or they can be dealt with simply as "exceptions" that have to be learnt by heart (exceptions are recognized as a valid category at the levels of phonology and morphology; the idea is also applicable within syntax and even within semantics).

The identification of S, A and P at the level of deep structure is made primarily on semantic grounds. Dixon points out that only A is actually identified in positive terms. S can be semantically either animate or inanimate and need not be perceived as an agent. Similarly, P cannot be equated with a semantic patient. Dixon contends that the identification of S, A and P is strictly reflected

14

INTRODUCTION

in the syntax and that each of these relations can
be identified through their individual syntactic
properties at both intermediate and surface levels.
The problem of transitivity could be considered
resolved, if rules were found which clearly identify
all three types of constituents. Individual
languages possess rules which single out S and A
(e.g. relativization in Malayo-Polynesian) or S and
P (e.g. antipassivization in ergative languages)[6] or
even S, A and P.[7] Rules which are restricted to S
and A in all languages have also been suggested
(S. Anderson 1976; Dixon 1979; Keenan 1976a).
However, although direct objects or Ps can be
identified by different syntactic criteria in
individual languages, the only syntactic rule which
appears to apply regularly to direct objects is the
passive. Therefore, in actual fact, all attempts at
defining direct objects universally and consequently
all universal definitions of transitivity are based
on the passive.
    Is there thus a mutual dependence between
passivization and transitivity or have linguists
failed to appreciate what transitivity actually
involves? Hopper and Thompson (1980) argue that the
latter is the case and that the solution lies in
a discourse approach to the problem.

1.2.2   Transitivity and Discourse

Hopper and Thompson contend that transitivity is not
an all or nothing notion, but rather a matter of
degree. According to Hopper and Thompson, clauses
can be ranked on a scale of transitivity determined
by the following parameters:

1) Participants   6) Affirmation
2) Kinesis   7) Mode
3) Aspect   8) Agency
4) Punctuality   9) Individualization of the object
5) Volitionality 10) Affectedness of the object

    For most linguists a canonical transitive clause,
as mentioned above, expresses an activity which is
"carried over" or "transfered" from an agent to a
patient. Hopper and Thompson state that the
enumerated parameters of transitivity relate to
different facets of the effectiveness or intensity
with which this action is transfered from one
participant to the other. Thus, a transfer can occur
only if two participants are involved (11a), not one
(11b) and only if the verb expresses an action (12a),

15

INTRODUCTION

not a state (12b).

    (11) a. John killed Betty.
         b. Betty died.
    (12) a. I hugged Sally.
         b. I like Sally.

A transfer is more effectively carried out if:

a) it is viewed from its endpoint (13a) than if it lacks an endpoint (13b).

    (13) a. John bought some beer.
         b. John is buying some beer.

b) there is no transitional stage between inception and completion (14a) than if the action is ongoing (14b).

    (14) a. Susan kicked him.
         b. Susan carried him.

c) the action is carried out purposefully (15a) than if it is unintentional (15b).

    (15) a. I wrote your name.
         b. I forgot your name.

d) the action is positive (16a) rather than negative (16b).

    (16) a. John drinks beer.
         b. John doesn't drink beer anymore.

e) the action is expressed in the indicative (17a) as opposed to the subjunctive, optative, hypothetical, imaginary or conditional (17b) mood.

    (17) a. I answered the question.
         b. If only I had answered the question.

f) the action is carried out by a NP which can be viewed as agentive (18a) rather than one which cannot (18b).

    (18) a. George startled me.
         b. The picture startled me.

The effectiveness of the transfer is also dependent on the object. If the object is individual, i.e. if it possesses one of the properties on the left

INTRODUCTION

in the chart below, the transfer is more likely to
be regarded as complete than if the object is non-
individual, i.e. it has the characteristics listed
on the right side.

<u>individuated</u>   <u>non-individuated</u>

proper   common
human, animate   inanimate
concrete   abstract
singular   plural
count   mass
referential, definite   non-referential

Compare (19a) with (19b) and (19c) with (19d).

(19) a. Clive wanted that car.
     b. Clive wanted fame and fortune
     c. Bette painted the Prime Minister.
     d. Bette painted bananas.

If only one part of the object is affected (20b) the
transfer will be less complete than if the whole
object is affected (20a).

(20) a. John drank the beer.
     b. John drank some beer.

Hopper and Thompson point out that one of the
consequences of their treatment of transitivity is
that some one-participant clauses, for example (21)
would have to be regarded as higher on the scale of
transitivity than certain two-participant clauses
like (22), since the former contain more high
transitivity features than the latter.

(21) a. The children danced.
     b. Susan left.
     c. Bill laughed.
(22) a. Mick likes beer.
     b. Sandra understands things.
     c. They respect intelligence.

The clauses in (21) are punctual, telic, and involve
actions which are volitional. Those in (22) have
only one of the high transitivity features i.e. two
participants. This apparent paradox, according to
Hopper and Thompson, accurately reflects the facts
of language.

Hopper and Thompson appear to be correct in
that the morphological marking and syntactic

INTRODUCTION

behaviour of nominals may depend on the above
mentioned parameters. This does not mean, however,
that their scale of transitivity always reflects
morphological and syntactic distinctions. Note, for
instance, that under Hopper and Thompson's analysis
(11a), (13a), (16a), and (12b) all differ in degree
of transitivity. The clause (11a) is very high on
the scale of transitivity for it has all of the
above mentioned high transitivity features. (13a)
lacks two features; the object is non-individual
and not affected. (16a) is missing the two features
in (13a) and is in addition non-telic. The clause
(12b) lacks four features: action, aspect, punctuality, and agency. Nevertheless, both morphologically and syntactically the clauses are identical.
All can, for instance, passivize. What then is
gained by making these distinctions? A scale of
transitivity would be justified if it were possible
to demonstrate both the syntactic effects of different degrees of transitivity and the uniform
behaviour of clauses with the same transitivity
value. As shown above, the degree of transitivity
of (11a), (13a), (16a) and (12b) appears to have no
effect on, for instance, passivization in English.
Examples such as (22) and (23) illustrate that
clauses equally high on the scale of transitivity
also do not behave syntactically in an identical
fashion.

(23)   John lacks courage.

Both the clauses (22) and (23) possess only one of
the above high transitivity features, namely two
participants. Yet, (22) has a corresponding passive
while (23) does not. If clauses with a low
transitivity ranking such as (22) appear to have
similar syntactic potential to the ones which are
highly transitive e.g. (11) and (12), something must
be amiss with the definition of transitivity or,
contrary to common belief, transitivity does not
play a decisive role in passivization.
     Hopper and Thompson presumably would argue that
the presence or absence of certain features does
not have the same consequences for transitivity in
all languages. Languages vary in the type of morphological distinctions they make and in the way that
these distinctions are reflected syntactically.[8]
Therefore, languages may also differ in the extent
to which syntactic rules, such as the passive, are
sensitive to transitivity. If so, then perhaps
linguists have been misguided in treating

18

INTRODUCTION

transitivity as the defining characteristic of the passive in all languages.

We have considered two approaches to transitivity which although not completely distinct, concentrate on different aspects of transitivity. How these two conceptions affect the definition of the passive and whether or not there is a mutual dependence between transitivity and the passive will be discussed in the following chapters.

1.3 Language Universals

It is generally recognized that in the words of Chomsky (1965:278) 'the main task of linguistic theory must be to develop an account of linguistic universals'. The quest for language universals is based on the assumption that cross-language analyses will eventually enable linguists to specify the range and type of possible linguistic processes, explain the existing relationship between them and consequently discover the constraints imposed on human language and possibly human cognitive capacity in general.

The studies on language universals have revealed that there are in fact very few strict universals and the ones that appear to exist are too general to be of any real interest. In the preceding discussion we have been using the terms *subject*, *direct object*, *transitive* and *passive* as if they belonged to the small set of strict universals. A brief word of explanation is therefore in order.

1.3.1 Subject/Object vs S, A, P

Ever since the time of Plato, linguists and philosophers have been using the terms *subject* and *object* assuming that the morphological, syntactic and semantic properties of all languages can best be described with reference to these terms. The difficulties with defining a direct object have been sketched above. The traditional definition of grammatical subject 'as the nominal constituent of the transitive clause which has the same grammatical properties i.e. position in the clause, case marking and control of verbal agreement as that of the intransitive nominal' also poses a number of problems.

Recent attempts of characterizing subjects universally (e.g. Keenan 1976a) have revealed that the above criteria do not identify the same type of NPs as subject in all languages (compare the Latin

19

INTRODUCTION

(25) and Avar (27) below) and may produce distinct
semantic results even within a single language (e.g.
case marking and verbal agreement may be in conflict
or nouns and pronouns may operate according to
different systems). In addition,morphological
properties may not coincide with the syntactic
behaviour of NPs (cf. S. Anderson 1976). Furthermore,recent studies have shown that the notion of
subject plays no major role in the syntax of some
languages e.g. Yidin[y] (Dixon 1977), Navajo and
Lakhota (Foley and Van Valin 1977), Tagalog
(Schachter, 1976, 1977), Greenlandic Eskimo
(Woodbury 1977), while the adequate description
of the morphological and syntactic properties of
other languages requires the recognition of three
syntactic primes, not just two.
    In view of the controversy surrounding the
notions subject and object, we propose to adopt the
Dixonian terms S, A and P. This system of
description facilitates language comparison, since
it enables reference to be made to three syntactic
primes irrespective of how a given language groups
these categories.[9] The following conventions will be
used in the remainder of this study:

    a) core categories S, A, P
    b) subject S/A
    c) absolutive S/P

We will avoid the term *direct object* whenever
possible. Like all other linguists we are faced
with the problem of deciding whether a NP is or is
not a P.[10] The terms *agent, patient, recipient,
benefactive* etc. will be employed to denote NPs
other than the core categories.

1.3.2   Transitivity and Ergativity

The universal status of transitivity has recently
been called into question particularly with respect
to ergative languages.[11]
    The term *ergative*, like the term *accusative*, is
primarily a morphological term defined with reference to grammatical case. In some case marking languages the same grammatical case is assigned to S
and A - the nominative - and a separate case to the
P - the accusative - as in Latin.

    (24) Milites   pugnaverunt
         soldier:nom:pl fight:perf:3pl
         'The soldiers fought'.

20

INTRODUCTION

(25) Milites   Darium   vicerunt
     soldier:nom:pl Darius:acc conquer:perf:3pl
     'The soldiers conquered Darius'.

These languages are termed accusative. In other
languages S and P appear in the same case - the
absolutive - while A takes another case - the ergative - as in Avar.

(26) Jas - al łimer - ∅   b - itl - ana
     girl-erg child - abs n - send - past
     'The girl sent the child'.

(27) Łimer - ∅   b - al   - ana
     child - abs n - come - past
     'The child came'.

Such languages are referred to as ergative.
    Just as the term *accusative* has been extended
to languages with no surface case marking such as
Thai or Mandarin, so the term *ergative* is also
used to describe languages which group S and P in
contradistinction to A by means of separate
particles i.e. prepositions (Tongan) or postpositions or by the sequence and form of pronominal
affixes on the verb e.g. Abkhaz and Abaza (Catford
1976). Note that in Avar,in addition to the case
marking,the identification of S and P is also shown
by means of the agreement affixes on the verb. In
both (26) and (27) the verb agrees with the neuter
noun łimer - child which is indicated by the neuter
affix b.
    Lately,in the wake of Dixon's (1972) grammar of
Dʸirbal,the terms *accusative* and *ergative* have also
been used in a syntactic sense. In the vast majority
of the world's languages the major syntactic rules
are formed with reference to S and A and thus the
justification for the term *subject*. These languages
are said to have accusative syntax. In a handful of
languages some syntactic operations are sensitive
to S and P (as in Dʸirbal) or single out the A and
thus function ergatively (Dixon 1972, 1979; Blake
1977). Suggestions have been made in the literature
that the notion of transitivity is not applicable to
ergative languages (Martinet 1962; Tchekoff 1973a,b;
Wagner 1978). It has been claimed that verbs in
ergative languages behave differently from verbs in
accusative languages and thus should be referred to
as *ergative verbs*. This claim is based on the fact
that in some ergative languages it is possible to

INTRODUCTION

"delete" the A of what would be regarded as a transitive verb in accusative languages as, for instance, in Avar (28) (Černy 1971:43) and Tongan (29) (Churchward 1953).

Avar

(28) a. Inssu-ca   cul-ø   qot-ula[12]
        father-erg   woods-abs cut-pres
        'Father chops wood'.

    b. Cul - ø   qot - ula
       wood-abs   cut - pres
       'Wood chops'.

Tongan

(29) a. Na'e tamate'i 'e Tevita 'a Koliate
        past kill   erg David abs Goliath
        'David killed Goliath'.

    b. Wa'e tamete 'i 'a Koliate
       past kill   abs Goliath
       'Goliath was killed (died)'.

Although similar sets of clauses can be found in English (30) and other accusative languages, this process is definitely restricted, while in ergative languages it appears not to be.[13]

(30) a. John moved the stone.
    b. The stone moved.

Mallinson and Blake (1980:9) quoting Claude Tchekoff point out that in Avar it is not only possible to delete the A, but, in fact, the majority of verbs require the expression of only one participant, while the addition of the other participant is optional. If this indeed is the case, is it feasible to speak of the transitive/intransitive distinction in a language such as Avar? If the term is used with reference to Avar it can only be done so tenuously.

What about other ergative languages? Does the deletability of the A warrant abandoning the transitive/intransitive distinction for these languages? Linguists such as Dixon (1977a, 1979) and Blake (1977, 1979c) argue that it does not and have shown that the notion of transitivity plays an equally important role in ergative languages as in accusative languages.

We do not exclude the possibility of a language with verbs which show a complete lack of orientation towards their nominal modifiers and which could not be treated in terms of the transitive/intransitive

22

INTRODUCTION

distinction. However, as up to date only one
language has been discovered which may possibly
fall into this category, namely Avar,we will assume
that the notion of transitivity and the problems
posed by it is valid for all languages.

1.3.3 The Passive

Although linguists speak of a universal characterization of the passive (Perlmutter and Postal 1977;
O'Grady 1981; Dryer 1982), there is no doubt that
the passive is not a language universal, for
irrespective of how it has been defined it has not
been attested in numerous languages of the
Australian continent, Polynesian languages such as
Tongan and Samoan, many Amer-Indian languages and
even in the European language Hungarian, just to
name a few.[14] Nevertheless, constructions called
passive have been reported in all the main language
families and in all the accepted language types
irrespective of the typological criteria used, be
it word order, morphological structure, marking of
S, A and P, subject vs topic prominence (Li and
Thompson 1976), or reference vs role domination
(Foley and Van Valin 1977; Schachter 1977).
     This is not to say that no correlation between
the passive and language type has been observed.
On the contrary, the passive is primarily associated
with accusative, subject prominent, reference
dominated languages. As these are the typological
characteristics of Indo-European languages,and the
term *passive* was adopted from Latin to describe
certain constructions in the well known European
languages, this is by no means surprising. The
passive is not, of course restricted to these
languages.
     It is difficult to determine the actual
distribution of the passive due to the lack of
consensus on what is a passive.[15] Even if the
more controversial passive clauses are disregarded
(e.g. those in the Philippine and Sino-Tibetan
languages),the fact that this construction is very
wide-spread is indisputable. The need for a cross-
language characterization is similarly unquestionable.

NOTES

     1. The terms *topic*, *focus*, *given* and *new* are
discussed in 7.1. The distinct pragmatic functions
of the agent and patient are a direct result of the

23

INTRODUCTION

change in constituent order characteristic of the passive in many languages.

2. In TG sentence structure is depicted in terms of labeled tree diagrams as (1c, d). Each sentence type is characterized by a particular tree configuration and each constituent of a sentence is associated with a given position on a tree. It is assumed that the relation between two clauses, which are perceived to be related, can be shown by reference to the change in the position of the constituents on the tree diagram. Compare (1c) and (1d).

3. An alternative representation of (1b) is as in (I). (Perlmutter 1980:199).

(I)
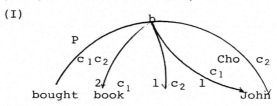

In such Relational Networks the grammatical relation of each constituent at each stratum or level is represented by a separate arc. The levels of structure are indicated by the coordinates c_1 c_2 c_3 etc. That John bears the "1"- relation at the first level and the chômeur relation at the second level is indicated by the fact that it heads (the arrow indicates the head of an arc) a "1"- arc with coordinate c_1 and a cho-arc with coordinate c_2. The fact that the book is a "2" at the first level and a "1" at the second is indicated by the fact that it heads a "2"-arc with coordinate c_1 and a "1"-arc with coordinate c_2. We will use the stratal diagrams and not the networks as in (I) for the former are more convenient for expository purposes. It is important to note that verbal tense, auxiliaries, agreement and linear precedence are not represented in either of the RG notations.

4. Although other grammatical relations are also recognized in RG (cf. Perlmutter and Postal 1983b:86-7), we will be dealing only with the following:

subject	direct object	indirect object	non-terms/obliques
1	2	3	benefactive locative

INTRODUCTION

                                        instrumental
                                        manner
                                        causal
                                        etc.
   5.   Of course it is possible in TG to postulate
an underlying word order distinct from the surface
word order. However, such a solution would be
completely *ad hoc* with no justification other than
saving the theory (cf. Mallinson and Blake 1980:28).
   6.   The antipassive is said to relate clauses
such as the following from Yidinʸ (Dixon 1977a:320).

II   a. Guri:li   bama:l   baga:l
        wallaby:abs   person:erg   spear:past
        'The man speared the wallaby'.

     b. Bama   gurilinjdja baga:djinju
        person:abs   wallaby:loc spear-a/p:past
        'The man speared the wallaby'.

As a result of the antipassive,an original A appears
in surface S function and an original P in an
oblique case, usually together with some form of
marking on the verb. In Yidinʸ the original P
appears in either the dative or locative and the
verb takes the derivational affix :dʸi-n. The
antipassive is attested in Chinook (Silverstein
1976), Pocoman (Smith and Stark 1976), Greenlandic
Eskimo (Woodbury 1977), and in languages of the
Australian continent such as Dyirbal (Dixon 1972),
Yidinʸ (Dixon 1977a), Kalkatungu (Blake 1979a),
Pitta-Pitta (Blake 1977), Warungu (Tsunoda 1974),
Kala Laɡau Langgus (Bani and Klokeid 1976) just to
mention a few. The term *antipassive* has.also been
used by Heath (1976) and Postal (1977) to cover
unspecified object clauses like (IIa, b) and
reflexive or reciprocal constructions such as the
French (IV) and (V).

III.   a. He drinks.
       b. Speed kills.

IV.   Pierre se   critiqu-e
       Peter   himself   criticize-pres:3s
       'Peter criticizes himself'.

V.   J'ai   fait se   critique-er
       I:nom-have   had himself criticize-inf
       Pierre
       Peter
       'I had Peter criticize himself'.

25

INTRODUCTION

We do not believe that the extension of this term to cover cases similar to (III), (IV) and (V) is warranted. If the loss of an underlying P is taken to be definitive of the antipassive as Heath and Postal suggest, then almost all languages will have an antipassive.

7.   In Welsh, for example, it is possible to identify S, A and P on the basis of relativization (Jones 1976:118). When S, A, and P are relativized they are placed in initial position and followed by a relative pronoun a and a relative clause. When any other NPs are relativized the particle y is inserted instead of a.

8.   Hopper and Thompson are of course correct that the distinctions made are always in the direction they predict. Thus, for instance, in Polish the direct object of (Va) shows up in the genitive in both the negative (VIb) and in (VIc) which is interpreted as a partitive.

VI. a. Jan-∅   kupił   to   win-o
      John-nom buy:past:3s this wine-acc
      'John bought this wine'.

    b. Jan-∅   nie kupił   tego
      John-nom no buy:past:3s this:gen
      win-a
      wine-gen
      'John did not buy the wine'.

    c. Nalej   mu   win-a
      pour:imp him wine-gen
      'Pour him some wine'.

To **give** another example, in Kalkatunqu (Blake 1979a) clauses which express an action that is being directed towards a goal as opposed to one that has been successfully completed are assigned intransitive type marking. Compare (VIIa) and (VIIb).

VI. a. Kupaŋuru-ṭu caa kalpin-∅   ḻai-ṇa
      old man-erg here young man-abs hit-past
      'The old man hit the young man'.

    b. kupaŋuru-∅ caa kalpin-ku   ḻai-mina
      old man-abs here young man-dat hit-imperf
      'The old man is hitting the young man'.

For further examples see also Hopper and Thompson (1980).

9.   Languages which Li and Thompson (1976) call

INTRODUCTION

topic-prominent (e.g. Lahu, Lisu) or neither *topic or subject prominent* (e.g. Tagalog, Ilocano) do not fit neatly into this categorization. Nevertheless, for the majority of languages the division into S, A, and P is convenient for descriptive purposes.

10. Some of the problems relating to the direct or indirect object status of nominals will be discussed in 2.2.7.

11. Foley (1976) also contests the universal status of transitivity by claiming that in Fijian all verbs are basically intransitive. He distinguishes between intransitive verbs with agent or experiencer subjects and those with patient subjects. Both type of verbs can be used transitively when a transitive suffix is added to the verb. According to Foley the transitive use of verbs is somehow derived or secondary. We do not have enough data at our disposal to be able to reject or accept Foley's analysis. However, the examples he gives do not provide conclusive evidence for regarding all verbs in Fijian as basically intransitive. Nevertheless this possibility cannot be ignored.

12. This verb belongs to a class of verbs which do not display agreement.

13. Linguists such as J. Anderson (1968), Lyons (1968) and Halliday (1970) refer to verbs such as: move, open, close, break etc. as *ergative* verbs. They claim that these verbs are basically intransitive and that their transitive use is derived. For an alternative interpretation of such verbs (cf. p. 77-8).

14. Some other languages which are claimed to lack a passive are: Enga (New Guinea), Tamang (Sino-Tibetan), Isthmus Zapotec (Oto-Manguean), Choctan (Muskogean), Washo (Hokan), Lisu (Lolo-Burmese).

15. Van Valin (1980), for example, distinguishes between grammatical passives and lexical passives the latter corresponding to what we refer to as anticausatives, (cf.p.77). Since the term *passive* according to Van Valin is also used for anticausatives, extreme caution is necessary when attempting to determine the distribution of the passive.

Chapter Two

THE PERSONAL PASSIVE

2.0   Introduction

Since the term *passive* is primarily associated with
what is known as the personal passive, we shall
examine the characteristics of this canonical construction before discussing the less typical passive
constructions. We therefore, begin with an overview
of the properties traditionally attributed to
personal passives, (2.1) and then proceed to determine the relationship between the personal passive
and transitivity (2.2). Some tentative conclusions
on the nature of the personal passive will be drawn
in 2.3 which will enable us to evaluate the status
of the controversial passives or non-actor focus
constructions in the Philippine languages in 2.4.

2.1   Properties of the Personal Passive

The properties given on p.1, typically viewed as
characteristic of the passive, refer to personal
passives. A construction is regarded as a personal
passive if it has:

        a)   an overt subject with semantic content
        b)   a corresponding active construction
        c)   the subject of the passive corresponding
             to the P of the active.

The Ngarluma clause (1b) (Hale 1968:14-15), the
Russian (2b) (Babby and Brecht 1975), and the
Dhangar-Kurux (3b) (Gordon 1973) are typical
examples of personal passives.

Ngarluma

28

THE PERSONAL PASSIVE

(1) a. Yukuru-∅   pilya-ṇa maŋkuḷa-ku
       dog-nom   bite-past child-acc/dat
       'A dog bit the child'.

   b. Maŋkuḷa-∅   pilya-ŋŋali-ṇa yukuru-la
      child-nom   bite-pass-past dog-loc/inst
      'The child was bitten by a dog'.

Russian

(2) a. Oleg-∅   otkry-l   kalitk-u
       Oleg-nom   open-past   gate-acc
       'Oleg opened the gate'.

   b. Kalitk-a   byla otkryta   Oleg-om
      gate-nom   was open:p.past   Oleg-inst
      'The gate was opened by Oleg'.

Dhangar-Kurux

(3) a. Een   kesari-n   naab-k-an
       I:nom   kesari-acc   thresh-past-1s
       'I threshed the kesari'.

   b. Kesari-∅   naab-r-a   engghay
      Kesari-nom   thresh-pass-past   I:gen
      xekkh   ti
      hand   by
      'The kesari got threshed by me'.

Passives such as (1b) where the verb takes a special affix, here (n)ŋali, are referred to as *synthetic* passives.[1] This type of passive contrasts with (2b) where in addition to a change in verbal morphology an extra verbal, here byla - a form of to be - is introduced. Passive constructions like (2b) are called *periphrastic*. The clause (3b) is similar to (1b) in that the passive verb differs from the active only in the presence of an additional affix- r - in the passive.[2] The affix r in Dhangar-Kurux may also function as a reflexive marker as in (4).

(4) Aas   xaa:s   - r   - a   - s
    he:nom   scratch - refl - past - 3s
    'He scratched himself'.

Therefore, clauses such as (3b) are sometimes called *reflexive* passives.

Personal passives in which the subject corresponds to a P in the active are by far the most common type of passive constructions. In fact, in

THE PERSONAL PASSIVE

many languages only such passives occur. In others
the subject of a passive clause may correspond to a
recipient in the active: English, Swedish (only
with the s-passive cf. 3.2.2), Classical Greek,
Sanskrit, Persian, Indonesian, Malagasy, Tagalog,
Quechua, Tzotzil, Huichol, Classical Nahuatl, Tiwa,
Nitinaht, Halkomelem, Japanese, Vietnamese,
Machiguenga, Bantu languages (Shona, Chicewa,
Kinyarwanda, Mashi, Maragoli, Chi-mwi-ni).
Languages such as English, Japanese, Vietnamese,
Indonesian, Tagalog, Malagasy, Huichol and the above
Bantu languages also allow a benefactive NP to
function as the subject of the passive. Instrumen-
tal NPs can appear as passive subjects in Malagasy,
Tagalog, Machiguenga, Kinyarwanda, Mashi, Maragoli,
Chi-mwi-ni and Quiche. In Palauan, Tagalog, Fijian,
Maori, Mashi, Maragoli, Thsiluba, Kinyarwanda,
Olutsootso, Chicewa, Mandarin, Sanskrit and English
some locative NPs may occur as subjects of the
passive. Languages like Palauan and Chi-mwi-ni
also allow subjects which would correspond to a
source in the active and others such as Halkomelem
have passive clauses with causal subjects.[3]
In addition to the three properties mentioned,
personal passives are seen to possess the following
two characteristics:

    a) they typically lack an overt agent
    b) they are morphologically and/or syntactically
       marked

We will consider the various cross-linguistic
manifestations of the personal passive in the light
of the enumerated properties and show that the only
property which passives actually do have in common
is the overt lexically-specified subject.

2.1.1 The Active Counterpart

Although actives and passives are not always
strictly synonymous particularly when quantifiers,
pronouns and modal auxiliaries are involved (cf.ch.8),
in the majority of instances the propositional
content of the passive can be expressed by an active
counterpart. This holds for both agentive and
agentless passives. The clauses (5a) and (6a), for
example, are likely to be interpreted as (5b) and
(6b) respectively.

      (5) a. Although Bob often lied to Mary, he was
           never punished.

30

THE PERSONAL PASSIVE

      b. Mary never punished Bob, although he often lied to her.

(6) a. Persuasion was not written with as much flair as Emma.
    b. Jane Austen did not write Persuasion with as much flair as Emma.

When an agentless passive is uttered in isolation the passive may be ambiguous in a way that the active is not. The entity responsible for <u>Janet's death</u> in (7a) may be a single individual (7b), a group of individuals (7c) or some other cause (7d), (7e).[4]

(7) a. Janet was killed.
    b. Someone killed Janet.
    c. Some people killed Janet.
    d. Lightning killed Janet.
    e. Boredom killed Janet.

Nevertheless, generally the linguistic or extra-linguistic context will allow us to establish the identity of the passive agent and thus the active subject even if albeit only partially or incompletely. However, in a number of Amer-Indian languages such as Jener and Tiwa from the Tanoan language group (Allen and Frantz 1978), Makah, Teseshat, Ucluelet, Kyquot, Chiclisit and Nitinaht from the Wakashan language group there are some passive constructions which do not have corresponding actives.[5]

In the Wakashan languages there are no active clauses with an A in third person and a P denoting first person. For instance, in Nitinaht (Klokeid 1976a:311), it is possible to say both (8a) and (8b), but (9a) is ungrammatical.

(8) a. Tcˈixwatsaʔap   ʔa   (ʔoxw)   bowatc   ʔaq
     frighten   dec   nom   deer   the
     ʔōyoqw   Ralph
     acc   Ralph
     'The deer frightened Ralph'.

    b. Tcˈixwatsaʔab-ˈt ʔa   (ʔoxw)   Ralph   ʔoxwTt
     frighten-pass   dec   nom   Ralph   by
     bowatc   ʔaq
     deer   the
     'Ralph was frightened by the deer'.

THE PERSONAL PASSIVE

(9) a. *Pixtcitł   ʔa (ʔoxw) John ʔōyoqw
    pinch   dec nom   John acc
    s(iyˈa)
    me
    ('John pinched me'.)

In order to express an event involving a third
person agent and a first or second person patient or
recipient the passive construction must be used (9b).

(9) b. Pixtcitł-ʔīt   s   ʔoxwīt John
    pinch   -pass I   by   John
    'I was pinched by John'.

A comparison of (8a) and (8b) shows that in the
passive the position of the NPs is inverted; the
active P which took the accusative preposition_
appears with the nominative marker ?oxw and thē verb
as well as the nominative preposition of the passive
agent take the affix -ʔit (subject to phonological
changes). Clauses in Nitinaht appear to be governed
by a chain-of-being hierarchy where first person
is considered to be higher than second or third.
The ungrammaticality of clauses, such as (9a), is due
to the fact that a Nitinaht subject must be higher
on the chain-of-being hierarchy than any other
nominal in the same clause.
  In Tiwa (Allen and Frantz 1978) passive clauses
are restricted to instances where the agent is third
person. Thus, while both the active (10a) and
passive (10b) are possible, (11a) and (12a) do not
have a passive counterpart.

(10) a. Seuanide-ø ø - liora - mu - ban
     man - nom 3s:3s-lady - see - past
     'The man saw the lady'.

   b. Liorade-ø   ø - mu - che - ban seuanide
     lady - nom 3s -see - pass-past man
     - ba
     - inst.
     'The lady was seen by the man'.

(11) a. I -   mu - ban
     1s:2s- see - past
     'I saw you'.

   b. *A - mu - che - ban na - ba
     2s - see - pass - past 1s - inst.
     ('You were seen by me'.)

32

THE PERSONAL PASSIVE

(12) a. Bey   - mu - ban
         2s:1s - see - past
         'You saw me'.

     b. *Te - mu - che - ban   ĩ - ba
         1s - see - pass - past 2s - inst.
         ('I was seen by you'.)

The A and P of an active clause are crossreferenced
on the verb in Tiwa. In (11a) i stands for first
person acting on second. The crossreferencing
pronoun bey in (12a) denotes second person acting on
first. In the case of third person acting on third,
as in (10a),the form of the pronoun is ∅. In the
Tiwa passive the agent in the instrumental case
appears in clause final position if the subject is
non-pronominal, and clause initially if the subject
is expressed only in terms of a crossreferencing
pronoun. Compare (10b) with (13b). In passive
clauses only the subject is crossreferenced on the
verb. The crossreferencing pronouns used are the
same as with intransitive clauses indicating that
the subject of a passive clause is an S (not an A)
and that the clause is intransitive. Unfortunately,
as the crossreferencing pronoun for third singular
is ∅, this is not very obvious in (10b). Compare
(13b) and (14b) with (15b) for a clear example
    When both NPs in a Tiwa clause are animate and
third person the passive is optional. When third
person acts on first or second person, the passive
is obligatory. Clauses such as (13a) and (14a) are
ungrammatical.

(13) a. *Seuanide-∅   mu - ban
         man   - nom ? see - past
         ('The man saw me'.)

     b. Seuanide-ba te - mu   - che - ban
         man - inst 1s - see - pass - past
         'I was seen by the man'.

(14) a. *Seuanide-∅   mu - ban
         man - nom ? see - past
         ('The man saw you'.)

     b. Seuanide-ba a - mu - che - ban
         man - inst 2s - see - pass - past
         'You were seen by the man'.

There are no crossreferencing pronouns which denote
third person acting on first or second person.

THE PERSONAL PASSIVE

(15) a. Te - 'aru - we
ls - cry - pres
'I'm crying'.

b. A - 'aru - we
2s - cry - pres
'You are crying'.

Allen and Frantz propose a chain-of-being hierarchy
for Tiwa, similar but not identical to Nitinaht, where
first and second person outrank animate third person
which in turn outranks inanimate third person.

Although Indo-European languages do not possess
chain-of-being hierarchies similar to those in the
above mentioned languages, passive clauses with
first or second person agents are rather unusual.
This is due to the fact that first and second person
pronouns tend to be taken as topics and, therefore,
are unlikely candidates for passive agents (cf.7.1.1)

The Amer-Indian languages are not the only
languages in which passive clauses do not always have
corresponding actives. Lexical adjectival passives
or *stative* passives like the following English
examples from Sinha (1973:619) are another case
in point.

(16) a. Certain kinds of wild life are
distributed throughout Alaska.

(17) a. You are hereby acquitted by the finding
of this court.

The clauses (17b,c) and (18b,c) can hardly be taken
as the active counterparts of (17a) and (18a).

(16) b. Forces of nature distribute certain
kinds of wild life throughout Alaska.

c. God distributes certain kinds of wild
life throughout Alaska.

(17) b. I acquit you by the finding of this court.

c. The finding of this court acquits you.

The clauses (17a) and (18a) differ substantially
from the other examples quoted in this section, for
the lack of a corresponding active is not due to
hierarchical restrictions, but as will be argued in
4.2 springs from the fact that they are actually
active not passive.

34

THE PERSONAL PASSIVE

2.1.2 The Passive as an Agentless Construction

It is often stated that the primary function of the passive is to avoid mentioning an agent. Poutsma (1926:101-2), for instance, says:

> The principal occasion of the use of the passive voice is the desire of the speaker to avoid mentioning the primary participants of the action, because not clearly known, or thought of no importance, or because involving the possibility of compromising him (or them).

Similar statements can be found in Jespersen (1933), Kruisinga (1925), Curme (1931) and the works of other traditional linguists. The same claims have been made more recently especially by Eckman (1974) and Haiman (1976).

In many languages passive clauses cannot appear with an overt agent, e.g. Latvian, Urdu, Kupia, Classical Arabic, Amharic, Igbo, Tera, Sonrai, Fijian, Atjnjamathanha, Cupeño, Cora, Huichol, Cahuilla, Shoshoni and Pepecano. In other languages the agent can, but need not be specified. Statistical data reveal that agentless passives are far more common than those with an agent. See for instance Huddleston (1971) and Krauthamer (1981) for data on English, Duskova (1972) for information on Czech and Brinker (1971) and Schoenthal (1976) for German.

However, in the Dravidian language Kota (Subbiah 1972) and the Austronesian languages Palauan (Josephs 1975; Wilson 1972) and Indonesian (Chung 1976a,b) it appears that passive clauses always occur with an agent.[6] Consider the following examples from Kota.

(18) a. A:n   puj - (n)   tavircpe:-n
     I:nom   tiger-acc   killed - 1s
     'I killed the tiger'.

     b. Puj-∅   en-a:l   tavircpe:-n
     tiger-nom I-inst   killed-1s
     'The tiger was killed by me'.

In Kota the P of the active appears in initial position in the passive and the agent is expressed in the instrumental case. There is no additional marking on the verb. The situation in Palauan is slightly more complex.[7] In active transitive clauses formed from perfective verbs, the verb agrees

35

THE PERSONAL PASSIVE

in person and number with the P.

(19) a. A sęchęlik a s-il-sęb-ii   a blai
        my friend   stem-past-burn-3s   house
        'My friend burned down the house'.

A separate set of suffixes is used to indicate this
agreement. In passive clauses formed from perfective verbs the verb agrees in person and number both
with the subject and the agent.

(19) b. A blai a lę-s-il-sęb-ii
        house 3s(hyp)-stem-past-burn-3s
        a sęchęlik
        my friend
        'The house was burned down by my friend'.

The agreement between the agent and the verb is
shown by a set of prefixes referred to by Josephs
as hypothetical prefixes. There is no additional
passive marking on the verb.
    In active clauses with imperfective verbs the
verb does not agree with any of the NPs.

(20) a. A Droteo a me -ng   -uiu a hong
        Droteo   vb.m.-imperf-read   books
        'Droteo is reading the books'.

In the corresponding passive the verb agrees only
with the agent.

(20) b. A hong a lo   -ng   -uiu a Droteo
        books   3s(hyp)-imperf-read   Droteo
        'The books are being read by Droteo'.

When the agent is first or second person it is
marked solely by the hypothetical pronouns.

(21)   A   a ku   - ng   - uiu
        books 1s(hyp) - imperf - read
        'The books are being read by me'.

Third person agents are typically specified as in
(19) and (20). Even if the agent is not expressed
by a specific NP in clause final position, it is
expressed by the hypothetical pronouns,which are
obligatory.
    Indonesian has two types of passive clauses;
a canonical passive (22b) (cf. p.53) and a
restricted passive (22c) (Chung 1976a:59-61).

THE PERSONAL PASSIVE

(22) a. Saja mem - batja buku itu
     I   tr - read   book the
     'I read the book'.

   b. Buku itu di   - batja (oleh) saja
      book the pass - read   by   I
      'The book was read by me'.

   c. Buku itu ku - batja
      book the I - read
      'The book, I read'
      'The book was read by me'.

In this second type of passive - the restricted
passive - the agent is obligatory. The subject of
the restricted passive must be definite and the
agent a first or second person pronoun. In (22c)
the NP book has been moved to initial position, the
verb appears in the stem form without the transitive
marker and the agent is optionally cliticized to the
verb in preverbal position.

In each of these languages the passive is
indicated exclusively by means of the agent which
is encoded in the verb. Although the operation of
syntactic rules clearly indicate that the P of the
active functions as the subject of the passive, the
agent retains one of its subject properties, namely
it governs agreement. The passive agent,therefore,
cannot be said to function as an oblique constituent
in these languages in the same sense as in English.

As passive clauses in these languages (only the
restricted passive in the case of Indonesian)
require an agent, it is no longer possible to say
that all passive clauses are basically agentless or
that the main function of the passive is to omit
specifying the agent. Josephs (1975:143), in fact,
states that in Palauan 'passive clauses are used
when the speaker feels it necessary to mention both
agent and patient, but focuses on the latter'.
Conversely,one could argue that the obligatory agent
retention puts into question the passive nature of
these clauses. This second line of argument is
undermined by the fact that even in languages which
freely allow the omission of the agent phrase some
passive agents are obligatory.

In the Bantu language Kinyarwanda, for example,
(Kimenyi 1980:135) passive agents which correspond
to semantically non-agentive subjects (23) or appear
with verbs that have cognate (24) or abstract
objects must be overt.[8]

37

THE PERSONAL PASSIVE

(23) a. Úmwáana   a-rwaa-ye   Ínkóróra
       child   3s-be-sick-asp   cough
       'The child has a cough'.

   b. Ínkóróra i-rwaa-w-e   n'úúmwáana
       cough   3s-be sick-pass-asp by child
       'The cough is had by the child'.

   c. *Ínkóróra i-rá - rwáa-w - e
       cough   3s-pres-be sick-pass-asp
       ('The cough is had')

(24) a. Umukoôbwa y-a-roos-e   inzosí mbi
       girl   3s-past-dream-asp dreams bad
       'The girl dreamed bad dreams'.

   b. Inzozí mbi z-a   -roos-w-e   'n
       dreams bad 3pl-past-dream-pass-asp by
       umukôobwa
       girl
       'Bad dreams were dreamt by the girl'

   c. *Inzozí mbi z -a -roos -w -e
       dreams bad 3pl-past-dream-pass-asp
       ('Bad dreams were dreamt')

In Olutsootso (Dalgish 1976a,b), another Bantu
language, the agent in passive clauses with locative
subjects is also obligatory (cf. p.72). Similarly
in Finnish, a language which possesses two types of
personal passive, the agent in what Östman (1981:
286) calls the "long passive" must be specified.

(25) a. Pojat   rakastivat   tyttoja
       boy:nom:pl   love:past:3pl girl:partit:pl
       'The boys loved the girls'.

   b. Tytot   olivat   poikien
       girl:nom:pl were   boy:gen:pl
       rakastamia
       love:pass:pl
       'The girls were loved by the boys'.

Interestingly enough even in a language such as
English in which the majority of passive clauses
found in the literature are agentless (70% –
Jespersen 1933: 121; 80% – Svartvik 1966) in certain
cases it is not possible to omit the agent in a
passive clause. Consider the following examples
from Mihailovic (1966:123-4).

38

THE PERSONAL PASSIVE

(26) a. On his death his daughter succeeded him.
b. On his death he was succeeded by his daughter.
c. *On his death he was succeeded.

(27) a. An even worse insult followed his first one.
b. His first insult was followed by an even worse one.
c. *His first one was followed.
d. *His first insult was followed.

(28) a. His parents brought him up.
b. He was brought up by his parents.
c. *He was brought up.
d. He was brought up in Cambridge.

(29) a. Miss Perkinson played the part of the mother.
b. The part of the mother was played by Miss Perkinson.
c. *The part of the mother was played.
d. The part of the mother was played well.

In (26) the omission of the agent phrase results in an incomplete message. In (27) the agent is not deletable for it is inanimate and not semantically agentive. When the verb <u>follow</u> is used with an animate agent no such restrictions hold. The agent in (28) and (29) can be omitted only if a prepositional phrase or adverbial is used instead of the agent. The optional character of the agent thus seems to depend on both the linguistic and extra linguistic context of utterance.

The problem of agent deletion or omission in languages like English is an extremely interesting one. We will return to this problem in our discussion of the pragmatics of the passive in ch.7.

2.1.3 Word Order and Morphological Marking of Passive Clauses

In the examples of passive clauses given so far the passive clauses differ from actives:

a) in terms of the order of NPs: English (ch.1, 1) Polish (ch.1, 8), Ngarluma (1), Russian (2), Dhangar-Khurux (3), Nitinaht (8), Tiwa (10), Kota (18), Palauan (19), Kinyarwanda (23).

b) by the appearance of a special marker on the verb

THE PERSONAL PASSIVE

(Ngarluma, Dhangar-Khurux, Nitinaht, Tiwa) or the use of a participle forms of the verb (English, Polish, Russian, Finnish)

c) by the presence of an additional verb (English, Polish, Russian, Finnish)

d) by a change in nominal marking (English, Polish, Russian, Finnish, Nçarluma, Dhangar-Khurux, Nitinaht, Tiwa, Kota).

None of these properties alone can be used as a basis for defining passive constructions for none features in all passive clauses.
It has already been pointed out in the discussion of Indonesian, Palauan and Kota that in these languages the passive verb does not take a special passive marker.[9] A change in the position of NPs is similarly not a universal feature of passive clauses for in languages such as Maithili (30), an Indo-Aryan language spoken in the Jakpur area of Nepal (Williams 1973:398), the Dravidian languages Kannada (Dryer 1981), Malayalam (Mohanam 1982:582) the Mayan languages Quiche (31), Cakchiquel (Norman 1978) and Tzotzil (Cowan 1969:9) and Basque (Lafitte 1962) the order of NPs in passive clause may be identical to that of active clauses.

Maithili

(30) a. Ram həmra ciTThi bhej-I-ək
       Ram me:dat letter send-asp-3s
       'Ram sent the letter to me'.

     b. Ram dwarə həmra ciTThi bhej-əl
        Ram by   me:dat letter send-pass
        gel   chəl
        go:asp:3s was
        'The letter was sent to me by Ram'.

Quiche

(31) a. X - ø - u - ramij lee chee lee achih
        asp-3sP-3sA-cut   the tree the man
        'The man cut the tree'.

     b. X - ø - rami - x lee chee r-umal lee
        asp-3sS-cut-pass the tree 3s-by the
        achih
        man
        'The tree was cut by the man'

THE PERSONAL PASSIVE

The Philippine languages Cebuano (Bell 1976;1983) and Kapampangan (Mirikitani 1972) as well as the Formosan languages Amis and Seediq (Starosta 1973) may also display similar order in actives and passives.[10]

The existence of languages such as Maithili, Tzotzil etc. in which active and passive clauses may display the same order of constituents is regarded by proponents of RG as primary evidence against Chomsky-type definitions of the passive i.e. in terms of word order and the preposing or postposing of NPs. As in these languages the order of NPs is identical in actives and passives, it is not possible to view the passive as a movement rule similar to the passive in English or other European languages. It should be noted, however, that in Slavic and Romance although the passive subject typically occurs clause initially and the passive agent clause finally, the positions of agent and patient may be the same as in the corresponding active as evidenced by the following examples from Polish and Spanish (Suñer 1982)

Polish

> (32) Przez studentów został ogłoszony
>   by   students became proclaim:p.part
>   strajk
>   strike
>   'A strike was proclaimed by the students'.

Spanish

> (33) Seran   transmitidos por television (...)
>   will:be broadcast   by   television
>   programas de castellano y   matematicas
>   programmes of Spanish   and mathematics
>   'Programmes of Spanish and mathematics
>   will be broadcast by television'.

The problem of the order of constituents in active and passive clauses will be resumed in our discussion of the pragmatics of the passive in ch.7.

In the vast majority of case marking languages both the NPs in active clauses undergo a change in case marking in the corresponding passive. The P of the active surfaces in the passive in the nominative case while the agent typically takes the instrumental case as in: Russian, Czech, Tiwa, Kannada, Tamil,

41

THE PERSONAL PASSIVE

Kota, Malayalam and Yindjibarndi. In a few languages the passive agent takes genitive (Classical Greek, North Russian, Lithuanian, Finnish, Armenian), or accusative/dative case marking (Lardil). The passive agent may also occur in the locative case (Ngarinjin), locative-instrumental (Ngarluma) and ablative (Armenian, Latin).

In some languages such as Greenlandic Eskimo, Gugu Yalandji and Imbabura Quechua the case marking of only one of the NPs is changed in the passive clause. In Greenlandic Eskimo (34) and Gugu Yalandji (35) the P of the active "retains" the same case marking in the passive by virtue of the fact that these languages are morphologically ergative i.e. both S and P take the absolutive case.

Greenlandic Eskimo

(34) a. Aŋut-ip arnaq - ∅   taku - vaa
man-erg woman - abs see - ind:3s:3s
'The man saw the woman.

b. Arnaq - ∅ aŋuti - $\begin{Bmatrix} mit \\ mut \\ mik \end{Bmatrix}$ taku -

woman-abs man - $\begin{Bmatrix} abl \\ al \\ inst \end{Bmatrix}$.   see -

$\begin{Bmatrix} tuu \\ niqur \end{Bmatrix}$-puq
pass-ind:3s
'The woman was seen by the man'.

Gugu Yalandji

(35) a. Danny-ngka mayi - ∅ nyadji - n
Danny-erg food-abs see-compl
'Danny saw the food'.

b. Danny-nda mayi - ∅ nyadji - dji - n
Danny-loc food-abs see - pass - compl
'The food was seen by Danny'.

The passive in Greenlandic Eskimo is built on the passive participle plus copula (q) a + u or on the abstract nominalizer - niq - meaning have with the suffix - qur. The passive agent is expressed by the ablative, allative, or instrumental (Woodbury 1977: 217). Note also that,as in Tiwa,the agreement suffixes indicate that the passive clause is intran-

42

THE PERSONAL PASSIVE

sitive. Compare (34b) and (36).

    (36) Aŋut-ǿ   autlar - puq
          man-abs go away - ind:3s
          'The man went away'.

In Gugu Yalandji (Hershberger 1964:47) the verb in
the passive appears with the suffix - dji - and the
agent takes the locative case.
    In Imbabura Quechua (37), in contrast to Eskimo
and Gugu Yalandji, it is the A of the active which
retains the same nominative case marking in the
passive (Cole and Jake 1978:81-2).

Imbabura Quechua

    (37) a. Ñuca - ca wawa - ta micu-chi-rca   - ni
            I:nom-top child-acc eat-caus-past - 1s
            'I fed the child'.

        b. Wawa - ǿ - ca ñuca - ǿ micu - chi -
            child-nom-top I- nom   eat-caus -
            shca   ca   - rca
            p.part be:3s-past
            'The child was fed by me'.

The Imbabura Quechua passive clause thus has two NPs
in the ǿ nominative. The -ca is a topic marker
which can be affixed onto any NP. In both the
active and passive clauses the verb agrees with the
subject.
    Changes in case marking cannot be viewed as a
universal feature of passive clauses, due to the
existence of languages such as Basque (38) in which
no such change occurs (**Perlm**utter and Postal 1977:398).

    (38) a. Piarres-ek egiń d -u -ǿ
            Peter-erg   made 3sP-have-3sA
            etchea-ǿ
            house-abs
            'Peter made the house'.

        b. Piarres-ek egina d -a   etchea-ǿ
            Peter-erg   made   3sS - is house-abs
            'The house was made by Peter'.

Although there is no change in nominal morphology in
the passive clause, the fact that the two clauses
(38a) and (38b) differ in structure is indicated by
the use of the intransitive auxiliary d-a, a form of
izan 'be', in (33b) contrasting with ukan 'have' in

THE PERSONAL PASSIVE

(38a) which appears in transitive clauses. Compare
(38b) with (39).

> (39) Aita-ø   ethorri d -a
>   father-abs come   3s-is
>   'The father has come'.

The intransitive auxiliary reveals that Piarresek
in (38b) is an S, not an A. Basque is a morphologically ergative language. Basque's ergativity can
be seen in both the case marking and crossreferencing pronouns.
 The crossreferencing pronouns are identical for
S and P NPs. In the example above (38) the third
person crossreferencing pronoun refers to etchea
'house'. The third person crossreferencing
pronoun for A NPs is ø as evidenced by (38a) and
also (40).

> (40) Aita-k   ikusi n -u ø
>   father-erg see   1sP-have-3sA
>   'The father has seen me'.

The examples of passive clauses cited above
reveal that languages differ in the number and type
of strategies utilized for marking passive constructions. In some languages, mainly the much discussed Indo-European ones, passive clauses differ
from their corresponding actives with respect to all
the four properties mentioned: word order, verbal
morphology, appearance of an additional verb and
case or prepositional marking of the nominals.
Passive clauses in other languages display only
some of these properties. But none of these
features is characteristic of all passive clauses.

2.2   Transitivity and the Personal Passive

Since it has always been tacitly assumed that
passive clauses are intransitive, this property of
the passive has rarely been discussed. Recently,
however, proponents of RG have singled out the
detransitivizing aspect of the passive as one of
the defining characteristics of this construction.
Postal (1977:275) states: 'Passive is a detransitivizing rule, since it allows an early direct object
to be a late subject and thus sanctions clauses
whose late strata do not contain direct objects.'
In the RG framework the intransitivity of passive
clauses is said to be a natural consequence of the
Chômeur Law previously the *Relational Anihilation*

44

THE PERSONAL PASSIVE

Law which states that: (Perlmutter and Postal 1983:9b)'if some nominal *Na* bears a given term relation in a stratum (c_i), and some other nominal *Nb* bears the same relation in the following stratum (c_i +1), then *Na* bears the chômeur relation in c_i+1'. In other words as the P of the active clause is promoted to subject in the passive the original subject is put en chômage. The resulting clause is intransitive.

Although this may not always be immediately apparent, Perlmutter and Postal's (1977) analysis appears to be quite correct with respect to passive clauses which do not have an obligatory agent and possess subjects corresponding to active Ps.[11] When only one obligatory participant is involved the passive is clearly intransitive. When the agent is overt the intransitivity of passive clauses is often indicated by morphological marking. For instance,in Tiwa (p.32) there are two sets of cross-referencing pronouns. One set is used for S NPs, the other set are portmanteau forms used for the particular combinations of A and P. In passive clauses (10b), (13b), (14b) the first set of pronouns is used signalling that the clauses are intransitive.

A similar situation exists in Alaskan Eskimo (Hinz 1944). Alaskan Eskimo has a complex system of verbal agreement. The agreement suffixes are phonologically fused with the particular mood suffixes. There are separate suffixes for nominals in S function and others for all the possible person and number combinations of A and P. The agreement suffix in the intransitive (41) is identical to that used in the passive clause (42).

(41) Mikilingok-ø   litnaurt-ok
    child-abs   learn-ind:3s
    'The child learns'.

(42) Tunto-ø   angût-mum   tokû-tsim-ok
    reindeer-abs man-terminalis kill-pass-ind:3s
    'The reindeer has been killed by the man'.

The passive in Alaskan Eskimo appears to be formed by the addition to the verb of the particles – umauk – tsimauk – ngauk – lutsek with the meaning 'have' or 'state of being'. The agent in the passive takes what Hinz calls the terminalis case or is not expressed at all.

In other languages such as Basque, Greenlandic Eskimo, Quiche, Cakchiquel, the Bantu languages

45

THE PERSONAL PASSIVE

(Chi-mwi-ni, Mashi and Maragoli) in transitive
clauses both A and P are marked on the verb by
separate crossreferencing pronouns or agreement
affixes. The presence of only one crossreferencing
pronoun or agreement affix on the verb in the Basque
(38) and Greenlandic Eskimo (34) indicates that
these passive clauses are intransitive. In addition
in Basque (but not in Greenlandic Eskimo) the form
of the crossreferencing pronoun is distinct from
that used in transitive clauses. The same holds for
Quiche (31) and Cakchiquel (43) (Norman 1978).

Cakchiquel

> (43) a. R-ik'in jun machät x - i - ru - sok -
>   3s with I   machete asp 1sP 3sA-wound
>   b'e - j ri   achin
>   inst-suf the man
>   'The man wounded me with a machete'.
>
>   b. R-ik'in jun machät x - i - sok - b'e -
>   3s-with I   machete asp-1sS-wound-inst
>   x   r-oma   ri achin
>   pass 3s-by   the man
>   'I was wounded with a machete by the
>   man'.

In these two languages, as in Basque, the crossreferencing pronouns operate according to an
ergative system i.e. one set of pronouns is used to
refer to S and P (∅ for third singular in Quiche,
i for first singular in Cakchiquel) and a separate
set is used for A NPs (u for third singular in
Quiche and ru for third singular in Cakchiquel).
The passive clauses in the two languages are intransitive. The verb being marked only for absolutive agreement with the S.
    There is therefore adequate support for the in-
transitivity of passive clauses with patient
subjects. The intransitivity of passives with
non-patient subjects is far more controversial.
    We will first examine the transitive/intransi-
tive status of passive clauses formed from
transitive or ditransitive verbs with recipient,
benefactive, manner or instrumental subjects
(2.2.1) and then proceed to discuss the controversial passive clauses formed from what appear to be
intransitive verbs (2.2.2).

46

THE PERSONAL PASSIVE

2.2.1   Transitive or Intransitive

Proponents of RG claim that only direct objects can become the subject of passive clauses. Therefore in RG all passive clauses with subjects corresponding to other than direct objects are derived not by a single passive rule, but rather by two rules. The first of these rules promotes the recipient, instrumental, locative etc. to a P and simultaneously demotes the original P to a chômeur (as a consequence of the *Chômeur Law* cf.p.45). The passive then promotes the derived P to subject and demotes the original subject to a chômeur. Under this analysis (44c) is derived from (44a) via (44b).

(44) a. Mary gave the book to John
     b. Mary gave John the book.
     c. John was given the book by Mary.

This is represented in (44d).

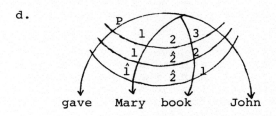

The passive clause is intransitive. It consists of only a "1" - <u>John</u> and two chômeurs - <u>the book</u> and <u>by Mary</u>.

The chômeur status of the passive agent is unquestionable, at least in most languages.[12] The chômeur status of the NP <u>the book</u> in (44) is far less evident. Perlmutter and Postal 1978, 1983b) Johnson (1974, 1977), Frantz (1977) and Klokeid (1977) present the following arguments as evidence that <u>John</u> and not <u>the book</u> is the P in (44b).

a) <u>John</u> immediately follows the verb which is the <u>unmarked</u> position for P NPs in English.
b) <u>John</u> like other P NPs is not preceded by a preposition in contrast to John in (44a).
c) <u>John</u> like other P NPs can appear as the subject of a passive clause (44c).

The NP <u>John</u> in (44b) is therefore considered to be

THE PERSONAL PASSIVE

promoted to P status by a rule called dative-
movement or indirect-object advancement. This rule
is said to apply not only to recipients but also
benefactive NPs as in (45).

(45) a. Susan bought a dress for Barbara.
b. Susan bought Barbara a dress.
c. Barbara was bought a dress (by Susan).

Further support for the fact that the subject of a
passive clause cannot correspond to the prepositional recipient or benefactive, but only to a basic
P or a P derived by dative-movement or indirect-
object advancement is given by (46).

(46) a. Harry revealed the facts to the F.B.I.
b. *Harry revealed the F.B.I. the facts.
c. *The F.B.I. was revealed the facts by
Harry.

The verb in (46a) does not allow dative-movement
and consequently the passive is also ungrammatical.
Verbs like add, describe, praise, entrust, produce,
demonstrate, dedicate, distribute, transfer, select,
allow, donate etc. behave in a similar fashion
(Green 1974). Relational grammarians and other
linguists as well argue that the ungrammaticality
of both (46b and c) would be unaccounted for if the
recipients or benefactives were allowed to be promoted to subject directly.
    This analysis obscures the fact that, as pointed
out by Ziv and Sheintuch (1979), the derived P in
(44b) and (45b) does not have all the syntactic
properties of P NPs in English, i.e.:

a)   It cannot be tough-moved like P NPs. Compare
     (47) and (48).

     (47) a. It is easy to please this girl.
          b. This girl is easy to please.

     (48) a. It is easy to tell this girl a story.
          b. *This girl is easy to tell a story.

b)   It cannot appear in the "of" phrase of
     gerundive nominals

     (49) a. They read books.
          b. The reading of books.

     (50) a. They give people presents.

48

THE PERSONAL PASSIVE

(50) b. *The giving of people presents.

c)   It cannot be relativized according to the same
     strategies as P NPs

(51)   The girl ⎧ ∅ ⎫ you met in the park
                  ⎨ that ⎬ is here.
                  ⎪ whom ⎪
                  ⎩ who ⎭

(52)   * The girl ⎧ ∅ ⎫ I gave flowers is here.
         *   ⎨ that ⎬
         *   ⎪ who ⎪
         ??   ⎩ whom ⎭

d)   It cannot always be topicalized like P NPs.

(53)   Very exotic drinks they served at the
         party last night.

(54)   ? My next door neighbour I give a cheque
         every month, (but my landlord, I pay only
         once every three months).

Ziv and Sheintuch (ibid) argue that the ungrammatical examples above cannot be explained by reference
either to the number of objects or by fact that the
NPs in question are derived and not basic Ps,because
these factors do not affect the syntactic behaviour
of other P NPs.[13]
     Under the analysis proposed by Ziv and Sheintuch
the prepositionless NPs immediately following the
verb in (44b), (45b), (48a) and (50a) are indirect
objects not Ps. They claim that only these NPs
can in fact be considered as indirect objects in
English. The prepositional NPs in (44a), (45a) and
(46a),according to Ziv and Sheintuch,are not indirect objects, but oblique NPs. A comparison of
the syntactic behaviour of these prepositional NPs
with other oblique NPs reveals that they behave
similarly. Consider,for instance,the following
examples:

(54) a. Bill gave presents to the children.
     b. Susan knitted a sweater for the baby.
     c. She played the sonata on this piano.
     d. I get on with that teacher.
     e. They studied by candlelight.
     f. Margaret sat at the desk.

The underlined NPs in (54a) and (54b) are according

49

THE PERSONAL PASSIVE

to most linguists indirect objects. Those in (54c, d, e and f) are usually considered as oblique. All these NPs behave identically under passivization (55), tough-movement (56) and relativization (57) and (58).

(55) a. *The children were given presents to.
    b. *The baby was knitted a sweater for.
    c. *This piano was played a sonata on.
    d. *That teacher is got on with.
    e. *Candlelight is studied by.
    f. *The desk was sat at.

(56) a. Children are easy to give presents to.
    b. The baby is hard to knit a sweater for.
    c. This piano is difficult to play sonatas on.
    d. That teacher is easy to get on with.
    e. Candlelight is impossible to study by.
    f. The desk is impossible to sit at.

(57) a. The children to whom Bill gave presents ...
    b. The baby for whom Susan knitted a sweater ...
    c. The piano on which she played the sonata ...
    d. The teacher with whom I get on ...
    e. The candlelight by which they studied...
    f. The desk at which Margaret sat ...

(58) a. The children Bill gave presents to ...
    b. The baby Susan knitted a sweater for ...
    c. The piano she played the sonata on ...
    d. The teacher I get on with ...
    e. The candlelight they studied by ...
    f. The desk Margaret sat at ...

If the prepositional NPs in (44a), (45a), (47a) and (54a,b) are not indirect objects, but rather oblique NPs and if the term *indirect object* is assigned only to the prepositionless NPs, as those in (44b) and (45b), then passivization in English cannot be restricted to P NPs. However, the prepositionless NPs in (44b) and (45b) immediately following the verb can only be treated as indirect objects if there is, in fact, a direct object - P - in the same clause. Whether the book and a dress in (44b) and (45b) can be regarded as a P is highly questionable. Ziv and Sheintuch fail to point out that these two NPs do not possess all the properties typically assoc-

50

THE PERSONAL PASSIVE

iated with P NPs in English. Although NPs such as
the books in (44b) can be relativized (59) and
topicalized (60),like P NPs,they cannot be passivized (61), undergo tough-movement (62) or appear in
the "of" phrase of nominalizations (63).

(59) The books $\begin{Bmatrix} \emptyset \\ \text{that} \\ \text{which} \end{Bmatrix}$ Mary gave John ...

(60) The books from Holland I gave my best
friend, but the books from Italy I left
for myself.

(61) *The books were given John by Mary.

(62) *These books are hard to give John.

(63) *The giving of books John.

The situation is therefore by no means as
straight forward as implied by Ziv and Sheintuch
and other linguists who advocate the same approach.[14]
Under their analysis it would be necessary to claim
that either (44b) and (45b) are intransitive because
there is no P; or that they are ditransitive, but
the P NP does not have all the properties of a P.
The first analysis is unacceptable. The second
analysis entails abandoning the generalization that
all P NPs can passivize. If NPs such as the books
and a dress in (44b) and (45b) are treated as P NPs,
the underlined NPs in (64) have to also be regarded
as Ps.

(64) a. The book contains references to the
passive.
b. The job involves work.
c. My bookshelf holds many interesting
books.

The underlined NPs in (64) behave syntactically in
a similar fashion to the alleged P NPs in (44b) and
(45b). They cannot be passivized (65) but they
relativize (66) and can be topicalized (67) like
P NPs.

(65) a. *References to the passive are contained
by this book.
b. *Work is involved by this job.
c. *Many interesting books are held by my
bookshelf.

51

THE PERSONAL PASSIVE

(66) a. The references to the passive $\left\{\begin{array}{l}\emptyset \\ \text{that} \\ \text{which}\end{array}\right\}$ the book contains were very helpful.

(66) b. The work $\left\{\begin{array}{l}\emptyset \\ \text{that} \\ \text{which}\end{array}\right\}$ the job involves will be good for you.

c. The interesting books $\left\{\begin{array}{l}\emptyset \\ \text{that} \\ \text{which}\end{array}\right\}$ my book-

shelf holds were bought in Australia.

(67) a. References the book contains, real information it does not.
b. Work the job involves, but money it does not.
c. Books my bookshelf holds, literature it does not.

These examples can be viewed either as confirmation of the P status of <u>the books</u> and <u>a dress</u> in (44b) and (45b) or the reverse depending on how the linguist regards the underlined NPs in (64).

Both Perlmutter and Postal's analysis of ditransitive clauses in English and the analysis suggested by Ziv and Sheintuch suffer from a number of deficiencies. If passivization is to be regarded as the major distinguishing characteristic of P NPs then Perlmutter and Postal's analysis has to be preferred. If on the other hand passivization is to be viewed as a possible, but not necessary property of Ps and is "permitted" to apply to other than P NPs, then the approach advocated by Ziv and Sheintuch could be adopted.

The data from other languages reveals that Perlmutter and Postal's analysis of passivization works well for some languages, while an analysis along the lines of Ziv and Sheintuch is more appropriate for others. Consider first the Indonesian examples from Chung (1976a,b;1977).

(68) a. Orang itu meng - irim - (kan) surat
man the tr - send - ben letter
kepada wanita itu
to woman the
'The man sent a letter to the woman'.

b. Surat itu di - kirim-(kan) kepada
letter the pass-send-ben to

52

THE PERSONAL PASSIVE

```
wanita itu (oleh) orang itu
woman  the  by    man   the
'The letter was sent by the man to the
woman'.
```

(68) c.
```
Orang itu meng -irim-i wanita itu
man   the tr -send-ben woman  the
seputjuk surat
a        letter
'The man sent the woman a letter'.
```

d.
```
Wanita itu di - kirim  - i sebuah
woman  the pass-send - ben a
surat (oleh) orang itu
letter by    man   the
'The woman was sent a letter by the man'.
```

In (68b), the passive of (68a), <u>surat</u> 'the letter' is
the subject. The passive agent appears in a prepositional phrase with <u>oleh</u>. The passive marker <u>di</u>
is prefixed to the verb. In (68c) dative-movement
has taken place. As indicated by (68a,b),recipient
NPs in Bahasa Indonesia are preceded by the preposition <u>kepada</u>. The verb in some cases takes the
benefactive suffix - <u>kan</u>. Dative-movement reverses
the position of the P and the recipient or benefactive, deletes the preposition <u>kepada</u> and for some
verbs replaces the benefactive suffix - <u>kan</u> by - <u>i</u>
or ∅. That <u>wanita itu</u> 'the woman' is indeed a P in
(68c) is evidenced by the fact that:

a) it occurs to the immediate right of the verb as
unmarked Ps do in Indonesian.
b) it is prepositionless, a characteristic of core
NPs in Indonesian.[15]
c) it can appear as the subject of a passive
clause,as in (70d).
d) it can become the subject of the second type of
passive (cf. p.37),as in (69a) (Chung 1976b:60).

(69) a.
```
Wanita itu saja kirim - i surat itu
woman  the  I   send - ben letter the
'The woman was sent the letter by me'.
'The woman I sent the letter'.
```

If dative-movement does not apply the recipient or
benefactive cannot appear as the subject of this
second passive.

(69) b.
```
*Wanita itu saja kirim surat  itu kepada
woman  the  I   send letter the to
```

THE PERSONAL PASSIVE

('The woman was sent the letter by me').
('The woman I sent the letter to').

e) it can be replaced by the reflexive - <u>diri</u> 'self'
(70a) which only replaces P NPs. (70b) is ungrammatical.

(70) a. Orang itu meng - irim- i diri seputjuk
man the tr — send-ben self a
surat
letter
'The man sent himself a letter'.

b. *Orang itu meng - irim - (kan) surat
man the tr — send - ben letter
kepada diri-nja
to self-his
('The man sent a letter to himself').

f) it can be relativized by the same strategy that
applies to core NPs, i.e. by deletion of the
relativized noun and addition of the complementizer
<u>jang</u> (71a). The NP <u>wanita itu</u> cannot be relativized
in the same manner if dative-movement has not taken
place (71b).

(71) a. Tidak seorang pun suka kepada wanita
not someone even like to woman
jang ajah saja kirimi surat
comp father my send-ben letter
'No one likes the woman who my father
sent the letter'.

b.*Tidak seorang pun suka kepada wanita
not someone even like to woman
jang ajah saja kirim surat (kepada)
comp father my send letter to
('No one likes the woman who my father
sent the letter to').

On the other hand the NP <u>surat</u> 'letter' in (68c)
cannot undergo any of the syntactic rules mentioned.
It cannot appear as the subject of the first (72) or
the second type of passive (73).

(72) *Surat itu di-kirim-i oleh wanita itu
letter the pass-send-ben by woman the
('The letter was sent by the woman').

(73) *Surat itu saja kirim-i kau
letter the I send-ben you

54

THE PERSONAL PASSIVE

(73) ('The letter was sent you by me').
      ('That letter, I sent you').

Similarly it cannot be replaced by the reflexive
- diri (74) or undergo relative clause formation
(75).

(74) *Orang itu meng-irim-i   seputjuk surat
       man   the tr - send-ben a   letter
       diri
       self
       ('The man sent a letter himself').

(75) *Saja me-lihat surat jang Ali kirim-i
        I   tr-see   letter comp Ali send-ben
       kakak   saja
       sibling my
       ('I saw the letter that Ali sent my
       sister').

The NP surat in (68c) is clearly in RG terms a
chômeur. Passive clauses like those in (68d) are
intransitive. They do not contain a P NP.
    In Chi-mwi-ni (Kisseberth and Abasheik 1977) the
situation is similar to that in Bahasa Indonesia.
However, whereas Indonesian has both clauses containing a patient P and a recipient or benefactive
(68a) and clauses in which recipients and benefactives are promoted to P (68c) by dative-movement,
Chi-mwi-ni is said to have only the latter. Clauses
such as (76a) are ungrammatical in Chi-mwi-ni.

(76) a. *Wa:na   wa -zi - pele zibu:ku mwa:limu
          children S/A-P - gave books   teacher
          'The children gave the books to the
          teacher'.

     b. Wa:na   wa - m - pele mwa:limu
          children S/A - P - gave teacher
          zibu:ku
          books
          'The children gave the teacher the
          books'.

(77) a. Wa:na   wa - zi - bozele zibu:ku
          children S/A - P   stole books
          'The children stole the books'.

     b. Zibu:ku   zi - bozela   na wa:na
          books   S/A were stolen by children
          'The books were stolen by the children'.

55

THE PERSONAL PASSIVE

As evidenced by (77a) the P in Chi-mwi-ni;

a) is crossreferenced on the verb
b) immediately follows the verb
c) may appear as the subject of a passive clause.

In (76b) it is mwa:limu 'teacher' which is cross-referenced and immediately follows the verb. Only mwa:limu can appear as the subject of a passive clause (78a). The clause (78b) is ungrammatical.

(78) a. Mwa:limu $\emptyset$ - pela   zibu:ku na wa:na
        teacher S/A gave books   by children
        'The teacher was given the books by the
        children'.

    b. *Zibu:ku zi - pela na wa:na   kwa
        books   S/A - gave by children to
        mwa:limu
        teacher
        ('The books were given to the teacher
        by the children'.)

Under Perlmutter and Postal's analysis dative-movement would have to be viewed as obligatory in Chi-mwi-ni. Examples such as those in (76b) strongly support Dixon's (1979) claim that in ditransitive clauses either the semantic patient or the recipient or benefactive may be a P. Under Dixon's proposal (76b) would be considered as a basic clause not derived by obligatory dative-movement.

Another language which can be conveniently analyzed along the lines proposed by Perlmutter and Postal is Shona (Hawkinson and Hyman 1974). In Shona, as in Chi-mwi-ni, there are no three participant clauses containing an agent, patient, recipient or benefactive where the patient functions as a P. Shona unlike Chi-mwi-ni also allows four participant clauses with an agent, patient, recipient and benefactive. In these instances it is always the benefactive NP which displays the properties of a P not the recipient. Shona is an SVO language or AVP in the terminology adopted here. P NPs like the other core NPs appear without prepositions (79a).

(79) a. Mùrúmé á - kà   - nyórá tsámbà
        man 3s(an)S/A-past - write letter
        'The man wrote a letter'.

P NPs can be topicalized and passivized as evidenced

56

THE PERSONAL PASSIVE

by (79b,c)

(79) b. Tsàmbà á - kà - yí - nyórá
letter 3s(an)S/A-past-3s(inan)-write
'The letter, he wrote it'.

c. Tsàmbà yá - kà - nyór - w - à
letter 3s(inan)S/A-past-write-pass-asp
né mùrúmé
by man
'The letter was written by the man'.

In ditransitive clauses the benefactive or recipient
NPs typically appear immediately after the verb
which takes the applied affix -er/ir. Only these
NPs can be topicalized or passivized.[16] In clauses
with both recipient and benefactive NPs the benefactive is placed immediately after the verb (80a),
can be topicalized (80b) and passivized (80c). The
recipient cannot. Note that the recipient appears
with the preposition ku.

(80) a. Mùrúmé á kà -nyór - ér - á
man 3s(an)S/A-past-write-appl-asp
mwàná tsàmbà kù mùkâdzí
child letter to woman
'The man wrote a letter for the child
to the woman'.

b. Mwàná mùrúmé á - kà - mú - nyór-
child man 3s(an)S/A-past-3s(an)-write-
ér - á tsàmbà kù mùkâdzí
appl-asp letter to woman ·
'The child, the man wrote him a letter
to the woman'.

c. Mwàná á - kà - nyór - ér - ẃ -
child 3s(an)S/A-past write-appl-pass-
á tsámbà né mùrúmé kù mùkâdzí
asp letter by man to woman
'For the child was written a letter by
the man to the woman'.

The semantic patient tsámbà 'letter' in (80a) again
cannot undergo any of these rules.

In all the three languages discussed so far
passive clauses are intransitive. The semantic
patient in ditransitive clauses (only after dative-
movement in Indonesian) does not have the morphologi-

57

THE PERSONAL PASSIVE

cal or syntactic properties of a P NP. Instead these properties are displayed by the semantic recipient or benefactive. Only the semantic recipient or benefactive can become the subject of a passive clause. Since the semantic patient does not function as a P, passive clauses formed from ditransitive verbs in these languages are intransitive.

Unfortunately the above analysis of passive clauses based on dative-movement cannot be applied so easily to all languages. Japanese, for instance, does not appear to have a rule of dative-movement. The passive can apply to both kozutsumi and Hanako in (81a),(Shimizu 1975:530-1).

> (81) a. Taroo ga   kozutsumi o   Hanako ni
> Taroo nom package   acc Hanako dat
> okuru
> send
> 'Taroo sends a package to Hanako'.
>
> b. Kozutsumi ga Taroo ni Hanako ni
> Package   nom Taroo by Hanako dat
> okurareru
> send:pass
> 'The package was sent to Hanako by Taroo'.
>
> c. Hanako ga   Taroo ni kozutsumi o
> Hanako nom Taroo by package   acc
> okurareru
> send:pass
> 'Hanako is sent a package by Taroo'.

There is no intermediate stage between (81a) and (81c) where the recipient loses its dative marker as in English or Indonesian. In (81a) the semantic patient has the postpositional marking and position of P NPs. In (81c) it retains its postpositional marking and also may retain its position. It cannot undergo passivization for passivization cannot apply twice to the same clause.[17] What then is the status of kozutsumi in (81c)? Is the clause transitive or intransitive?

Defenders of the intransitive theory could argue that kozutsumi in (81a) has been demoted by an obligatory rule of dative-movement as in Chi-mwi-ni and Shona, but that it has not lost its morphological marking or the ability to passivize. This would entail abandoning the claim that passivization applies only to P NPs which few linguists are pre-

58

THE PERSONAL PASSIVE

pared to do. In any case the obligatory dative-movement analysis does not in fact work for Japanese, because not all recipients or benefactives can be passivized (Howard and Niyekawa - Howard 1976). The verbs <u>utta</u> 'sell', <u>katta</u> 'buy', <u>ageta</u> 'give', for instance, only allow the semantic patient to occur as the subject of a passive clause.

(82) a. Satoo-san wa   Tanaka-san ni
       Sato   top   Tanaka   dat
       syepado   o   utta
       German shepherd   acc   sold
       'Sato sold Tanaka a German shepherd'.

   b. Ano syepado   wa   Satoo-san
      that German shepherd   top   Sato
      kara Tanaka-san ni   urareta
      by   Tanaka   dat sell:pass
      'The German shepherd was sold to Tanaka by Sato'.

   c. *Tanaka-san wa   Sato-san ni syepado
       Tanaka   top   Sato   by German
          o   urareta
       shepherd acc sell:pass
       ('Tanaka was sold a German shepherd by Sato').

It is difficult to argue that these verbs are exceptions to dative-movement for there is no real evidence for dative-movement in the first place. It appears that the passive can apply directly to recipient NPs in Japanese. Does this mean that (81c) has to be regarded as transitive?

The only way this conclusion could be avoided is if it is assumed that when a recipient or benefactive NP of ditransitive clauses becomes the subject of a passive clause in Japanese (and Kinyarwanda, Mashi, Maragoli which will be discussed below) both the former A and the P are demoted, i.e. that the derivation of (81c) is not (81d) but (81e).

(81) d.

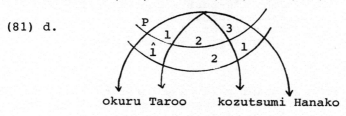

THE PERSONAL PASSIVE

(81) e.

P, 1 2 3 / 1̂ 2̂ 1

okuru   Taroo   kozutsumi   Hanako

The fact that passivization does not apply twice to
the same clause can be viewed as partial justification for the derivation in (81e). Such a derivation
although possible for Japanese cannot, however, be
postulated for the Bantu languages Kinyarwanda, Mashi,
Maragoli, Chicewa or Haya since in these languages
the semantic patient in clauses corresponding to (81c)
retains its characteristic P properties.

In Kinyarwanda (Gary and Keenan 1977, Kimenyi
1980), for example, both recipients and benefactives
possess exactly the same properties as P NPs, namely:

a)   they are not marked by prepositions
b)   they can be pronominalized by an infix which
immediately precedes the verb root and agrees in
noun class with the controller
c)   they can be reflexivized by inserting an invariant -i-
d)   they can appear as the subject of a passive
clause
e)   they can be relativized.

These common properties are illustrated in the following examples from Gary and Keenan (ibid). Only
clauses with P and recipient NPs are given. Note
that, as in Shona, the affix er / ir is attached
to the verb whenever a recipient or benefactive is
present.[18]

a)   lack of prepositional marking

  (83) Yohani y-ø - oher - er - eje
     John 3s-past - send - appl - asp
     Maria Ïbaruwa
     Mary letter
     'John sent a letter to Mary'.

b)   pronominalization

  (84) a. Yohani y - a-y- oher-er -eje Maria
     John 3s - past 3s send-appl-asp Mary
     'John sent it to Mary'.

60

THE PERSONAL PASSIVE

   b. Yohani y - a   - mw - oher - er -
      John   3s - past - 3s pass send-appl -
      eje ibaruwa
      asp letter
      'John sent her the letter'.

c)   reflexivization

   (85) a. Yohani y - ∅ -   i - kubis - e
         John   3s - past-refl- strike asp
         'John struck himself'.

       b. Yohani y - a - yi - oher - er -
         John   3s -past - refl- send - appl -
         eje ibaruwa
         asp letter
         'John sent himself a letter'.

d)   passivization

   (86) a. Ibaruwa y - ∅   - oher -er   -ej - w -
         letter 3s - past - send -appl -asp-pass-
         e   Maria na Yohani
         asp Mary by John
         'The letter was sent to Mary by John'.

       b. Maria y - ∅ - oher - er - ej -
         Mary 3s - past- send - appl - asp -
         w   - e ibaruwa na Yohani
         pass - asp letter by John
         'Mary was sent a letter by John'.

e)   relativization

   (87) a. N - a -bon-ye ibaruwa Yohani y - ∅ -
         ls-past-see-asp letter John 3s-past-
         ohér - er -eje Maria
         send - appl-asp Mary
         'I saw the letter that John sent Mary'.

       b. N - a - bon - ye Maria Yohani y - ∅ -
         lst-past-see-asp Mary John 3s-past-
         ohér-er -eje ibaruwa
         send-appl-asp letter
         'I saw Mary to whom John sent a letter'.

The NP ibaruwa in the passive clause (86b) can be
relativized (86c) and pronominalized (86d) indicating that it has not lost its P properties.

61

THE PERSONAL PASSIVE

    (86) c. Ibaruwa Maria y - ∅   ohér - er - ej -
         letter Mary 3s-past-send - appl-asp-
         w - e
         pass-asp
         'The letter that Mary was sent'.

         d. Maria y - ∅ - y - ohér - er   - ej -
         Mary 3s-past - 3s - send - appl - asp -
         w - e
         pass - asp
         'Mary was sent it'.

Passive clauses such as (86b) and their equivalents
in the other Bantu languages mentioned have to be
considered as transitive. There is no dative-
movement and when the recipient or benefactive is
promoted to the subject of a passive clause the P NP
continues to behave like a P. It is not possible
to say that dative-movement is obligatory and that
is why there are no clauses in the language where
the recipient or benefactive NPs are headed by a
preposition and do not have all the properties of
P NPs, because such an analysis would not account
for the fact that ibaruwa in both (83) and (86b)
does not lose any of its P properties. Passive
clauses with instrumental subjects in Kinyarwanda
(88a) and Maragoli (89) and manner and accompaniment NPs in Mashi (90a) similarly have to be regarded as transitive.

Kinyarawanda

    (88) a. Ikaramu y-∅-andik   - ish - ij -
         pen   3s -past-write - appl - asp -
         w   - e   ibaruwa na Yohani
         pass-asp   letter by John
         'The pen was written with a letter by
         John'.

Maragoli

    (89)   Ikalamu ya-handik - ir - w - a ibalwa
         pen   3s -wrote - appl-pass-asp letter
         'The pen was written-with a letter'.

Mashi

    (90)   Obusime   bwa-ganir-ir   - w - a -
         happiness 3s -told - appl-pass-asp -

62

THE PERSONAL PASSIVE

```
mo      abana    endibi
man     children story
'In a happy way were told the children
stories'.
```

The above clauses are said to be derived by first
advancing the instrumental or manner NP form an
oblique position in the clause to immediate postverbal position with simultaneous deletion of the
accompanying preposition and then promoting these
constituents to subject. Thus (88a), for example,
is derived from (88b) via (88c).

```
(88) b. Yohani  y-∅ - andik - se   ibaruwa
        John    3s -past-write-asp letter
        n-ikaramu
        with-pen
        'John wrote the letter with a pen'.

     c. Yohani  y-∅ - andik-ish-ije     ikaramu
        John    3s -past-write-appl-asp pen
        ibaruwa
        letter
        'John wrote-with the pen a letter'.
```

In (88c) the instrumental NP and the patient possess
the characteristics of P NPs in Kinyarwanda. Both
can be pronominalized, reflexivized, topicalized,
relativized and passivized. Note again the applied
suffix. When the instrument is promoted to subject
via the passive as in (88a) the patient retains all
of its P properties. The same applies to the patients in the Maragoli (89) and Mashi (90a). Such
passive clauses, like those with recipient and
benefactive subjects, provide strong evidence against
the claim that all passive clauses are intransitive.
   As recipients and benefactives and also instrumental, manner and accompaniment NPs (the latter
only after oblique-advancement) in the respective
Bantu languages possess the properties of P NPs,
Gary and Keenan (1977) argue that the languages
should be analyzed as allowing two or even three Ps
(89b) or (91) in the same clause.
Maragoli
```
(89) b. A - ganir-ir-a      obusime    abana
        3s -told-appl-asp happiness children
        endibi
        stories
        'She told in a happy way the children
        stories'.
```

THE PERSONAL PASSIVE

Mashi

(91) A-yerek-er-a John omwana
   3s -showed-appl-asp John child
   ensanamu
   picture
   'He showed the picture to the child
   for John'.

Such an analysis would save the generalization that the passive can apply only to Ps. It would constitute a viable solution to the problem if the passive were in fact confined to Ps. The discussion in 2.2.2 will reveal that this generalization cannot be maintained for in the Bantu languages oblique NPs can be passivized directly without prior advancement to "2". Moreover, since under Gary and Keenan's proposal it would still be necessary to distinguish between those Ps which can appear with mono-transitive verbs and those Ps which can occur only in ditransitive clauses with the applied affix, we see little justification for their analysis.

The status of recipients, benefactives, instrumentals, and manner and accompaniment NPs in the Bantu examples discussed is indubitably an issue in need of further investigation. However, even if all these NPs were to be regarded as Ps, passive clauses such as (86), (88a), (89) and (90a) have to be treated as transitive. The Bantu data have forced Perlmutter and Postal (1983b) to accept this conclusion.[19]

It must be pointed out that a transitive analysis of the passive clauses discussed above entails a re-evaluation of the status of A NPs. If the existence of a P NP implies the presence of an A NP, then Maria in (86b) has to be treated as an A. If Maria is taken to be an A this A is not semantically equivalent to an A in active clauses. In active clauses an A NP is a potential controller or agent. In this passive clause it is a recipient, while in other passives it could be a benefactive, manner, instrumental or accompaniment NP. Therefore, if the transitivity of (86b) is accepted it will be necessary to make a distinction between basic and derived A NPs.

2.2.2 The Personal Passive and Intransitive
   Clauses.

It is a well known fact that passive clauses can be formed not only from transitive and ditransitive verbs, but also from verbs which look like intran-

64

THE PERSONAL PASSIVE

sitive verbs as, for example in English.

(92) a. George Washington slept in this bed.
b. This bed was slept in by George Washington.

(93) a. The whole committee has argued over this plan.
b. This plan has been argued over by the whole committee.

Typical transitive verbs in English take non-prepositional objects. Note that one of the arguments for the "direct objecthood" of recipients or benefactives in clauses which have undergone dative-movement (cf. p.47) was the lack of prepositional marking. However, in view of the fact that most linguists define transitivity in terms of passivization, they argue that although clauses such as (92a) and (93a) seem to be intransitive, they are in fact either transitive or derived transitive.

Chomsky (1965), for instance, claims that <u>in this bed</u> in (92a) and <u>over this plan</u> in (93a) should be generated directly in the VP as in (94) and be treated as direct objects, while the underlined NPs in (95) and (96) which do not have a corresponding passive should be attached directly to "S" as in (97).

(94)
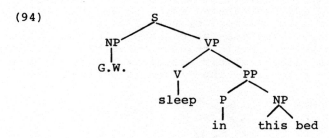

(95) a. John stepped up <u>the ladder</u>.
b. *The ladder was <u>stepped up</u> by John.

(96) a. Mark dashed into <u>the room</u>.
b. *The room was <u>dashed into</u> by John.

THE PERSONAL PASSIVE

(97)
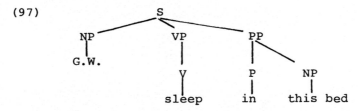

Lakoff (1970) proposes that NPs which can be passivized should be generated in deep structure as direct objects and that the prepositions should be introduced after passivization has applied by a rule called preposition spelling. Johnson (1974) considers the prepositions in (92a) and (93a) to be predicates and the NPs which follow them as direct objects. He gives the following underlying structure for (93a)-type clauses.

(98)
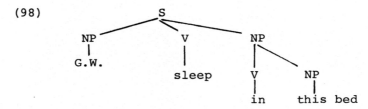

The surface structure is said to be derived by a rule of predicate raising which raises the verbal preposition to the role of verbal particle of the matrix verb. The passive can apply to the direct object like with basic transitive verbs. Perlmutter and Postal (1978) simply postulate a rule of oblique advancement to "2". Thus (93b) is derived as in (99)

(99)
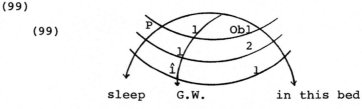

Perlmutter and Postal's proposal differs from that of the other linguists in that (93a) is not considered to be transitive. Only the passive (93b) is derived via a transitivizing rule.

All of these proposals, except for that of

THE PERSONAL PASSIVE

Chomsky, suffer from the same deficiency. There is no evidence that any of the suggested rules have taken place. For instance, as pointed out by Riddle et al. (1977), if Johnson's (1974) analysis were correct then the preposition should behave like a particle and undergo optionally particle-movement. But it does not. Compare (100) and (101).

(100) a. Margaret looked up the address.
b. Margaret looked the address up.

(101) a. Max flew under the bridge.
b. *Max flew the bridge under.

Lakoff's (1970) proposal on the other hand entails that clauses such as (93c) should be acceptable.

(93) c. *George Washington slept this bed.

Again they are not. Perlmutter and Postal's (1978) analysis is questionable in the sense that the change from an oblique relation to direct object is not accompanied by a change in structure. In other words the rule is completely vacuous. It functions exclusively for the convenience of the linguists.

The position adopted by Chomsky is more promising. A number of linguists have suggested that whether or not a NP is conceived as being a direct object (P) depends on its use in the given linguistic and situational context. Riddle et al (1977), for example, state that:

the prepositional phrase tends to function as a direct object just in case it in itself is crucial to the complete description of the activity expressed in the verb, rather than merely indicating the time or place of an activity.

In (102) America is not likely to be affected in any detectable manner by the fact that Ann lived there, whereas the popularity of this cabin in (103) could well be enhanced by the numerous visits from dignitaries.

(102) a. Ann has lived in America.
b. *America has been lived in by Ann.

(103) a. Many famous dignitaries have lived in this cabin.

THE PERSONAL PASSIVE

(103) b. This cabin has been lived in by many
famous dignitaries.

The notion of affect thus according to Riddle et al.
(1977) is the main criterion which characterizes
direct objects. A similar view is shared by
Bolinger (1977) who claims that a NP will be regarded as a direct object and a clause as transitive
if the NP is viewed as genuinely affected by the
action of the verb.[20] He states that transitivity
'is not a feature of verbs, but a feature in them,
put there on occasion of use'.

The above analysis which treats NPs accompanying
superficially intransitive verbs as direct objects
or Ps just in case they can passivize appears to
work well for English. It can also be applied, for
instance, to Maori. In Maori, according to Chung
(1978), there are three classes of verbs: canonical
transitive, middle transitive and intransitive.
Canonical transitive verbs describe events which
produce a direct effect on the direct object.
Middle transitive verbs involve events that do not
affect the direct object immediately. In Maori the
P of a transitive verb is marked with the accusative
preposition i (104), that of middle transitive with
either i or ki (105) and (106). Intransitive verbs
may optionally co-occur with oblique NPs. The
examples (107) and (108) show that the prepositions
used with locative and source NPs have the same form
as those which occur with P NPs.

(104) a. Ka   inu   te tangata i   te wai
         t/asp drink the man   acc the water
         'The man drinks the water'.

(105) a. E   mōhio ana   te tangata ki te
         t/asp know prog the man   acc the
         reo Māori
         lg   Maori
         'The man knows the Maori language'.

(106) a. Kua   kite a   Hōne i   te hōiho
         t/asp see prop   John acc the horse
         'John saw the horse'.

(107) a. Ka   haere au i   te māunga
         t/asp go   I on the mountain
         'I walk on the mountain'.

(108) a. Ka   haere au ki te māunga
         t/asp go   I to the mountain

THE PERSONAL PASSIVE

'I go to the mountain'.

The clauses (104) - (107) have corresponding passives while the passive of (108a) is ungrammatical.

    (104) b. Ka   inu   - mia te wai e te
            t/asp drink - pass the water by the
            tangata
            man.
            'The water is drunk by the man'.

    (105) b. E   mōhio - tia ana te reo Māori
            t/asp know - pass prog the   Maori
            e te tangata
            by the man
            'The Maori language is known by the
            man'.

    (106) b. Kua kite - a   te hōiho e a
            t/asp see - pass the horse by prop
            Hone
            John
            'The horse was seen by John'.

    (107) b. Ka   haere - tia te   māunga e au
            t/asp go   - pass the mountain by me
            'The mountain has been walked on by me'.

    (108) b.*Ka   haere - tia te māunga e au
            t/asp go   - pass the mountain by me
            ('The mountain has been gone to be me'.)

The NP promoted to subject via the passive loses its prepositional marking and is placed in the position immediately after the verb. The agent is preceded by the agentive preposition e and the verb takes a form of the suffix -Cia. The difference between (107) and (108) is similar to that between (102) and (103) in English. The mountain in (107) presumably is viewed as affected by being walked on while in (108) it is not affected in a similar fashion. Chung (1978:174) sums up the above examples in the following manner. 'Assuming that the affected locatives of (107) are surface direct objects of their associated underlying intransitive verbs, the facts of (104) - (108) argue that the passive is restricted to NPs that are direct objects'. Obviously,it could just as well be argued that they are direct objects in the first place. The same cannot be said for Chicewa (Trithart 1975, 1979).

THE PERSONAL PASSIVE

Compare the following examples.

    (109) a. Jóni a - ná - (yí) - nyamul - a
            John 3s - past - (3s) - carry - asp
            m - phásá
            cl - mat
            'John carried the mat'.

         b. M - phásá i - ná - (yí) - nyamul-
            cl - mat 3s - past - (3s) - carry -
            idw - a ndí Jóni
            pass -asp by John
            'The mat was carried by John'.

    (110) a. Jóni a - ná - (pá) - khal - a
            John 3s - past - (on) - sit - asp
            pa - m - phásá
            on - cl - mat.
            'John sat on the mat'.

         b. *Jóni a - ná - (yí) - khal - á
            John 3s - past - (3s) - sit - asp
            pa - m - phásá
            on - cl - mat
            ('John sat on the mat'.)

         c. M - phásá i - ná - (yí) - khal - idw-
            cl -mat 3s - past - (3s) - sit - pass-
            á ndí Jóni
            asp by John
            'The mat was sat on by John'.

In Chicewa P NPs typically appear in postverbal
position, are not marked by a preposition and are
crossreferenced on the verb. Locative NPs are
preceded by a preposition. This preposition not the
NP is optionally crossreferenced on the verb.

    According to Trithart (1979), locative NPs differ
from all other NPs (including P NPs) in that they
can be pronominalized via verb final cliticization
as in (111).

    (111) A - ná - khál - á po
           3s-past - sit - asp - on there
           'He sat there'.

Unfortunately, Trithart does not state which pronominalization strategy is applied to other NPs.
Both the P NPs in (109a) and the locative NP in
(110a) can become the subject of a passive clause.
All subjects in Chicewa are obligatorily cross-

THE PERSONAL PASSIVE

referenced on the verb. In passive clauses like
(109b) the former P NP can be crossreferenced as
well. Thus the same NP is crossreferenced twice.
The clauses (109b) and (110c) differ only with
respect to the basic transitivity of the verb.
Although the subject in (110c) corresponds to a
locative in (110a), the crossreferencing pronoun in
(110c) is a P pronoun not a locative one.

The above examples provide strong evidence for
the analysis of passive clauses proposed by
Perlmutter and Postal. As P NPs differ from locative NPs not only morphologically, but also syntactically, if m-phásá in both (109a) and (110a) is
treated as a P, these differences will not be
accounted for. Under Perlmutter and Postal's
analysis m-phásá in (110a) is regarded as a locative.
The passive (110c) is derived by first advancing
the locative to "2".

However, neither Chomsky's (1965) nor Perlmutter
and Postal's (1978) analyses can be applied to
Hibena (Speed Hodges and Stucky 1979), Mashi
(Gary 1977a,b) Olutsootso (Dalgish 1976a,b) or
Malagasy (Keenan 1976b).[21] Access to passivization
cannot be taken as an argument for the P status of
a NP in these languages because locatives in Hibena
and Olutsootso and both locatives and instrumentals
in Mashi and Malagasy can advance directly to subject. Consider the following examples from
Olutsootso (Dalgish 1976a,b).

(112) a. Esie en-deer - aanga eBi-taBo
     I   ls-bring- t/asp cl.8-book
     mu-shi-iro
     loc-cl. 7-market
     'I bring the books in the market'.

     b. Mu-shi-iro   mu-leer-uung- w -
     loc-cl.7-market loc-bring-t/asp-pass-
     a - mwo eBi-taBo   neende esie
     asp-loc cl.8-book by   I
     'In the market is brought the books
     by me'.

(113) a. ABa-xasi   Ba-tsiits-aanga ha-mu-
     cl.2-women cl.2-go-t/asp loc-cl.3
     chela
     river
     'The women go near the river'.

71

THE PERSONAL PASSIVE

(113) b.   Ha-mu — chela ha-tsii -Buung-w-a-
           loc-cl.3 river loc-go - t/asp-pass-asp
           ho   neende aBa - xasi
           loc   by   cl.2 - women
           'Near the river is gone by the women'.

Core NPs in Olutsootso occur with a noun class
prefix. As indicated in (112a) and (113a) subject
NPs are crossreferenced on the verb. The form of
the crossreferencing affix, as in other Bantu
languages, depends on the noun class prefix of the
subject NP. Locative NPs take one of three prefixes:
ha- referring to general location 'near;, 'at',
xu- meaning 'on', 'onto', and mu- denoting 'in',
'inside'. In the passive (112b) and (113b) the
verb appears with a locative prefix indicating that
a locative is the subject of the clause. In addition a locative suffix is attached to the verb which
agrees with the derived subject. The passive marker
in Olutsootso is the infix u which becomes w by
glide formation. The agent of the passive, which
according to Dalgish cannot be deleted when locatives are passivized, appears in a prepositional
phrase with neende. The verb in (112a) is transitive, the one in (113a) under any definition of
transitivity not totally dependent on the passive
would have to be regarded as intransitive. The
locative NP does not behave syntactically like a P
NP which is manifested by its behaviour under pronominalization. In Olutsootso pronominalization of
P NPs involves a feature copying and deletion
process. An object prefix Bi - in (112c) agreeing
with the pronominalized NP in class appears after
the subject prefix on the verb and the pronominalized NP is deleted.

(112) c.   Esie en-Bi-leer   -aanga mu - shi
           I   ls-3pl-bring -t/asp loc -cl.7
           iro
           market
           'I bring them in the market'.

The pronominalization of locative NPs does not
result in the appearance of object prefixes. The
clauses (112d) and (113c) in which an object prefix
is inserted are ungrammatical.

(112) d.   *Esie en-mu-leer   - aanga eBi taBo
            I   ls-loc-bring - t/asp cl.8 books
            ('I there bring the books').

72

THE PERSONAL PASSIVE

(113) c. *ABa-xasi   Ba - ho   tsiits - aanga
        cl.2-women cl.2-loc go   - t/asp
        ('The women there go').

Rather when locatives are pronominalized the appropriate locative suffix is attached to the verb as in (112e) and (113d).

(112) e. Esie en-deer   aanga-mwo eBi - taBo
        I   1s-bring t/asp-loc cl.8-books
        'I bring the books in there'.

(113) d. ABa-xasi   Ba - tsiits - aanga - ho
        cl.2-women cl.2 - go   - t/asp   loc
        'The women go near there'.

Dalgish argues that verbs like: <u>tsiits</u> 'go', <u>cheend</u> 'travel, <u>mool</u> 'crawl', ku 'fall', <u>siil</u> 'jump', <u>siinji</u> 'stand', <u>tuux</u> 'come', ixal 'sit', and <u>rul</u> 'come out' which can only be followed by locative NPs could be regarded as transitive, if transitivity is defined on the basis of whether or not *terms* in the RG sense can follow the verb. He claims that locative NPs can be considered as *terms* in Olutsootso for similarly to terms:

a)   they take a class prefix while oblique NPs do not
b)   they may govern certain agreement phenomena: verbal locative suffixation, adjectival agreement and relativization marking
c)   they may hold grammatical relationships with their verbs in the sense that verbs can be marked to agree with locative NPs as subjects and dislocated objects
d)   they can be relativized
e)   they can occur as subjects and in some instances as direct objects of their verbs and thus undergo raising and tough-movement.

Dalgish states that if the test for transitivity is whether *terms* can follow verbs it is still necessary to distinguish between those verbs which can occur only with locative NPs and canonical transitive verbs. Under Dalgish's definition of transitivity, passivization of locative NPs in Olutsootso could be viewed as a natural consequence of their status as *terms*. Unfortunately, in other languages NPs which can be passivized do not display properties of *terms*. In Mashi (Gary 1977a,b), for instance, instrumental and locative NPs do not control any agreement

73

THE PERSONAL PASSIVE

phenomena, they cannot be topicalized or under
normal circumstances relativized. Thus it is not
possible to restrict passivization to *terms* universally, even if this notion is extended to encompass
NPs other than Ps (direct objects) and recipients
and benefactives. Note that Dalgish totally rejects
the idea of treating locative NPs as either basic
or derived Ps.

All the above mentioned linguists adhere to a
multiple level theory of clause structure. As it
is no longer fashionable to postulate abstract
underlying representations or abstract intermediate
structures, they have great difficulties with
restricting the passive to P NPs in all languages.
Linguists who recognize only one level of structure
face similar problems. If they assume that the
subject of a passive clause must be a P in the corresponding active, they are forced to differentiate
between a number of different P NPs: patient P NPs,
recipient P NPs, benefactive P NPs, locative P NPs
etc. These distinctions must be made because the
respective NPs have different morphological and
syntactic properties in most languages. If on the
other hand they assume that passive subjects need
not correspond to active Ps, they have to determine
the factors governing the passive. Some attempts
to do so will be discussed in ch.6.

The data, especially from Kinyarwanda, Mashi,
Maragoli and Olutsootso, prove that the passive
cannot be restricted to P NPs if P NPs are defined
by a cluster of morphological, syntactic and
semantic properties and not just in terms of the
passive. Only if P NPs and transitivity are defined
exclusively in reference to the passive, can passivization be viewed as an universal test for transitivity. It is hard to see anything wrong with such
a proposal. However, if it is assumed that a NP
can become the subject of a passive clause just in
case it is perceived to be a P, all attempts to
attribute certain other P properties to this NP have
to be abandoned. In other words, passivization can
be used as a test for transitivity only if it is
assumed that it is determined by transitivity.
Linguists who are not prepared to make this assumption have to accept the fact that although passivization is a reliable indicator of transitivity and
P NPs in the large majority of languages, it cannot
be used as a universal test for transitivity.

THE PERSONAL PASSIVE

2.3 Some Tentative Conclusions

In this chapter a number of properties attributed
to personal passives have been analyzed. We hope to
have shown that personal passives cannot be defined
universally in terms of word order, case marking,
verbal morphology or agentlessness. Nor can they
be restricted to transitive verbs whether basic or
derived or defined exclusively with reference to
P NPs.
    The only feature which unites all the passive
constructions discussed in this chapter is the non-
agentive character of the subject. This property
of passive clauses does not, however, suffice to
distinguish them from clauses such as (114).

    (114) a. John received a present.
          b. That suit fits you well.
          c. John resembles Fred.
          d. Mary is old.
          e. John died.

It cannot therefore be used as a basis for a
definition. How then can the passive be defined?
It appears that there are two courses of action
available. Either all hope of defining the passive
universally is abandoned or the term *passive* has to
be restricted in such a way that a definition will
be possible. We opt for the latter solution.
    In our discussion of the properties of the
personal passive we have been continually comparing
the passive to the active. That there is a direct
relationship between the active and the passive is
undeniable. That this relationship needs to be
expressed is similarly unquestionable. Must the
passive therefore be defined in relation to the
active? In our opinion there is no other alternative.
Only the juxtaposition of the active and the passive
can serve as a basis for a definition. A comparison of the two constructions reveals that:

    a) the subject of a passive clause corresponds
        to a non-subject in the active
    b) the overt or implied agent of a passive
        clause corresponds to a possible subject
        of an active clause.

These are the two characteristics which the personal
passives considered in this chapter share the only
exceptions being the Nitinaht (9b), the Tiwa (14b)
and the English (16a). The Nitinaht and Tiwa

75

THE PERSONAL PASSIVE

passive clauses do not constitute real counter – examples to the above characterization of the personal passive for although (9b) and (14b) do not have corresponding actives, passive clauses with third person participants do. The lack of actives corresponding to (9b) and (14b) is an incidental gap due to the specific constraints of the two languages and does not undermine the existence of a direct relationship between actives and passives. The English (16a) on the other hand cannot be dismissed in a similar fashion. In ch.4 it will be argued that consequently such clauses are not passive.

The relationship between actives and passives is typically expressed by means of a passive rule. This rule is said to demote the subject NP of the active to an oblique relation in the passive or delete it and simultaneously promote a non-agentive NP to subject. The statement of the relationship between the active and the passive in terms of such a passive rule is regarded by many linguists as untenable,for it implies that passive clauses are derived from actives or structures underlying actives. Psycholinguistic investigations suggest that this is not the case (Brown 1973; Maratsos and Abramovitch 1975). Therefore,linguists such as Shopen (1972), Freidin (1975a) and Bresnan (1978, 1982b), just to name a few, prefer to generate both actives and passives independently and relate the two constructions in the lexicon by means of a lexical or derivational rule. Nevertheless, irrespective of how the passive is generated in a grammar the actual relationship between the active and the passive remains the same. As our concern is not with how the relationship between actives and passives should be captured in a grammar, but rather with the nature of this relationship, the passive will be referred to as being derived by a passive rule. This view of the passive is adopted purely to facilitate description. No claim pertaining to the derivational priority of the active is intended.

The passive as a transformational or relational rule is generally conceived of as being composed of two "parts"; a promotion and a demotion. Some linguists regard promotion as the primary property of the passive (Chomsky 1965; Johnson 1974, 1977; Frantz 1977;Perlmutter and Postal 1977, 1978, 1983b), while others consider the demotion property of the passive as basic (Alisova 1969; Khrakovsky 1973; Keenan 1975; Comrie 1977a).

THE PERSONAL PASSIVE

Linguists who treat the passive primarily as a process of demotion view the promotion of a NP to subject as a secondary property of the passive which does not necessarily have to occur whenever passivization takes place. Owing to the fact that the promotion of NPs to subject is regarded as a possible but not necessary consequence of the passive, the definition of the passive does not depend on the original morpho-syntactic status of the promoted constituent. If a subject is demoted to an oblique position in the clause, then the construction is a passive irrespective of whether a P, recipient, benefactive, instrumental, locative NP or no NP is promoted to subject.[22] For those linguists who treat the passive primarily as a promotional rule, the morpho-syntactic status of the promoted NP is crucial since the passive is defined with reference to this NP.[23] Perlmutter and Postal originally defined the passive as a rule which promotes only direct objects to subject. Now they have acknowledged that in some languages recipient and benefactives may be promoted to subject directly as well. However, the passive is still, under their analysis, restricted in that it can only apply to direct objects and some recipients and benefactives.

As passivization cannot in actual fact be confined to P NPs and recipients or benefactives, both the promotional and demotional analyses appear to be equally appropriate. Under both approaches the problem of determining the exact structures to which the passive can apply has to be dealt with. The demotional analysis is preferable only in that it handles impersonal passives, which will be discussed in the next chapter, more adequately than the promotional view.

Under both the promotional and demotional definitions of passivization clauses such as (115) and (116) would also have to be regarded as passive.

(115) a. John moved the stone.
      b. The stone moved.

(116) a. Bill closed the door.
      b. The door closed.

Then term *anticausative* is used by Kholodovic (1969), Masica (1976) and Comrie (1977b) to describe the above type of clauses where an intransitive verb is derived from a basically transitive one with the P of the transitive verb corresponding to the S of the intransitive. There is nothing in either of the two

77

THE PERSONAL PASSIVE

definitions of passivization which would exclude
clauses such as the above. Naturally, in English
the verbal morphology of passive clauses is distinct
from that of anticausatives. This is not the case
in Russian, for instance, (Babby and Brecht 1975;
Comrie 1977b). Compare the following examples.

Russian

    (117) a. Anton - ∅   otkry-1   dver'
            Anthony-nom open-past door-acc
            'Anthony opened the door'.

         b. Dver'   otkry - la - s
           door-nom open-past-refl
           'The door opened'.

    (118) a. Oleg-∅   otkry-val   kalitk-u
            Oleg-nom open-imperf gate-acc
            'Oleg was opening the gate'.

         b. Kalitk-a otkryvala - s   Oleg-om
           gate-nom open-imperf-refl Oleg-inst
           'The gate was being opened by Oleg'.

The verb in the anticausative clause (117b) is
marked by the suffix <u>sja/š</u>. In the imperfective
passive (118b) the same suffix is used to mark the
verb as passive. The two clauses differ in that
whereas (118b) can occur with an agent, (117b) cannot. Passive clauses do not take an overt agent
in all languages. Therefore, the lack of an overt
agent cannot be regarded as the distinguishing
feature of anticausative and passive constructions.
Nevertheless, there is a difference between the two.
Although passive clauses need not have or in some
languages cannot have a specified agent, the existence of some person or thing bringing about the
situation is implied. The subject in passive clauses
is depicted as "bearing no responsibility" for
the situation or state in which it is in even if
logically it can or must be regarded as somehow
responsible (but cf. p.133). Anticausative constructions conversely express a situation which
appears to be brought about spontaneously. The
subjects in (115b) and (116b) seem to "bear responsibility" for the action expressed by the verb.
Although in reality <u>stones don't move</u> nor doors
<u>open or close</u> of their own accord, in the anti-
causative they are presented as if they did. The

78

THE PERSONAL PASSIVE

only agent which can be expressed in the anti-causative construction is the reflexive pronoun itself or themselves (in the plural) (119a). Note that a reflexive pronoun cannot typically appear in a passive clause (119b).

(119) a. The door opened itself.
b. *The door was opened by itself.

In fact a reflexive agent is somehow inherent in the anticausative.

If the implied agent of the passive clause is the only feature which distinguishes passives from anticausatives,any definition of personal passives has to include a statement about the agentive character of this construction.

2.4 The Passive in Philippine Languages.

The analysis of personal passives presented in this chapter has shown that personal passives have three properties in common:

a) they have a subject which corresponds to a non-subject in the active
b) the action or event expressed by the verb is brought about by some person or thing which is not the subject.
c) the person or thing if not overt is at least strongly implied and can function as a potential subject of the active.

Having established the above properties of personal passives it is now possible to discuss the status of the controversial non-actor focus constructions in the Philippine and Formosan languages and the cases of obligatory agent retention in the Austronesian languages, Indonesian and Palauan, and in the Dravidian language, Kota. Before proceeding to the main point of the discussion we will first briefly look at the structure of the clause in Philippine-type languages.

2.4.1 The Structure of the Philippine Clause

In contrast to the typical Indo-European languages the languages of the Philippines indicate by means of affixes on the verb what is the semantic role of the NP which in the majority of languages would be regarded as subject.[24] Consider the following

THE PERSONAL PASSIVE

examples from Tagalog (Schachter 1977).

(120) a. Mag   salis   ang babae
act(?) - will give   woman
ng bigas sa sako para sa bata
    rice   sack   child
'The woman will take rice out of a
the sack for a the child'.

   b. Aalis -   in   ng babae ang bigas
will take - pass(?) woman   rice
sa sako para sa bata
    sack   child
'A/the woman will take the rice out
of the sack for a the child'.

   c. Aalis -   an   ng babae ng bigas
will take - pass(?) woman   rice
ang sako para sa bata
    sack   child.
'A/the woman will take some rice out
of the sack for the child'.

   d. Ipag   - salis   ng babae ng bigas
pass(?)- will take   woman   rice
sa sako ang bata
    sack   child
'A/the woman will take some rice out
of a the sack for the child'.

In (120a) the verb prefix indicates that the
"subject" NP is an actor.[25] The _in_ suffix in (120b)
signals a patient subject while the _an_ _ipag_ affixes
indicate a locative and benefactive in subject
position. NPs in Tagalog are marked for semantic
roles by a set of prepositions. When a NP appears
in "subject" position its preposition is replaced
by _ang_ for common nouns, _si_ for singular proper
nouns and _sina_ for plural proper nouns.

    In recent years there has been a considerable
amount of controversy over the status of clauses
such as (120b,c,d). Linguists such as Bloomfield
(1917), Blake (1925), Constantino (1970), Perlmutter
and Postal (1978), Garry and Keenan (1977), Hopper
and Thompson (1980) and Givón (1981) use the label
passive to describe clauses like these. Wolfenden
(1961), Ramos (1974), de Guzman (1978) on the other
hand have suggested that terms like _objective voice,
dative voice, locative voice_ etc. should be used
instead. Other linguists like Otanes (1970),

80

THE PERSONAL PASSIVE

Hidalgo (1970), Schachter and Otanes (1972), Naylor (1975), Schachter (1976, 1977), Foley (1976), Foley and Van Valin (1976, 1977), Muller and Schwartz (1981) contend that the term *focus* should be used in preference to *voice*, to describe the organization of the Tagalog clause. They claim that ang is not the marker of subjects, but rather that it indicates 'a NP brought into sharp perspective so that the attention of the listener is drawn closer to that constituent which is presumably in the speakers mind' (Hidalgo 1970:27). This NP is called *topic*, (Schachter, Otanes, Hidalgo) or the *referential peak* (Foley, Van Valin). The affixation on the verb is considered to be an indicator of the **seman**tic role not of the subject, but the referential peak or topic. Clauses like (120b) are said to be in goal or patient focus while those in (120c) and (120d) in directional or locative focus.

Most linguists who advocate an analysis of Philippine clauses in terms of a focus system claim that the focus system cannot be equated with an active/passive distinction in languages like English, for in contrast to English, no NP in a Tagalog clause can be considered as subject. This is indeed correct if a subject NP is viewed as the central grammatical relation in terms of which a language operates. However, under a more modest interpretation of the term it is possible to distinguish a subject. The properties commonly displayed by subjects in the much discussed European languages, indispensibility, control of coreferential deletion and reflexivization, addressee of imperatives, are associated with two distinct constituent types in Philippine languages - the topic or referential peak marked by ang in Tagalog, and the actor. In actor focus constructions, i.e. when the actor is the topic, all these properties are manifested by the same constituent. If the actor focus construction, is taken as the basic unmarked construction, the NP which is the topic - actor can be regarded as an S or an A. In other than actor focus clauses the NP marked by ang could be treated as the subject.

This is the analysis advocated by Perlmutter and Postal, Givón and Mulder and Schwartz for Tagalog, Bell (1983) for Cebuano and **Schwartz** (1976) for Ilocano. Linguists such as Schachter, Otanes, Foley and Van Valin on the other hand maintain that such an analysis cannot be substantiated. The main argument against recognizing a subject in Phillipine -type languages is that in terms of frequency and

THE PERSONAL PASSIVE

morphological marking the actor focus constructions
cannot be considered as basic clauses. In Philippine-
type languages when what would be considered to be a
P in an active transitive clause is definite, the
patient/goal focus construction is preferred. Hence
from the point of view of frequency it is the patient/
goal focus and not the actor focus which appears to
be basic. Schachter, Otanes, Foley and Van Valin
consider this to be compelling evidence against the
subject analysis. Mallinson and Blake (1980:53),
however, argue that from the morphological point of
view all the focus constructions are equally marked
or unmarked and consequently none can be considered
as the basic construction. They regard the ang-
nominal as subject irrespective of semantic role.
Thus although they differ from Perlmutter and Postal,
in not treating the actor focus clauses as basic
clauses, like Perlmutter and Postal, they do regard
the subject relation as valid for Philippine-type
languages. Although the ang-nominal possesses the
full set of subject properties only if it is
simultaneously the actor, Mallinson and Blake do not
consider this to be evidence against the subject
status of this constituent. The fact that it is
the actor which controls reflexivization, for
example, is taken to be an idiosyncracy of the
Philippine-type languages. Perlmutter and Postal
(1977, 1978) and Bell (1983) deal with the problem
of reflexivization in Tagalog and Ilocano respectively (the same facts hold for Ilocano) by claiming
that it is controlled not by the surface subject -
the ang-nominal - but by the initial subject which
by definition is the actor. Whichever of these
analyses is chosen, the fact remains that subject
NPs in Philippine languages are not identical
syntactically to subjects NPs in other languages.

2.4.2   Passive or Active

Assuming that a subject can be distinguished in
Philippine languages, can the non-actor focus
constructions be called passive? According to the
three properties enumerated on p.79 they can.
Nevertheless, the non-actor focus constructions
differ from typical passive clauses in three respects:[26]

   a) they exhibit a very high text frequency
   b) the agent is usually overt

THE PERSONAL PASSIVE

      c) they are highly transitive according to the
      ten parameters of Hopper and Thompson (1980).

a) The text frequency of passive clauses in a
language such as English is very low, in comparison
to that of patient/goal focus constructions in the
Philippine languages.[27] Hopper and Thompson (1980)
attribute the high text frequency of patient/goal
focus clauses in the Philippine language to the
fact that these languages utilize voice as a means
of discourse foregrounding and backgrounding,where
foreground is understood as the material which
supplies the main points of discourse and *background*
the part of a discourse which does not immediately
and crucially contribute to the speaker's goal, but
merely assists, amplifies or comments on it.[28] In
the Philippine languages the patient/goal focus constructions are strongly correlated with foregrounding. According to Hopper and Thompson affected and
individuated objects are much more likely to occur
in the foreground of discourse than in the background. One of the distinguishing features of
individuated constituents is definiteness and referentiality. As the topics in patient/goal focus
constructions are definite, Hopper and Thompson
argue that the Philippine languages represent an
extreme case where the statistical correlation
between definite objects and foregrounding has re-
sulted in a specialization of non-actor focus to
denote foregrounding.

b) The agent in non-actor focus clauses, again in
contrast to the passive agent in a language like
English is nearly always overt. In addition, as
mentioned above, it controls reflexivization and
therefore does not behave like a typical chômeur in
RG terms.

c) As the non-actor focus clauses typically occur
with a specified agent, the <u>ang</u> nominal is definite
and referential and the verbs tend to be punctual,
non-actor focus clauses are highly transitive. The
high transitivity of these clauses is,according to
Hopper and Thompson,again connected with their foregrounding function. Hopper and Thompson analyzing
a number of narrative texts in terms of their ten
parameters of transitivity, found that foregrounded
clauses average 8.0. points, while background clauses
only 4.1. points. These figures indicate that
there is a strong correlation between transitivity
and foregrounding and intransitivity and background-

THE PERSONAL PASSIVE

ing. Passive clauses in English on the other hand possess few of the high transitivity features and tend to be associated with backgrounding and not foregrounding.

The similarities between passive clauses and non-actor focus clauses are unquestionable. Do the differences between the two constructions warrant abandoning the term *passive* to describe the latter? This is largely a matter of interpretation.

In order for the relational definition to apply, the actor focus clauses have to be treated as basic. Similarly under Givón's definition of the passive. Givón (1979a:186) states:

> Passivization is the process by which a non-agent is promoted into the role of "main topic" of the sentence. And to the extent that the language possesses coding properties (position, case or prepositional marking, verbal agreement) which identify main topics as subjects and distinguishes them from topics, then this promotion may also involve subjectivization.

Givón quotes the Philippine non-actor focus clauses as examples of the passive *par excellence*. They can only be passive if the non-actors are viewed as being promoted to topic, not if this position is assumed to be their basic one. The fact that the Philippine languages have clauses in which the actor is the only possible topic e.g. transitive clauses with non-definite objects, such as (121), (Schachter and Otanes 1972) and intransitive clauses (122) (ibid), can be viewed as support for treating actor focus clauses as basic.

(121)   K   -um - ain si Juan   ng   isda
           act(?)-ate   John   fish
           'John ate some fish'.

(122)   Um   - upo si Juan
           act(?) - sat   John
           'John sat down'.

It must be noted, however, that there are also intransitive clauses with patient/goal or locative focus that do not permit an alternative actor focus[29] The situation is thus a very complex one.

If the term *passive* is abandoned with respect to the non-actor focus clauses in the Philippine languages, must it also be abandoned for the clauses

84

THE PERSONAL PASSIVE

in the Austronesian languages mentioned and also Kota? The clauses in these languages are similar to the Tagalog ones in that they are all highly transitive according to the ten parameters of Hopper and Thompson due to the obligatory agent, which retains some of its morphological subject properties and in Indonesian even syntactic subject properties. Since Indonesian has canonical passive clauses and unquestionable active ones, the second type of passive can hardly be disqualified on the same basis as the Tagalog clauses. There thus remains the case of the other two languages. The data on Kota is insufficient to allow anything conclusive to be said. In Palauan the subject of the passive does not have to be definite. Passivization can apply only to patient and some locative source or casual NPs. Consequently, its distribution is not comparable to that in the Philippine languages and, therefore, the arguments applied to the Philippine languages do not hold.

If passive clauses are "permitted" to have obligatory agents and be transitive in the sense of Hopper and Thompson in the three languages mentioned and also in Maori, is it feasible to abandon the term *passive* for the Philippine non-actor focus clauses? We think not.

Under a passive analysis of the Philippine non-actor focus clauses, the Philippine languages represent yet another case of direct advancement to "1", in RG terms, of recipients, benefactive, source, locative and instrumental NPs. Perlmutter and Postal (1978) appear to be quite happy to accept this.

The unusual properties of passive clauses in the Philippine languages and the other Austronesian languages mentioned have recently led linguists to claim that these languages are ergative, in the process of becoming ergative or were previously ergative (Egerod 1975; Payne 1982; Cooreman et al. 1983). A passive to ergative drift has been postulated for a number of Polynesian languages by Chung (1977, 1978) and S. Anderson (1977) who contend that ergative languages like Tongan and Niuean were originally accusative and possessed passive clauses which were reinterpreted as active ergative. This reinterpretation involved the loss of passive marking on the verb (or a reanalysis of a passive affix as a transitive affix) and the reanalysis of the passive agent as the active subject. The subject properties of the passive agent, whether morphological or syntactic, in Indonesian, Palauan and the Philippine languages, as well as the high dist-

THE PERSONAL PASSIVE

ribution of the passive in the latter could be viewed as evidence for this change. Nevertheless, the above languages cannot be treated as ergative under a synchronic analysis if the term *ergative* is used in the morpho-syntactic sense described in ch. 1.[30]

NOTES

1. The terms *inflectional* and *derivational* are also used to refer to such passives. However, we will continue to use the accepted terminology.

2. In Dhangar-Kurux neuter nouns are not crossreferenced on the verb, hence the lack of a crossreferencing pronoun in (3b).

3. The list is not meant to be exhaustive.

4. The agent of the agentless passive may also be ambiguous as to the inclusion of the speaker/writer and/or addressee (cf.7.2), while the active is not.

5. Dryer (1976) maintains that in the Algonkian language Ojibwa, as in Tiwa, passive clauses are obligatory if the patient is first or second person and the agent third person. The constructions he cites are not generally considered to be passive and, therefore, due to lack of adequate data, they are not quoted herein. Some linguists also regard the Athabascan language Navajo (Hale 1973) as having an obligatory passive; when both of the participants are third person, but differ in animacy, only the animate participant can occur as subject. The passive status of these type of clauses is also open to question (cf. Frishberg 1972). If the Philippine non-actor focus clauses to be discussed in 2.4 are taken to be passive, then these languages must similarly be seen as possessing passive clauses which lack active counterparts.

6. Achenese (Lawler 1977) is another Austronesian language often cited as having obligatory agent retention. The verb, as in Kota, agrees with the agent both in the active (Ia) and the passive (Ib)

```
I a. An+?  agam  nyan ji-nging        uring
       child male  that 3(younger)-see person
       agam nyan
       male that
       'The child saw the man'
```

THE PERSONAL PASSIVE

I b. Ur+ing agam nyan ji-nging   le an+?
    person male that 3(younger)-see by child
    agam nyan
    male that
    'The man was seen by the child'.

Note that there is no passive verbal morphology.
The agent appears in final position and is preceded
by the preposition le. The passive nature of (Ib)
has been questioned by Durie (1983), among others,
who claims that no change in grammatical relations
is involved in such clauses. We are in no position
to assess which analysis is the more appropriate one
and therefore do not include Achenese in the discussion.
    7.   The structure of the Palauan verb is par-
ticularly complex. Typically active verbs are
preceded by a verb marker, however, when a past
tense morpheme is infixed into the stem, as in (19a),
the verb markers are deleted. There is no perfective affix. The imperfective infix has a number of
forms depending on the verb. There is no marking
for present tense. The past tense marking again
depends on the verb. Passive verbs appear without
a verb marker and consist of a hypothetical pronoun,
optional tense or aspect marker, stem and, with
perfective verbs, subject agreement marker which
has the same form as the object agreement suffix of
active perfective verbs, ii for third person singular
in (19a,b). The agent crossreferencing pronouns and,
in fact, the verb forms in the passive are called
"hypothetical" by Josephs (1975), for they are
typically used in conditional clauses to express a
hypothetical situation or event. The pronouns have
a number of variant forms depending on tense and
aspect. The particle a before the verbs and nouns,
according to Josephs, introduces a VP or NP.
    8.   Kinyarwanda is very unusual in allowing the
objects of verbs such as have, weigh, measure and
cost and cognate objects to be passivized. (Kimenyi
1980:128). Kinyarwanda, similarly to Indonesian,
also possesses a non-canonical passive which
disallows agent deletion (Kimenyi ibid: 141-6).
This passive is restricted to cases where the verb
has only two arguments which are full NPs not be-
longing to the same semantic category (e.g. animate).
However, this is an impersonal passive not a personal
one. Although the former subject looses its subject
properties, the only subject properties acquired by
the P are verb agreement and initial position.
    9.   There is also no passive verbal marking in

THE PERSONAL PASSIVE

the Kinyarwanda impersonal passive mentioned in fn.8 and in the similar non-canonical Swahili passive (Whiteley 1968, Givón 1972:274). If Foley's (1976) analysis of Fijian is accepted (cf. ch.1, fn.8) and the affixes on the verb are taken to be transitive affixes not passive ones, as claimed by Clark (1973), then Fijian is yet another language with no passive verbal morphology. According to Gerdts (1980), the verbal suffix -m in the Halkomelem passive (a Salish language spoken in British Columbia) is similarly not a passive marker, but an intransitivizing suffix found in other intransitive clauses.

10. The passive status of what are commonly known as focus constructions in the Philippine and Formosan languages is highly questionable (cf.2.4).

11. The languages with obligatory agents in the passive will be discussed in 2.4.

12. Under the earlier versions of RG, a chomêur by definition could not bear any grammatical relation to the verb. This view had to be modified due to the fact that in languages like Palauan, Kota and also Kapampangan, the passive agent shows agreement with the verb. In addition, in the Philippine languages and also North Russian for example, the passive agent performs an active role in the operation of syntactic rules.

13. The examples (56) to (63) are taken from Ziv and Sheintuch (1979).

14. Ziv and Sheintuch quote the following linguists who advocate a similar approach: Onions (1904), Poutsma (1926), Jespersen (1927), Kruisinga (1931), Fries (1952), Halliday (1968) and Quirk et al. (1972).

15. Note, however, that the P demoted by dative movement in (68c) is also prepositionless. Some Bahasa-Indonesian speakers claim that the by-phrase in a passive clause similarly need not be always preceded by the preposition oleh.

16. Hawkinson and Hyman (1974) state that the semantic patient may be topicalized or passivized in some ill defined circumstances.

17. Costa (1975) claims that passivization can apply twice in Italian (cf.5.2). Timberlake (1982) gives an example of an impersonal passive of a personal passive in Lithuanian and according to Keenan (1982), so does Noonan (1978) from Irish.

18. The affixes er, ir, ish and i are attached to the verb in the Bantu languages whenever a recipient, benefactive, instrument, locative, manner or accompaniment NP loses its prepositional marking and acquires the syntactic properties of a P NP.

88

THE PERSONAL PASSIVE

This affix is typically referred to as the applied affix.

19.   Perlmutter and Postal actually only regard passives with recipient and benefactive subjects as transitive. They contend that (88a), (89) and (90) are intransitive. Under their analysis, when an instrument, manner or accompaniment NP is promoted to "2", as in (88c), for example, the original "2" is demoted to a "3". They are "forced" to adopt such an analysis in view of the *Stratal Uniqueness Law* which is: 'no stratum can contain more than one "1"-arc, one "2"-arc or one "3"-arc' (Perlmutter and Postal 1983b:92). Their solution while appropriate for the Kinyarwanda (88c), both "2s" and "3" having the same morphological and syntactic properties, runs into problems once clauses with both patients and recipients, as well as a derived "2s" are considered, such as (89) or (91). If the original "2" is demoted to a "3", (89) and (91) would possess two "3s", breaking the *Stratal Uniqueness Law*.

20.   The notion of affect will be discussed in more detail in 6.1. It must be pointed out that not all direct objects can be seen to be affected by the action portrayed, nor are all affected NPs direct objects.

21.   The structure of the Malagasy clause is in many ways similar to that of the Philippine languages. Keenan (1976b) argues that, unlike in the Philippine languages, it is possible to distinguish a subject and that what he regards as the goal voice (clauses with patient or recipient subjects), circumstancial voice (clauses with locative, instrumental and benefactive subjects) and intermediary voice (clauses with "weak" instrumentals) can in no way be regarded as basic. Whether this indeed is the case is debatable.

22.   This is not quite correct. The clauses must have an implied or overt agent as well. This will be discussed presently.

23.   Although generally speaking there is not *a priori* reason why the passive should be stated in terms of the morpho-syntactic status of the promoted NP, Perlmutter and Postal attempt to do so because they want to distinguish the passive from clauses such as (V), which they claim involve sporadic advancement to "1"   (cf. p.209 ch.6).

V. a. $5 bought a lot of heroin in 1827.
   b.   1939 found the U.S. on the brink of disaster.

THE PERSONAL PASSIVE

24. The remarks below do not apply to at least one of the Philippine-type languages, namely Chamorro (Topping 1973) which has non-focus clauses as well as focus clauses. Although the verbal affixes, as in Tagalog, indicate the semantic role of the NP in focus, the focus clauses are not basic clauses, according to Topping, but fullfil the function of English clefts. Compare the non-focus (VIa) with the actor focus (VIb) and (VIc) and the patient/goal focus (VId).

VI. a. Si Juan ha li'e' i palao'an
        Juan he saw the woman
        'Juan saw the woman'.

    b. Si Juan I - um - i'e'   i palao'an
        Juan - act/foc - saw the woman
        'Juan is the one who saw the woman'.

    c. Si Juan man-li'e'   palao'an
        Juan act/foc   - saw woman
        'Juan is the one who saw a woman.

    d. L-in-i'e   i palao'an as Juan
        - gl/foc - saw the woman   Juan
        'It was the woman that Juan saw'.

The man- prefix in (VIc) as opposed to the -um- infix in (VIb) is used when the object in actor focus clauses is indefinite. Unlike in Tagalog, patient/goal focus clauses are not obligatory when the object is definite, even within the focus systems. (VIa) is not a left-dislocated clause (cf.7. 1.2), but an unmarked transitive clause. All subjects in non-focus clauses occur with a coreferential pronoun. (cf. Topping for details). Since the non-focus clauses in Chamorro are basic, the problems with establishing a subject do not arise. However, whether or not the patient/goal focus clauses and the ma- clauses (VII) (Topping uses the label passive to describe the latter) should be regarded as passive, is another question.

(VII). Ma-   lalalatde i patagon
        pass?   scold   the child
        'The child is being scolded.

The ma- clauses do not occur with a coreferential pronoun and the agent, according to Topping, is never expressed overtly.
    Cooreman (1982) and Cooreman et al. (1983) give

90

THE PERSONAL PASSIVE

quite a different analysis of Chamorro clause structure. They regard (VIa) as ergative, (VIb) as an alternative non-ergative, but less frequent transitive clause, (VIc) as antipassive and (VId), as well as (VII), as passive. A similar analysis is suggested for Tagalog (cf.fn.30).

25. Although most NPs which fall under the category actor are agentive, the term is also used to refer to experiencers or even abstract NPs.

26. The same holds for Maori (Chung 1978). Although Maori clause structure is more similar to Indo-European clause structure than that in the Philippine languages, in the sense that it is possible to distinguish S, A and P, passive clauses occur more frequently than active ones, and in narratives appear to be the norm for canonical transitive clauses. Nevertheless, Chung argues that the passive in Maori is a passive in the RG sense and demonstrates that it can be conveniently dealt with in terms of changes in grammatical relations. In addition, in contrast to the Philippine languages the passive agent does not possess any subject properties. Chung attributes the frequency of the passive in Maori to the fact that it is a late rule which takes affect only after conditions on other rules (i.e. Equi-NP deletion, relativization and clefting) have been satisfied. Despite the exceptionally high text frequency, passive clauses, according to Chung, should be considered as derived from the active.

27. The text frequency of the English passive is, however, relatively high as compared to other European languages (cf. ch.7)

28. Hopper (1981) makes the same claim for Classical Malay.

29. Bell (1983) suggests that within RG such clauses can be dealt with if they are derived from underlying unaccusative structures (cf.6.2) She also points out that the identification of actor nominals with the underlying grammatical subject is not equivalent to the claim that the initial subject is the actor in all sorts of sentences, because in verbless sentences (equational, attributive and existential) there is no actor.

30. Cooreman et al. (1983), however, regard the Tagalog patient/goal focus clauses as either ergative or passive and the actor focus clauses as antipassive. Ergative and passive clauses are distinguished in terms of word order; verb-agent-patient clauses being regarded as ergative and patient-verb-agent clauses as passive. _Ang_ is

91

THE PERSONAL PASSIVE

considered to be the marker of the absolutive and
ng/nang as either ergative or oblique.

Chapter Three

IMPERSONAL PASSIVES

3.0   General Remarks

What is an impersonal passive has been a point of
contention for some time. Most linguists regard
impersonal passives as subjectless constructions.
Others hold that impersonal passives do have a
subject, but only either a dummy one like the Dutch
er (2b) or a covert indefinite human one. In addition, linguists differ in the importance they
assign to verbal morphology. For some, a clause
must have passive verbal morphology (whatever that
is) in order to be classified as an impersonal
passive. Others make no such restriction. As a
result, constructions which have been labeled as
impersonal passives by some linguists have been
called active by others.
  Impersonal passives in contrast to personal
passives have not been widely discussed or documented. They appear to be less common than personal
passives. However, future research may reveal that
they are far more frequent than was previously
thought. Impersonal passives have been attested in
all branches of Indo-European and in the Finno-
Ugric, Altaic, Dravidian, Niger-Congo, Nilo-Saharan,
Yuman and Uto-Aztecan families.
  Few attempts have been made to classify the
type of impersonal passives found in natural languages. The most comprehensive classification in
the existing literature is that of Khrakovsky (1973:
67) who divides impersonal passives into four broad
groups on the basis of the presence or absence of
a form word in subject position, and the type of
verbal morphology used:

a) Impersonal passives without an overt subject
and verbal morphology distinct from that used in

93

IMPERSONAL PASSIVES

the closest corresponding active as, for instance, in Turkish (George and Kornfilt 1977:70).

(1) a. Hasan-ø   otobüse-e   bin-di
      Hasan-nom   bus-dat   board-past
      'Hasan boarded the bus'.

     b. Otobüse-e   bin-il-di
      bus-dat   board-pass-past
      'The bus was boarded'.

The NP <u>otobüse</u> does not have the nominative marking typical of subject NPs in Turkish. Nor does it govern subject-verb agreement. The verb in the passive clause appears with the passive affix <u>il</u> or <u>in</u> subject to vowel harmony.[1] No agent can be expressed in the Turkish impersonal passive.[2]

b) Impersonal passives with a form word in subject position and verbal morphology distinct from that used in the closest active counterpart as in Dutch (Kirsner 1976:387).

(2) a. De   jongens   fluiten
      the boys   whistle
      'The boys whistle'.

     b. Er   wordt   door   de   jongens
      there become by   the   boys
      gefloten
      whistle:p.part.
      'There is whistling by the boys'.

The verb in (2b) is in the past participle form, accompanied by the auxiliary verb <u>worden</u> 'become'. The subject of the active clause appears in a prepositional phrase with <u>door</u> in the passive.

c) Impersonal passives without an overt subject and active verbal morphology, for instance, in Russian (Khrakovsky 1973:67).

(3) a. Burj-a   povali-la   derev-o
      storm-nom knock over-past tree-acc
      'The storm knocked over the tree'.

     b. Bur-ej   povali-lo   derev-o
      storm-inst knock over-past:n. tree-acc
      'The tree was knocked over by the storm'.

IMPERSONAL PASSIVES

The NP derevo is not promoted to subject. It
retains its final position in the clause, and does
not govern verbal agreement. The subject of the
active clause is no longer in the nominative, but
rather in the instrumental, the case of passive
agents. The verb is in the third person singular
neuter form. The verbal morphology of the clause
is not thus as in canonical passive constructions.
Compare (3b) with (2b) in chapter two.

d) Impersonal passives with a form word in subject
position and active verbal morphology, as in French.

(4) a. Il vendit la maison
       He sold   the house
       'He sold a house'.

    b. On vendit la maison
       one sold   the house
       'The house was sold'.

Impersonal passives of the first type are by
far the most common and simultaneously the least
controversial. The passive status of the remaining
three has been questioned by one linguist or another.
The French on-clauses in particular, as their
equivalents with man in German and uno in Italian
are not generally considered to be passive. Nevertheless, they can be viewed as passive under some
definitions of the term.
What all the above clauses have in common is the
lack of a specified subject. Whether this is a
sufficient criterion for labeling them passive is
an issue which will be taken up in 3.2.
Since impersonal passives are typically viewed
as lacking a subject, they are seen as primary
evidence for the demotional definition of the passive mentioned in ch.2.3. Although the demotional
analysis is by no means uncontroversial, its merits
will be argued for throughout this chapter. In 3.1
two of the characteristic features of impersonal
passives will be discussed. The particular type of
structures called impersonal passive will be evaluated with respect to both the presence of a subject
and their passive status in 3.2. The final section
will be devoted to an appraisal of the promotional
and demotional definitions of the passive.

95

IMPERSONAL PASSIVES

3.1 Characteristics of Impersonal Passives.

Impersonal passives are said to differ from personal passives in two major respects i.e. in relation to transitivity and in relation to the type of agent that they may convey. Whereas personal passives are typically regarded as being restricted to transitive verbs, impersonal passives are primarily associated with intransitives.[3] The agent of personal passives may be human, animate, abstract or a natural force, while agents of impersonal passives are claimed to be restricted to humans.

It will be demonstrated below that neither the first, nor the second characteristic holds cross-linguistically. However, whereas the restriction to intransitives can be shown to be quite evidently invalid, the impersonal passive does appear to display a strong predilection for human agents.

3.1.1 Impersonal Passives and Transitivity

Many linguists assume that if a language has both personal and impersonal passives, the personal will be restricted to transitive verbs, the impersonal to intransitives. This is not the case. However, in German, Dutch, Latin and Turkish, such a distinction does appear to hold i.e. under some definitions of transitivity. Consider the following examples from German.

(5) a. Er   töte-te   den   Löwen
    he:nom kill-past:3s the:acc lion:acc
    'He killed the lion'.

    b. Der   Löwe   wurde von ihm
    the:nom lion:nom became by him
    getötet
    kill:p.part
    'The lion was killed by him'.

    c. *Es wurde   den   Löwen
    it became   the:acc lion:acc
    getötet
    kill:p.part
    ('The lion was killed').

(6) a. Der   Lehrer   half   dem
    the:nom teacher:nom help:past the:dat
    Schüler
    pupil:dat
    'The teacher helped the pupil'.

IMPERSONAL PASSIVES

(6) b. *Der   Schüler   wurde   vom   Lehrer
the:nom pupil:nom became by:the teacher
geholfen
help:p.part
('The pupil was helped by the teacher').

c. Es wurde   dem   Schüler
it became the:dat   pupil:dat
geholfen
help:p.part
'The pupil was helped'.

(7) a. Wir   tanz-ten   gestern
we-nom dance-past:1pl yesterday
'We danced yesterday'.

b.   ?

c. Es wurde   gestern   von   uns
it became   yesterday by   us
getanzt
dance:p.part
'There was dancing by us yesterday'.

d. Gestern   wurde   getanzt
yesterday became   dance:p.part
'Yesterday there was dancing'.

Under the most widely accepted view, transitive
verbs in German are verbs which take an object in
the accusative. Verbs which take an object in the
dative (6a) or verbs which require only one obligatory NP (7a) are regarded as intransitive. Thus,
a transitive clause, such as (5a), has a personal
passive counterpart (5b), but not an impersonal one
(5c). Conversely, from the intransitive (6a) or
(7a) only an impersonal passive can be formed, (6c)
and (7c). Note that the NP dem Schüler in (6c) is
not promoted to subject. This NP retains its dative
marking. The third person singular neuter pronoun
es is placed in clause initial position if no other
NP precedes the verb. Compare (7c) and (7d). Both
in the personal and impersonal passive, the verb
appears in the past participle and a form of the
auxiliary werden 'become' is introduced. An agent
may be expressed in both personal and impersonal
passives, but is less common in the impersonal passive than the personal one. The agent is preceded
by the preposition von if it is animate and/or regarded as "actively responsible" for the action expressed by the verb. If the agent is inanimate and

IMPERSONAL PASSIVES

not "actively responsible", the preposition <u>durch</u> is used.

In other languages, both personal and impersonal passives can be formed only from verbs which are regarded as transitive. In Kannada (Cole and Sridhar 1976), for instance, the transitive clause (8a) has a personal (8b) and an impersonal (8c) passive counterpart. The intransitive (9a) has neither.

(8) a. Krishna-∅-nu   Rāma-nannu
       Krishna-nom-3s Rama-acc-3s
       kond-an-u
       kill-3s-past
       'Krishna killed Rama'.

   b. Krishnanu-indu Ramu-∅
      Krishna 3s-inst Rama-nom
      ko-pattu-nu
      kill-pass-past
      'Rama was killed by Krishna'.

   c. Rama-nannu   kollālayitu
      Rama-acc:3s   kill:become:past
      'Rama was killed'.

(9) a. Magalu-∅   hādid-al-u
       daughter-nom   sing-3s-past
       'The daughter sang'.

   b.   ?

   c. *Hadalayitu
      sing:become:past
      ('There was singing').

The verbal morphology of the Kannada impersonal passive, unlike in German, is not the same as in the personal passive. The personal passive is formed by infixing the verb <u>padu</u> 'to experience', 'to suffer' the impersonal by infixing āgu 'to become' (Andronov 1969; Sridhar 1980).   Although an agent can be expressed in the personal passive, it is not possible to do so in the impersonal passive.

In languages such as Finnish, Lithuanian and Ute, impersonal passives are not dependent on the transitivity of the verb. The Finnish clauses (10b) and (11b) are both grammatical, (Whitney 1973; Comrie 1975, 1977a).

98

IMPERSONAL PASSIVES

Finnish:

    (10) a. Maija-ø   söi   kala-n
           Maija-abs eat:imperf:3s fish-acc
           'Maija ate the fish'.

        b. Syötiin   kala
           eat:pass.part fish
           'The fish was eaten'.

    (11) a. Me   elä-mme   hauskasti täällä
           we:nom live-pres:1pl pleasantly here
           'We live pleasantly here'.

        b. Täällä eletään   hauskasti
           here   live:pass.part pleasantly
           'One lives pleasantly here'.

The verb in the impersonal passive appears in its
passive participle form, which is constructed by
adding an/än, taan/tään to the infinitive stem, or
by vowel substitution, depending on the mood, aspect
and tense of the verb   (Atkinson 1969: 80-82).
The passive verb is not inflected for person. No
distinction between first, second and third person
can be made. This has been traditionally viewed
as one of the basic properties of impersonal passives. Although the NP kala in (10b) loses its
accusative marking in the passive, it does not function as a subject. It cannot govern verbal agreement and does not have the syntactic properties of
a subject.[4] When a clause like (12a) with a pronominal P is put into the impersonal passive (12b),
the pronominal NP appears in the accusative not the
nominative case.

    (12) a. Maija   söi   sen
           Maija:nom eat:3s it:acc/gen
           'Maija ate it'.

        b. Syöttiin   sen
           eat:pass.part it:acc/gen.
           'It was eaten'.

The accusative pronoun can be conjoined with the
unmarked (nominative, absolutive) NP of the impersonal passive, as in (13), indicating that both
NPs are Ps, (Comrie 1975:116).

99

IMPERSONAL PASSIVES

(13) Mikko ja minut otettin
Mikko and I:acc receive:pass.part
ystävällisesti vastuan
friendly manner
'Mikko and I were received in a friendly
manner'.

The case marking of non-pronominal NPs does not,
therefore, indicate as clearly as pronominal case
marking that no promotion has taken place in the
impersonal passive. As in Kannada, the verbal morphology in the impersonal passive differs from that
of the personal passive. Compare (10b) and (11b)
with (25b) in ch.2. The agent cannot be expressed
in the Finnish impersonal passive.

Impersonal passives, like personal passives,
cannot be defined with respect to the basic transitivity of the verb. They cannot be viewed as intransitive counterparts of the personal passive in
any sense. The transitivity of the verb does,
however, affect impersonal passives, but in relation
to the properties of the agent, not as a factor
determining their occurrence.

3.1.2 The Agent of Impersonal Passives

Impersonal passives, like personal passives, may
occur with or without an overt agent. Crossling-
uistic studies reveal that agentless impersonal
passives tend to predominate.

In the following languages impersonal passives
cannot take an overt agent: Ute, Nez-Perce, Mojave,
Kannada, Kolami, Bengali[5], Arabic, Turkish, Maasai,
Spanish, Italian. All these languages, apart from
Ute, Kolami, Bengali and Arabic, also possess personal passives which, with the exception of Nez
Perce, allow the expression of an agent. Thus
although languages exist in which both personal and
impersonal passives are agentless, there are no
languages which allow an agent in the impersonal
passive while not permitting one in the personal.
The lack of a specific agent and not the absence
of a subject is, in fact, for some linguists (e.g.
Frajzyngier 1982; Östman 1981) the feature determining their impersonal status.

The agent of impersonal passives in languages
which allow the overt expression of this constituent is typically human. The only exceptions come
from Russian, Lithuanian and Welsh (cf.6.1.2). In
the first two languages the agent may be a natural
cause and in Welsh an animate, but not necessarily

IMPERSONAL PASSIVE

human entity. Interestingly enough, with the exception of Lithuanian the only examples of impersonal passives with non-human agents are those formed from transitive verbs. All the instances quoted in the literature of impersonal passives of intransitive verbs either occur with a human agent or imply human agency.

Frajzyngier (1982) regards this as the basic characteristic of impersonal passives of intransitive verbs, which not only distinguishes these structures from personal passives, but also from impersonal passives of basically transitive verbs. He argues that impersonal passives of intransitive verbs differ in both function and syntactic properties from those formed from transitive verbs and consequently cannot be treated as the same phenomenon. Frajzyngier contends that the primary function of impersonal passives of intransitives is the indication of an unspecified human agent and thus questions the grammaticality of all passives of intransitives with an overt agent, suggesting that they should be viewed as presentative structures similar to the English there-clauses. This could be a potential analysis for languages with dummy constituents in the impersonal passive, such as German or Dutch, but not for Hindi or Bengali, which do not have surface dummies. Frajzyngier's claim will be considered in more detail in 3.2.3. For the present it will be enough to point out that the validity of his hypothesis is considerably undermined by the fact that the vast majority of impersonal passives of transitive verbs also contain verbs denoting human activities. Although impersonal passives of intransitive verbs appear to be confined to human agents, this particular characteristic does not necessarily entail treating them as a phenomenon distinct from their transitive counterparts.

3.2. The Subject of Impersonal Passives

The issue which lies at the core of the three most recent discussions of impersonal passives, namely Comrie (1977a), Perlmutter and Postal (1978) and Frajzyngier (1982) is whether or not these constructions possess a subject. Three solutions to the above problem have been proposed; that impersonal passives:

a) are subjectless
b) possess a dummy subject

IMPERSONAL PASSIVES

c)   have an indefinite human subject.

Each of these suggestions will be discussed in turn.

3.2.1   The Subjectless Analysis

Impersonal passives have been traditionally regarded as subjectless, since they do not possess a NP
with the morphological characteristics typical of
subject NPs. In the Russian (3b) and Kannada (8c),
given above, the only candidates for subject are
not in the nominative case, but in the accusative.
In Turkish, (1b) the relevant NP is in the dative,
not the nominative. In Finnish, (10b) the nonpro-
nominal NP is in the nominative, but does not govern
verbal agreement. Similarly, in Maasai (Keenan
1976a; Hollis 1970) although the P of the active
clause appears in postverbal position in the passive
typical of subjects, it does not govern verbal
agreement and retains its accusative tone marking.
Compare the following examples.

(14)   Aá-dol   nánú
       3s:1s-see   I:acc
       'He sees me'.

(15)   A-dol   nanú
       1s-see   I:nom
       'I see him'.

(16)   Aá-suj   nánú
       3s:1s-follow I:acc
       'I am followed'.

When third person acts on first or second person
singular, the prefix is áá. Note that in the passive clause, the same pref̄ix is used indicating that
nánú has not been promoted to subject.
   However, the morphological marking of NPs does
not always coincide with their syntactic properties.
Morphology and syntax may be in conflict. In Icelandic (Einarsson 1945; Cole et al. 1978) subject
NPs occur in clause initial position, take the
nominative case and govern subject verb agreement.
P NPs appear in postverbal position and take the
accusative case. With some verbs such as hjalpa
'help', hilfa 'spare', gegna 'obey', neifa 'deny',
tyna 'lose', etc. the postverbal NP is in the dative case. With other verbs like voenta 'expect',

102

IMPERSONAL PASSIVES

oska 'wish', bidja 'ask', sakna 'miss', ga 'look after', the postverbal NP is in the genitive. In Icelandic, as in the other languages mentioned previously, clauses with dative or genitive objects have been traditionally regarded either as middle or intransitive.

Icelandic is said to have both a personal and impersonal passive. Personal passives are formed by passivizing accusative objects (except in double accusative constructions), impersonal passives by passivizing dative or genitive objects or recipients (in ditransitive clauses). Compare the personal passive (17b) with the impersonal passives (18b), (19b) and (20b) (Einarsson 1945).

(17) a. Jòn   tòk   kett-i
    John:nom take:past:3s cats-acc
    'John took the cats'.

  b. Kett-ir   voru tekin-ir   af
    cats-nom were take:p:part-nom:m:pl by
    Jòni
    John
    'The cats were taken by John'.

(18) a. Jòn   kasta-di   stein-um
    John:nom   throw-past:3s stones-dat
    'John threw the stones'.

  b. Stein-um   var kasta-d   af Jòni
    stones-dat was throw:p.part.n:s by John
    'The stones were thrown by John'.

(19) a. Jòn   beið   min
    John:nom   await:past:3s I:gen
    'John waited for me'.

  b. Min   var beðið   af Jòni
    I:gen was await:p.part.n:s by John
    'I was awaited by John'.

(20) a Jòn   gaf   mér   bokin-a
    John nom give:past:3s I dat book-acc.
    'John gave me the book'.

  b. Mér   var gefin   bokin-a af
    I:dat was give:p.part.n:s book-acc by
    Jòni
    John
    'I was given a book by John'

103

IMPERSONAL PASSIVES

Both personal and impersonal passives are formed
by adding the verb vera 'to be', or verða 'to become' and placing the verb in the past participle.
The passive agent is optionally expressed in an
af - phrase. In personal passives the passivized
NP displays all the morphological properties of a
subject. It appears in sentence initial position,
takes the nominative case and governs agreement in
person and number with the auxiliary verb and case,
gender and number with the past participle. In the
impersonal passive, the dative, or genitive NPs do
not lose their case marking. They do not govern
agreement with either the auxiliary or the past
participle. The past participle is in the neuter
singular. (Einarsson 1945; Andrews 1982). Thus
the clause initial NP in the impersonal passive
only has the position characteristic of subjects.
   Cole et al. (1978) argue that although the
dative and genitive NPs of the impersonal passive
do not possess the morphological characteristics of
subject NPs, syntactically these NPs behave like
subjects. Like other subjects, they can be deleted
by Equi-NP-deletion (21), undergo subject-to-object-
raising (22) and control reflexivization (23), Cole
et al. (1978:45-46).

(21) Ég vonast til að verða bjardað
     I hope comp aux V/dat/(supine)
     'I hope to be saved'.

(22) Ég tel   þeirra   hafa verið
     I believe them-gen aux aux(supine)
     beðið
     V/gen/(supine)
     'I believe them to have been visited'.

(23) Honum   voru seldir   drengirnir   af
     he:dat aux ,sold(part) boys:the(nom) by
     fraendum   sínum/hans
     relatives refl anaphoric
     'He was sold the boys by his self's rela-
     tives'.

What then is the syntactic status of dative and
genitive NPs in the Icelandic impersonal passive?
Which properties of subject NPs should be assigned
priority in deciding whether a NP is or is not a
subject, the morphological or the syntactic? As
discussed previously, traditionally morphology was
viewed as the primary indicator of the syntactic
status of NPs. Nowadays, linguists tend to identify

104

IMPERSONAL PASSIVES

NPs on the basis of their syntactic behaviour. If the syntactic properties of the dative and genitive NPs in Icelandic are taken as basic, then the Icelandic impersonal passive will have to be regarded as actually a personal passive.[6]

Consider now the case of Hindi. Hindi, like Icelandic, is said to possess both a personal and impersonal passive (Pandharipande 1978; Imai 1978). The personal passive is restricted to transitive verbs (24), the impersonal to intransitive verbs (25).

(24) a. Laṛkā   ciṭṭhiyā̃   paṛhtā he
        boy:m:3s letter:f:3pl reads:m aux:3s
        'The boy reads the letters'.

     b. Laṛke   se ciṭṭhiyā̃   paṛhī
        boy:m:3s by letter:f:3pl read:f:3pl
        jātī   hẽ
        go:f:3pl aux:3pl
        'The letters are read by the boy'.

(25) a. Laṛke   nahī̃ soe
        boys:m:3pl not   sleep:m:3pl
        'The boys did not sleep'.

     b. Laṛkõ   se soyā   nahī̃ gayā
        boys:m:3pl by sleep:m:3s not went:m:3s
        'It was not slept by the boys'.

In a passive clause, the verb appears in its perfective form, the auxiliary jānā 'to go' is introduced and the agent, if present, is followed by the postpositions se, ke, dwārā, zariye. When the auxiliary honā 'to be' is present in the active clause, it follows the auxiliary jānā in the corresponding passive. Note that the word order is the same in active and passive clauses.

In the personal passive (24b) the NP ciṭṭhiyā̃ is said to be the subject. In the impersonal passive no NP is regarded as subject. The NP ciṭṭhiyā̃ in (24b) is considered to be the subject, because it is unmarked and governs subject verb agreement. However, the subject of a personal passive need not have either of these two properties. Hindi has distinct case marking in the perfective and imperfective. In the perfective, A NPs are marked with the ergative postposition ne and S NPs are unmarked. In the imperative both S and A NPs are in the ∅ nominative case. P NPs in imperfective and perfective clauses can optionally take the accusative ko if they are definite. Otherwise they are unmarked. Verbal

105

IMPERSONAL PASSIVES

agreement in Hindi is quite complex. According to Saksean (1978) and Amrilavalli (1979), the verb agrees with the NP which is not overtly marked i.e. it agrees with the subject in imperfective clauses as in (24) and the S or P in perfective clauses as in (25a) and (26).

(26) Rām-nē rōṭī khā-ī
Ram-erg bread:f:3s ate:f:3s
'Ram ate bread'.

If both A and P are marked the verb is put into the neutral third person masculine singular as in (27a).

(27) a. Rām-nē rōṭī ko khā-yā
Ram-erg bread:f:3s ate:m:3s
'Ram ate the bread'.

In the personal passive, the passivized NP controls verbal agreement only if it is not marked as in (24b). If a clause like (27a) is passivized (27b) then the verb is in the third person masculine singular.

(27) b. Rām-se rōṭī ko khā-yā gayā
Ram by bread:f:3s ate:m:3s went:m:3s
'The bread was eaten by Ram'.

The passivized NP in (27b) has no morphological subject properties. It does not occur in clause initial position; it is marked by ko and does not govern subject verb agreement. Is this passive clause not actually an impersonal passive? The syntactic behaviour of the so called passive subject whether marked or unmarked indicates that this may well be the case.

According to Kachru et al. (1976), subject NPs in Hindi have the following syntactic properties:

a) they may control reflexivization
b) they may control Equi-NP-deletion
c) they may control conjunctive particle formation (CPF)
d) they are accessible to Equi-NP-deletion
e) they are accessible to CPF
f) they are accessible to raising.

The passive subject has only the first two properties. Klaiman (1978) argues that, in actual fact, the ability of passive subjects to control Equi-NP-deletion is rather dubious. He questions whether

IMPERSONAL PASSIVES

the only example given by Kachru et al. (1976) of
Equi-NP-deletion controlled by a passive subject is
an instance of Equi. He also argues that control
of reflexivization in Hindi cannot be regarded as
an exclusive property of subjects, because clauses
like (28), in which the controller is an underlying
recipient, also exist in Hindi.

(28) Mrs. Brown ko apnī bacī dikhāil gai
Mrs. Brown to own baby girl shown went
'Her own baby girl was shown to Mrs. Brown'.

It thus appears that the former P NP in the personal
passive is not promoted to subject. Are these clauses
then examples of impersonal passives? Klaiman
(1978) contends that they are not, since the so
called passive agent continues to function like a
subject, and, therefore, cannot be regarded as a
demoted constituent. He bases his claim on the
fact that the agent in the passive may control Equi-
NP-deletion, CPF and reflexivization. The ability
to control reflexivization is not a compelling
argument because according to Klaiman, this characteristic is not restricted to subjects.[7] That
leaves Equi-NP-deletion and CPF. Consequently, the
clauses (24b) and (27b) are open to two possible
interpretations. Either they are passive and the
passive agent continues to display two subject properties, or they are active with a subject lacking
the remaining four properties. The facts of Hindi
indicate that the second interpretation is not a
viable one. First of all, it has already been
shown that in some languages passive agents may
possess certain morphological (Palauan) and syntactic (Tagalog) subject properties. Thus, Hindi
would not be an exceptional case. Secondly, if (24b)
and (27b) are not passive, what are they? They
cannot be regarded as clauses which have undergone
topicalization, since the NPs in question are already in initial topic position. They do not perform a focusing function either. Finally, the
agent phrase in a passive clause, according to
Saksena (1978), is never obligatory, and in some
cases may not, in fact, be expressed. (29) and (30)
with an agent, are regarded by Saksena as ungrammatical.

(29) (*Rām-se) gāṛī-mē calā jā rahā hɛ
Ram-by train-in was go prog aux
'The train is being gone in (*by Ram)'.

IMPERSONAL PASSIVES

(30) (*Rām-se) davā   khāī jā-nī cāhiyē
     Ram-by medicine ate to go should
     'The medicine should be taken'.

Thus, the agent can hardly be considered as subject.
    In this brief section it has been shown that
some clauses referred to as impersonal passives
definitely do not have a subject, while others in
fact do, and consequently qualify as personal rather
than impersonal passives. So far only fully referential NPs have been considered. We now turn to
what are known as dummy subjects.

3.2.2 Dummy Subjects

In the Dutch (2b) and German (6c) and (7c) impersonal passives, the clause initial position, the subject position, is occupied by a dummy pronoun, er
and es respectively.[8] The Dutch er has the morphological form of the locative deictic there, while
the German es has the form of the third person singular neuter personal pronoun. These pronouns have
no meaning and no referent. A similar situation can
be observed in Swedish (31) (Oksaar 1972:95) and in
Danish (32) (Thomas 1926:191).

Swedish
    (31) a. Någon   skjut-er ute
            somebody shoots outside
            'Somebody shoots outside'.

         b. Det skjut-s   ute
            it shot-pass outside
            'There is shooting outside'.

Danish
    (32) a. De   læse ikke i Dag
            they read not in day
            'They are not reading today'.

         b. Det læse-s   ikke i Dag
            it read-pass not in today
            'There is no reading today'.

In Swedish, as in German, the third person singular
neuter pronoun det is used in the impersonal passive. Danish allows the locative deictic der 'there'
and the third person singular neuter pronoun det as
well. Both Swedish and Danish have two passive constructions, a periphrastic passive formed with the
auxiliary verb become , bli in Swedish and blive

108

IMPERSONAL PASSIVES

in Danish, and an s-passive formed with the active verb and the clitic s - a relic of the third person reflexive pronoun sik. Only the personal s-passive has a corresponding impersonal passive. According to Kayne (1975) and Postal (1982), French also possesses an impersonal passive as in (33b).

(33) a. Ils lui   ont tiré dessus
        they he:dat have shot above
        'They shot at him'.

    b. Il lui   a été tiré dessus
        it he:dat has been shot above
        'He was shot at'.

The dummy constituent il, which has the form of the third person masculine pronoun, appears in this construction.[9]

As the dummy pronouns in these languages occur in typical subject position, it is necessary to consider whether they could be viewed as subjects. The es of the German impersonal passive occurs only in initial position and only in matrix declarative clauses (Breckenridge 1975; Groves 1979). When an adverb immediately precedes the verb, as in (7d), es cannot appear. If es were a subject, it should be allowed to be moved to the postverbal position, like sie in (34b).

(34) a. Sie gehen heute in die Oper
        they go:pl. today to the opera
        'They are going today to the opera'.

    b. Heute gehen sie in die Oper
        today go:pl. they to the Opera
        'Today they are going to the opera'.

However, (35b) is ungrammatical.

(35) a. Es wurde gestern   getanzt
        it became yesterday dance:p.part
        'There was dancing yesterday'.

    b. *Gestern   wurde es getanzt
        yesterday became it dance:p.part
        ('Yesterday there was dancing').

Es is never found in embedded clauses. A clause, such as (36), with an embedded es is again ungrammatical, while without the es it is perfectly well-formed.

109

IMPERSONAL PASSIVES

(36) a. Er sagte,dass (*es) den   Kindern
        he said that (*it) the:dat children:dat
        geholfen   wurde
        help:p.part became
        'He said that (*it) the children were
        helped'.

Question formation in German as in English involves
a rule of subject auxiliary inversion exemplified
in (37b).

(37) a. Die   Kinder   wurden von der
        the:nom children:nom became by the
        Polizei gesehen
        police   see:p.part
        'The children were seen by the police'.

     b. Wurden die   Kinder   von der
        became the:nom children:nom by the
        Polizei gesehen?
        see:p.part
        'Were the children seen by the police'?

Es cannot undergo this rule.

(38) Wurde (*es) den   Kindern   geholfen?
           (*it) the:dat children:dat help:p.part
     'Were the children helped?'

The distribution of er in the Dutch, det in the
Swedish and der and det in the Danish impersonal
passive is not as restricted as in German. These
constituents can occur in embedded clauses as in
(39) from Dutch (Kirsner 1976) and (40) from Danish
(Thomas 1926).

Dutch

(39) Ik begon te zien dat er   niet geleefed
     I began to see that there no live:p.part
     'I began to see that life did not go on'.

Danish

(40) De   siger at der   ikke danse-s
     they say   that there no dance-pass
     'They say that there is no dancing'.

They are not deleted when an adverb is placed in
initial position.

110

IMPERSONAL PASSIVES

Swedish

    (41) Här skjut-s   det
         here shot-pass it
         'Here there is shooting'.

Danish

    (42) I dag danse-s   der   ikke
         today dance-pass there no
         'Today there is no dancing'.

In Dutch, however, when an adjunct of place appears
initially, _er_ is deleted (Smit and Meijer 1966).

    (43) In de kantoren werd   (*er)   geleefed
         in the offices became (*there) live:p.part
         'In the offices there was dancing'.

Similarly, when an agent phrase is preposed, _er_
cannot be postposed.

    (44) Door de   studenten wordt (*er)   gestaukt
         by   the students become (*there) strike.
         p.part
         'By the students there is striking'.

The distribution of the Danish, Swedish and Dutch
dummy pronouns is more subject-like than the German es.
    The fact that the above dummy constituents lack
all or the full set of subject properties suggests
that they are not, in fact, subjects. Proponents
of RG are compelled to consider dummies as subjects
because in RG it is assumed that all clauses must
have a final "1" -arc(subject) even if this "1"
is not realized on the surface. This principle of
RG is known as the _Final "1" - Law_ (Perlmutter and
Postal 1983b:100). For Perlmutter and Postal the
actual syntactic properties or distribution of the
above dummy pronouns is irrelevant. Since, for
example, the NP den Kindern in (36) or (38), or the
adverbials in (31b), (35a) cannot be regarded as
subjects, and the clause must contain a subject,
the dummy nominals are the only candidates for the
role. Obviously, if it is assumed that subjectless
clauses do exist, there is little justification for
Perlmutter and Postal's analysis.
    In essence, whether the dummy pronouns are
viewed as empty grammatical markers or subjects,

IMPERSONAL PASSIVES

depends not on their distributional and syntactic
properties, but on the assumptions made about
clause structure in general.

3.2.3   Indefinite Active Subjects

According to Khrakovsky (1973), the French on (46)
and German man-clauses (47b) are passive.

German

(45) a. Der   Arbeiter   baut   das Haus
the:nom worker:nom build the house:acc
'The worker built the house'.

b. Man   baut   das   Haus
one(?) build the:acc house:acc
'One built the house'.

Presumably he would also consider the Swedish and
Dutch man/men and the Spanish and Italian uno-
clauses in the same light.

Spanish

(46) Uno desea   la   felicidad
one desire:pres:3 the   happiness
'One desires happiness'.

All these clauses have been traditionally regarded
as active indefinite or active impersonal clauses.
They differ from typical active clauses in that the
agent of the clause is either indeterminate or unspecified.   In this sense, man, on, and uno-
clauses are said to resemble agentless passives. In
fact, in many grammars man-type constructions are
viewed as alternatives to the passive.   However,
they are not typically equated with passive clauses.
The primary reason why they are considered to
be active and not passive is the lack of passive
verbal morphology.   The absence of passive morphology is not really a good argument for the active
status of these clauses, because the term *passive
verbal morphology* is in many respects arbitrary.
In German, Dutch, Swedish, French and Spanish the
verb in a canonical passive clause appears in the
past participle, together with an auxiliary verb.
In addition to the periphrastic passive, all of
these languages, with the exception of Dutch,

112

IMPERSONAL PASSIVES

possess another construction, where the verb is in
the active and is accompanied by a morpheme either
synchronically or diachronically identical to a
reflexive morpheme as in (47) from Swedish and (48)
from French.

Swedish

    (47) Mañga böcker läste-s av mina vänner
          many books read-pass by my   friends
          'Many books are read by my friends'.

French

    (48) Les   maisons détruites   se
          the:pl houses destroy:past:f:pl refl
          rebâtir-ont
          rebuild:fut-3pl
          'The houses (which were) destroyed will
          get built again'.

Although the verbal morphology here is distinct
from that of the canonical passive, these clauses
are also referred to as passive clauses. Polish on
the other hand possesses constructions such as (49)
and (50) which display passive verbal morphology,
but are typically regarded as active.[10]

    (49) Po   obiedzie   poda-no   kawę
          after dinner:loc serve-part:n coffee:acc
          'After dinner coffee was served'.

    (50) U nich   zwykle siedzi   się   do
          at they:gen usually sit:pres:3s refl. to
          rana
          morning
          'One usually stays at their place till the
          morning'.

The above clauses differ from personal passives in
the absence of the passive auxiliary and in taking
a special impersonal participial ending in no or to
in the past tense, and a reflexive particle się in
the present. Unlike personal passives, they never
occur with an overt agent and are restricted to
verbs denoting human activities. Although the
verbal morphology is historically passive, these
clauses are rarely regarded as passive in synchronic descriptions of Polish. Verbal morphology cannot, therefore, be treated as the basic criterion

IMPERSONAL PASSIVES

of passiveness. If verbal morphology is disregarded, what then is the difference between passive clauses and man-type constructions?

Linguists who contend that passive clauses should be derived by a passive transformation and who view the promotional aspects of the passive as basic, would argue than man-type-clauses cannot be passive because no nominal is promoted to subject. Linguists who consider subject demotion as the primary function of the passive cannot use this as an argument. Whether man-type-clauses are to be treated as active or passive depends on the status attributed to the constituents man, on and uno. Khrakovsky claims that (45a) and (45b) differ in that man, in contrast to der Arbeiter, is not the semantic agent of the clause, but rather a grammatical marker with no semantic content. Khrakovsky (1973) defines the passive as a construction in which the semantic agent is not the subject. The agent in a passive clause may be designated lexically, but in an oblique position or it may be covert. In active clauses on the other hand the agent is always designated on the lexical level. If man is an empty grammatical marker which only indicates that the lexically designated agent has been removed from subject position and lost its subject status, man-clauses are passive. However, is it semantically empty or does it in fact have a semantic referent, but a very general one? Linguists disagree on this point. Most linguists claim that man, on and uno denote indeterminate human agents. They argue that these constituents cannot simply be regarded as grammatical markers, since they behave syntactically like subjects. The German man, for example, unlike the impersonal passive es is not restricted to the initial position of matrix clauses (51) (Zydatiss 1974:43).

> (51) Ein Bündel Korrespondenz   fand   man
>   a   bundle correspondence find:past one
>   in der Küche
>   in the kitchen
>   'A bundle of correspondence was found in
>   the kitchen'.
>   'Someone found a bundle of correspondence
>   in the kitchen'.

It can follow the verb when an adverb is placed initially (52) and undergo subject auxiliary inversion (53).

114

IMPERSONAL PASSIVES

(52) Hier tanzt   man gut
     here dance:pres one well
     'Here one dances well'.

(53) Geht   man in die Oper   oft?
     go:pres one in the Opera often
     'Do people go to the opera often?'

Kayne (1975) also points out that on differs from
the impersonal il. On according to Kayne, is a
subject clitic. Like other clitics, it undergoes
subject-clitic-inversion, cannot be modified or
contrastively stressed and cannot be separated from
the verb. Harris (1976) presents similar arguments
and concludes that on functions as a 'sort of unmarked personal pronoun denoting an unspecified or
unspecifiable person, while il is simply a fully
unmarked slot filling subject position'. If man,
on and uno denote a general, nonspecific agent,
how do these clauses differ from impersonal agentless passives?

Frajzyngier (1982) claims that, in fact, they
do not. As mentioned in 2.1.3 he contends that
impersonal passives of intransitive verbs do
possess a subject, an unspecified human one, which
is indicated by the structure of the whole sentence
and are thus both functionally and semantically
equivalent to active clauses, not only of the man-
type, but also those with first or third person
plural subjects such as the following from French
(54) and Polish (55).

French

(54) Nous mangeons   des grenouilles en France
     we   eat:pre:1pl   frogs   in France
     'We eat frogs in France'

Polish

(55) Tam   grają   "Człowieka z   żelaza"
     there play:pres:3s man   from iron
     'They're playing "Man of iron" there.

Impersonal passives of intransitive verbs, according
to Frajzyngier, are passive only in form. He states
(ibid:288-9):

    While their function is active, they differ
    from other active sentences in having an in-
    definite human subject; the active sentences
    have a specified subject, human, non-human,

IMPERSONAL PASSIVES

animate non-animate. These sentences differ
from impersonal sentences in the same feature,
except that impersonal sentences indicate the
lack of any subject in the semantic structure
of the sentence. They differ from passive
sentences (in Frajzyngier's terminology both
personal and impersonal passives of transitive
verbs) in specifying some feature of the semantic subject, while the passive sentences do
not specify the semantic subject in any way.

It is evident from the above statement that man-
type clauses and those like (54) and (55) are
neither active nor impersonal in Frajzyngier's
terms, for while not possessing a specified subject
they do indicate an indefinite human one. Both
Khrakovsky (1973) and Frajzyngier regard agentless
impersonal passives (in the case of Frajzyngier
only those formed from intransitive verbs) as being
equivalent to man-type clauses. Khrakovsky (ibid)
interprets this similarity as an indication of
their passive nature, while Frajzyngier interprets
both as being active-like. The data lend themselves
to either interpretation. If it is assumed that
agentless impersonal passives lack a subject and
that man-type clauses are basic clauses, then man-
type clauses differ from impersonal passives in
having an agent subject, while the latter do not.
If on the other hand impersonal passives are seen
to possess an agent subject, then they are not
passive.
    Assuming that Frajzyngier is correct, what then
is the status of impersonal passives of transitive
verbs? Is it feasible to suggest that in Finnish
(56) is passive and (57) active, for example,
(Östman 1981:287)?

    (56) Poikaa   rakaste-ttin
         boy:partit:s love-pass.part:past
         'The boy was loved'.

    (57) Tanssi-ttiin
         dance-pass.part:past
         'It was danced'.

Frajzyngier does not specify what he understands by
the term *transitive* and consequently it is not at
all clear how he would view impersonal passives
such as the German (6c) with intransitive two participant verbs. Surely, it would be difficult to
argue that they are passive when the agent is overt

116

IMPERSONAL PASSIVES

and active when no overt agent is present. Frajzyngier's division of impersonal passives in terms of
transitivity is of dubious value. Nevertheless,
Frajzyngier and Khrakovsky are both correct in
pointing out the ambivalent nature of agentless
impersonal passives and man-type clauses with respect to the active/passive dichotomy. The status
of these constructions is not as clear as Comrie
(1977a) and Perlmutter and Postal (1978) imply.
Under both Comrie's and Perlmutter and Postal's
definition of the passive, the impersonal passives
quoted in this chapter, including the controversial
Polish examples (49) and (50), qualify as passive.
All these structures plus the man-type clauses
fall under Givón's (1979a) conception of passivization. As for Givón (ibid:186) 'passivization
is the process by which a non-agent is promoted
into the role of "main topic" of the sentence',
whether or not man, on or uno are indefinite human
subjects or empty grammatical markers is irrelevant.
Since they are indefinite and non-referential, they
cannot be regarded as topics, (but cf. 7.1). The
clauses must, therefore, be viewed as possessing
non-agent topics which, according to Givón, is the
defining characteristic of passive clauses.
  Quite evidently detailed analyses of impersonal
passives and indefinite active constructions have
to be carried out before a definite decision on the
exact status of these constructions is reached.

3.3   The Impersonal Passive: Promotion vs Demotion

Perlmutter (1978a) and Perlmutter and Postal (1978)
contend that all impersonal passives, like personal
passives, can be accounted for in terms of a promotional analysis. The only difference between the
two, is that in the case of impersonal passives,
the promoted NP is a dummy. According to this view,
impersonal passives such as the Dutch (58a) should
be derived as in (58b).

      (58) a. Er   wordt   door de kinderen op het
              there become by   the children on the
              ijs   geschaatst
              ice   skate:p.part
              'It is skated by the children on the
              ice'.

117

(58) b.

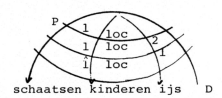

schaatsen kinderen ijs   D

The first stratum consists of a "1"-de kinde-and the locative phrase. In the second stratum a dummy NP bearing the "2" relation to the verb is introduced. This dummy NP is promoted to "1" in the third stratum and the original "1" is simultaneously demoted to a chômeur. The dummy is realized as er. The clause (58a) is derived from an underlying intransitive clause. Impersonal passives formed from basic transitive verbs, like the Welsh (59b), are derived in a similar fashion (Jones and Thomas 1977). This is illustrated in (59c).

(59) a. Mi   welodd John y   blant
       particle see   John the children
       'John saw the children'.

   b. Gwel-wyd y   plant   gan John
      see-pass the children by   John
      'The children were seen by John'.

   c.

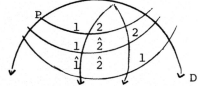

When the dummy "2" NP is introduced at the second stratum, the original "2"-blant-ceases to bear the "2" relation to the verb and becomes a "2" chômeur. This is a consequence of the *Chômeur Law* (p.44-5) and the *Stratal Uniqueness Law* (cf.ch.2 fn.19). Thus, in the impersonal passives of transitive clauses there are two chômeurs, not just one as with intransitive clauses.

Perlmutter and Postal's analysis of impersonal passives suffers from two main deficiencies. First of all, in the majority of languages, as in the Welsh (59b) example, there are no dummy subjects in the impersonal passive. Secondly, the original "2" of basic transitive clauses does not appear to function as a chômeur.

IMPERSONAL PASSIVES

Perlmutter and Postal are undaunted by the fact that dummies do not appear in the impersonal passives of most languages. They dispose of this fact in a very simple fashion. Speaking about Turkish Perlmutter states, 'No dummies appear overtly in Turkish sentences. With this generalization incorporated in the grammar of Turkish the surface distribution of dummies in Turkish is accounted for' (Perlmutter 1978:176). However, the same generalization cannot be made for Welsh. Perlmutter and Postal (1983b:102), in fact, give the following example illustrating that Welsh has dummy constituents in surface structure.

> (60) Yr oedd hi yn bwrw glaw ddoe
>   was she   throw rain yesterday
> 'It was raining yesterday'.

Pairs of clauses like (61a,b) where a dummy constituent is used instead of indefinite subjects, can be found in Welsh as well as in English, Dutch, Swedish etc.

> (61) a. 'Roedd damwain neithiwr
>   was   accident last night
>   'There was an accident last night'.
>
>   b. 'Roedd yna ddamwain neithiwr
>   was   there accident last night
>   'There was an accident last night'.

The lack of a dummy in the Welsh impersonal passive does not, therefore, spring from a language specific constraint, as in Turkish, but rather would have to be accounted for independently.

Note that for languages with no surface dummies in the impersonal passive it would not be feasible to argue that the dummy is incorporated in the verb, for if anything, the verb in the impersonal passive, as in the personal passive, implies the presence of an agent, not a hypothetical non-agent subject.

The second piece of evidence against Perlmutter and Postal's proposal comes from impersonal passives of basically transitive clauses. If Perlmutter and Postal's interpretation of impersonal passives is correct, then the P of a corresponding active transitive clause should be reduced to a chômeur in the impersonal passive. It should thus no longer bear the "2" relation to the verb, and consequently lose its characteristic morphological and syntactic properties.

IMPERSONAL PASSIVES

However, in languages which allow impersonal passives of basically transitive clauses, there is no evidence of demotion. The NP <u>plant</u> in the Welsh impersonal passive (59b) does not display the characteristics of oblique nominals, its status being rather that of a P. Although it resembles a subject in not undergoing soft mutation, typical of P NPs, unlike subjects, it does not govern agreement. Pronominal NPs on the other hand, as in Finnish (12b), appear in their P form. In Russian (3b), Kannada (8c) and Ute (62b) (Givón 1979a:192) the morphological marking of the P doesn't change.

(62) a. Taʔwóci tupúyci tiráabi-kya
man:nom rock:acc throw-past
'The man threw the rock'.

b. Tuypúyci tɨráabi-ta-x̂a
rock:acc throw-pass-past
'The rock was thrown'; 'Someone threw the rock'.

Similarly in Mojave (Langacker and Munro 1975)

(63) a. John-č nʸ - tapuy-m
John-nom 1s/P - kill-past
'John killed me'.

b. Nʸ - tapuy-č-m
1s/P -kill-pass-past
'I was killed'.

Mojave subject NPs are marked with the nominative suffix - <u>c</u>. P NPs are unmarked. Core NPs are crossreferenced on the verb. With third person NPs the pronominal prefixes are ∅. But first and second person NPs have a separate prefix for subjects <u>ʔ-</u> and another for P NPs <u>nʸ</u>. Oblique NPs are not crossreferenced. As evidenced by (63b), the same form of the prefix is used in the impersonal passive as with active P NPs. The crossreferencing pronouns in Dho-luo (Dalgish 1977), a Nilo-Saharan language spoken in Tanzania and Kenya, also indicate that there is a "2" and not a "2" chômeur in the impersonal passive. The neutral constituent order of Dho-luo is SVO, but various permutations are allowed. As in Mojave, core NPs are crossreferenced on the verb. The same crossreferencing pronouns are used for subject and P NPs except in the third person singular where <u>o</u> denotes subject NPs and <u>e</u>

120

IMPERSONAL PASSIVES

P NPs. The subject pronouns are prefixed to the verb, the P are suffixed. Non-pronominal NPs are not crossreferenced. Compare (64), (65) and (66).

(64) Otieno goy-nga   nyithind
     Otieno beat-t/asp children
     'Otieno beats (is beating) the children'.

(65) a. Otieno goy-a-nga   an
        Otieno beat-1s/P-t/asp I
        'Otieno beats me'.

(66)   An a-goy   goy-nga   nyithind
        I 1s/S/A - beats-t/asp children
        'I beat the children'.

In the passive of (65a) - (65b) - the initial NP - an - is crossreferenced like a P.

(65) b. (An) - i   - goy-a-nga   gi Otieno
        I   - pass - beat-1s/P-t/asp by Otieno
        'I am (being) beaten by Otieno'.

In Finnish, non-pronominal P NPs in the impersonal passive do not appear in the accusative case, but rather in the nominative. The data from Finnish relativization reveals that this NP is indeed a P NP. In Finnish, the relative clause is normally post-posed after the head noun with the relative pronoun in initial position (67) (Karlsson 1972).

(67) Tyttö jonka tapasin   oli kaunis
     girl who met:imperf:1s was beautiful
     'The girl whom I met was beautiful'.

When either the subject or the P of the relative clause is coreferential with the head noun, the relative clause may be preposed to prenominal position as in (68b) and (69b).

(68) a. Poika joka tanssi   pöydällä
        boy   who dance:imperf:3s table
        oli sairas
        was sick
        'The boy who danced on the table was sick'.

     b. Pöydällä tanssinut poika oli sairas
        table   dance:part boy was sick
        'The on the table danced boy was sick'.

IMPERSONAL PASSIVES

(69) a. Poika jonka näin   tanssi
        boy   who see:imperf:1s dance:imperf:
           pöydällä
        3s table
        'The boy who I saw danced on the table'.

     b. Näkemäni poika tanssi   pöydällä
        see:part boy   dance:imperf:3s table
        'The seen boy danced on the table'.

When the relative clause is preposed, the verb in
the relative clause is put into a participle form.
In addition, the coreferential part of the relative
clause is deleted and the order of constituents permuted. Consider now the examples below.

(70) a. Hän ei ollut luennolla joka pidettin
        he not be   lecture   which hold:pass.
           eilen
        part y/day
        'He wasn't at the lecture which was
        held yesterday'.

     b. Hän ei ollut eilen   pidetylla
        he not be   yesterday hold:part
        luennolla
        lecture
        'He wasn't at the yesterday - held
        lecture'.

(71) a. Läksy joka luetaan   on pitkä
        lesson which read:pass.part is long
        'The lesson which is being read is long'.

     b. Luettava läksy on pitkä
        read:part lesson is long
        'The read lesson is long'.

In (70a) and (71a) the NPs luennolla and läksy are
corereferential with the "deleted" NPs of the relative clause. The relative clauses are impersonal
passive constructions and thus the "deleted" luennolla and läksy are not subjects. The fact that
both relative clauses may be preposed (70b) and (71b)
argues that luennolla and läksy in the impersonal
passive must be P NPs and not chômeurs.
    Perlmutter and Postal's analysis of impersonal
passives could be saved if they were prepared to
abandon the *Stratal Uniqueness Law*. Then the original "2" would not have to be demoted to a chômeur

122

IMPERSONAL PASSIVES

when the dummy is introduced at the second stratum.
As it stands, their analysis cannot be accepted.
Note also that it cannot be claimed that the "2" is
demoted to a "3", not a chômeur. There is absolutely no evidence of such a demotion. In any case,
an analysis incorporating the demotion of "2" to
"3" would again break the *Stratal Uniqueness Law*,
since in languages such as Kolami (72) (McNair and
McNair 1973:170) impersonal passives formed from
ditransitive verbs would have two "3s".

Kolami

> (72) Pill ang pustok siy-uD   edd-in
>   girl to book   give-pass become-past
>   'The book was given to the girl'.

The above examples clearly show the deficiencies of
Perlmutter and Postal's proposal.
    If impersonal passives are subjectless, then
the passive cannot be defined universally in terms
of NP promotion. However, if it is assumed that
when the agent is demoted some other constituent
must be interpreted as topic, the passive can be
viewed as "creating a new topic". In personal passives the topic is the subject.[11] With impersonal
passives on the other hand any of the verbal arguments may be the topic or in fact the verb itself,[12]
as in the German (73) and Dutch (74).

German

> (73) Es wurde gelacht
>   it became dance:p.part.
>   'There was laughing'.

Dutch

> (74) Er   wordt gefloten
>   there become whistle:p.part.
>   'There is whistling'.

Nevertheless, this cannot be regarded as the defining characteristic of the passive, for under such
a definition of passivization there would be no way
of distinguishing the passive from topicalizations.
Although as mentioned in ch.2.4, the passive may
have evolved out of topicalizations, it nevertheless
must be distinguished from these constructions in
any synchronic analysis.

IMPERSONAL PASSIVES

The above facts support Keenan's (1975) and Comrie's (1977a) demotional view of the passive. Further evidence for the demotional analysis of impersonal passives will be presented in 6.1.2 and 6.3. It will be shown that the promotional analysis is incompatible with the 1-AEX (cf.p.179), one of the RG principles governing permissible clause structure.

NOTES.

1.   The suffix -in which has the morphological form of the reflexive suffix is used mainly with verbs whose stem already ends in /l/ or in a vowel.

2.   Mulder (1976:299), however, gives the following example of an impersonal passive clause with an overt agent.

I Adam-a çocuk-ø tarafɨndan vur-ul-du
   man-dat child-nom by   hit-pass-past
   'The man was hit by the child'.

3.   Other linguists argue that impersonal passive clauses formed from intransitive verbs simply do not exist. Statha - Halikas (1977:586) states: 'The impersonal intransitive is at best irrelevant to the question of promotional vs demotional characterizations of the passive, for it is not a passive, to begin with, but clearly an impersonal clause'.

4.   Comrie (1975) claims that non-pronominal NPs in Finnish only take accusative marking if they are accompanied by an A NP in the same clause. If they occur in constructions with no overt A, as in imperatives and impersonal passives, they take the nominative or, in Comrie's terminology, the absolutive case. Timberlake (1975:213) argues that this is not, in fact, the case. He states that both constructions in which the A and P are in the nominative, and constructions in which the P is in the accusative, despite the fact that there is no A in the same clause, can be found in Finnish. However, there do not appear to be any clauses in which an accusative NP is anything other than a P.

5.   The Bengali become-passive occurs with an agent under specific conditions (Klaiman 1981).

6.   Note also that the Icelandic clauses (18b), (19b) and (20b) invalidate Keenan's (1976a) claim that coding properties of subjects are always acquired prior to all syntactic properties. Faroese, (Cole et al. 1978; Lockwood 1964) provides another counterexample to Keenan's claim.

124

IMPERSONAL PASSIVES

7.   The passive agent controls reflexivization
in Lithuanian and Tagalog. Hindi, therefore, would
not be unique in this respect.

8.   This es must be distinguished both from
the meterological es as in (II) and what is commonly
known as the presentative es (Kirsner 1973; Hertzron
1975:382) as in (III)

    II.   Es regnet
           it rain:pres
           'It is raining'.

    III. Es kamen   die Männer
           it come:past the men
           'The men came'.

The same applies to the Swedish, Danish, Dutch der,
det.

9.   Impersonal passives are not discussed in
any of the standard French grammars e.g. Fraser and
Squair (1962), Grevisse (1976), Mansion (1962) and
Mueller et al (1968). However, Kayne (1975) and
Postal (1982) maintain that they do exist and that
the impersonal passive il must be distinguished from
the presentative il. We have not been able to establish conclusively whether such a distinction is
warranted. As our informants claim that these constructions are very rare in French and some even
doubt whether they are grammatical, we will not include the French il in the ensuing discussion.

10.   The Polish (49) and (50) are treated as
passive by Comrie (1977a). Although the general
consensus is that they are active, they exhibit
similar characteristics to impersonal passives in
other languages. We presume that Polish linguists
have disregarded the possibility of a passive analysis because unlike, for instance, in German the
verbal morphology differs from that in canonical
passive clauses and no agent is ever permitted. However, since neither distinct verbal morphology nor
the presence of an agent are characteristic of passive clauses universally, these constructions may be,
in fact, passive.

11.   As mentioned in 2.1.3, the patient need not
be the topic in e.g. the Slavic or Romance languages.
(cf. also ch.7).

12.   This is not the case in all languages. In
Ute (Givón 1982), for example, the verb cannot occur
without an argument.

Chapter Four

THE PERIPHRASTIC PASSIVE

4.0 Introduction

Periphrastic or analytic passive constructions are
characteristic of Indo-European languages. They
are also found in the Dravidian, Hamito-Semitic,
Sino-Tibetan and South American Indian languages.
In the vast majority of languages the periphrastic
passive is constructed by the addition of a form of
the verb to be (e.g. English, Spanish, Polish, Finnish, Lithuanian, Baluchi, Urdu, Quechua) or become
(e.g. German, Swedish, Latvian, Kupia, Kolami, Hindi,
Nez Perce). In a few of the Indo-Aryan languages
(e.g. Bengali, Hindi, Gujarati, Maithil, Ossetian)
as well as in Italian and Gaelic the passive can be
formed with the verb to go. In such diverse languages as Welsh, English and Tzeltal the verb
receive/get is employed in this capacity. The
South-East Asian languages; Vietnamese, Thai, Cambodian and Burmese and the Dravidian Tamil and Kannada
form passive clauses with a verb meaning to suffer/
to undergo. Come appears in the Kurdish Kashmiri,
Maithil and Italian passive. Even the verb to eat
may be used in this sense with a limited number of
verbs in Sinhalese and Dhangar-Kurux.
 The status of the constituents be, become, go
etc. in passive clauses has long been a problem.
Are they to be considered simply as grammatical
markers of the passive, auxiliary verbs or main
verbs?
 Since many languages possess more than one periphrastic passive e.g. a be and become passive (e.g.
Swedish, Latvian, Polish, Finnish, Nez Perce) a be
and get passive (e.g. English) or a become and go
passive (Bengali), which are not freely interchangeable, the first solution appears to be inappropriate.
In 4.1 some of the differences between various peri-

126

THE PERIPHRASTIC PASSIVE

phrastic passives in individual languages will be briefly illustrated. An attempt will be made to show that despite notable differences between passive clauses containing distinct auxiliary verbs within a given language, no consistent property can be associated with one auxiliary as opposed to another cross-linguistically.

The second, auxiliary verb analysis is the most widely accepted. It has been contested on the one hand by linguists such as Ross (1967), McCawley (1971), Huddleston (1969, 1976), Pullum and Wilson (1977) and Hudson (1984) who consider all auxiliaries as intransitive verbs taking sentential complements, and on the other by linguists who regard specifically the passive auxiliary as a main verb, for instance, Hasegawa (1968), Lakoff (1971), Bouton (1973), Fiengo (1974), Wasow (1977) and Radford (1977). Under this analysis the passive is a complex sentence.

In the well known European languages the passive verb appears as a past participle, a form of the verb which may also function as a deverbal adjective, rendering periphrastic passives superficially similar to predicative adjective constructions. This superficial similarity has induced various linguists to interpret past participles in passive clauses as adjectives e.g. Friedin (1975a), Wasow (1977), Lightfoot (1979) and Chomsky (1980).[1]

Both the complex sentence analysis and the adjectival analysis impose a stative interpretation on the be-passive which sets this particular passive apart from other passive constructions. The stative nature of the be-passive will be the topic of 4.2. It will be argued that the stative/actional division is inapplicable to passive clauses since both elements are present in the passive, constructions called *stative* passives not being in fact passive at all.

The complex sentence analysis of periphrastic passives in itself has no direct bearing on the characterization of the passive espoused herein, because the actual relationship between the active and the passive remains the same irrespective of whether the passive is a complex or simplex structure. Even if the derivation of the passive does not involve promotion and/or demotion, the correspondence of the passive subject to a non-subject in the active and the active subject to an oblique relation in the passive still obtains. However, some linguists have suggested that the periphrastic passive in the South-East Asian languages should not be

THE PERIPHRASTIC PASSIVE

defined in relation to a corresponding active, but
in purely structural terms as 'a structure containing a complement verb which requires that at least
one NP of the complement clause be coreferential to
the subject of the matrix clause', (Truitner 1972;
Clark 1974a,b). The *raison d'être* for this definition of the passive, as in the case of the similar
complex sentence analysis proposed for periphrastic
passives in the well known European languages, is
the alleged equivalence of the passive auxiliary
with the homophonous main verb of other constructions. Since under the above structural definition
of the passive no reference to a corresponding
active is made, it entails classifying clauses such
as (1) and its Thai, Vietnamese and Japanese equivalents as passive.

(1) John had his books stolen by a thief.

4.3 will, therefore, be devoted to a discussion of
whether the complex sentence analysis is the only
possible alternative for passive clauses in the
South-East Asian languages.

4.1   The Passive Auxiliary

The constituents be, become, go etc. in passive
clauses have been traditionally treated as auxiliary
verbs on a par with aspectual auxiliaries such as
the English perfective have or progressive be. Auxiliaries, as opposed to lexical verbs, are seen as
constituting a closed set of grammatical verbs functioning primarily as bearers of verbal inflections
with little or no semantic content. They are used
concomitantly with another verbal form and together
with this form they constitute a new semantic unit.
    The passive be, become, go etc. as auxiliary
verbs do not carry a lexical meaning. They do,
nevertheless, contribute to the semantics of the
clause. The precise nature of this contribution,
however, remains unclear, in some instances being
only very tenuously related to the possible semantics of the auxiliary.
    The characteristics associated with passive
clauses containing particular auxiliary verbs appear
to be language specific. Some of the differences
between passive clauses with distinct auxiliaries
within individual languages will be illustrated
below.

THE PERIPHRASTIC PASSIVE

4.1.1   Different Auxiliary Verbs

The use of a given auxiliary verb in languages which
possess more than one such constituent is determined
by a variety of semantic, syntactic and stylistic
factors. Polish, Dutch, Icelandic, German and
Finnish, for example, all distinguish between a
passive with be and become. However, in each language the two passive constructions are governed by
different factors and are used for distinct purposes.
     In Polish the become - passive is used only
with perfective verbs. The imperfective (2b) is
ungrammatical.

> (2) a. Pokój został pomalowany   w
>   room   become paint:p.part:perf. in
>   zeszłym roku
>   last   year
>   'The room was painted last year'.
>
>   b.*Pokój został malowany   w
>   room become paint:p.part:imperf in
>   zeszłym roku
>   last   year
>   ('The room was painted last year')

The be - passive is not restricted in a similar
fashion.

> (3) a. Pokój był pomalowany   w   zeszłym
>   room   was perf:paint:p.part in last
>   roku
>   year
>   'The room was painted last year'.
>
>   b. Pokój był malowany   w   zeszłym
>   room   was imperf:paint.p.part in last
>   roku
>   year
>   'The room was painted last year'.

Since the become - passive is confined to perfective verbs, it stresses the result of the action.
The be - passive when associated with an imperfective verb underlines the habitual or continuous nature of an activity. With perfective verbs on the
other hand the be - passive conveys an additional
remote or disjoint in time meaning not found with
the become - passive (Sullivan 1976:139). Thus (3a)
implies that the room already needs painting again
while (2a) does not.

THE PERIPHRASTIC PASSIVE

The occurrence of the Dutch become - passive and the be - passive, as in Polish, depends on aspect. However, whereas in Polish the become - passive is used with perfective verbs, in Dutch it is the be - passive which occurs in perfective tenses (Smit and Meijer 1966:49; Lagerwey 1968:495).

(4) a. Vroeger   werden huizen vaak van
       formerly become houses often of
       natuursteen gebouwd
       stone   build:p.part
       'Formerly houses were often built of
       stone'.

    b. Het huis is fenslotte gebouwd
       the house is finally   build:p.part
       'The house has finally been built'.

The auxiliary is also used to form the active perfect tenses of some intransitive verbs such as go, stay, meet, become, arrive. There is thus no formal distinction between the active perfects of these verbs and the passive perfects of all other verbs.

In Swedish and Icelandic the be and become-passives are said to differ in that the former emphasizes the resultant state, while the latter the process. The dominance of the stative element in the Swedish be-passive and the actional element in the become-passive can be seen by the preference of the be-passive for the stative adverbial phrase (Platzack 1980:67).

(5) a. Dörren var öppnad i/? på tio sekunder
       door   was opened for/in ten seconds
       'The door was opened for/in ten seconds'.

    b. Dörren blev öppnad *i/på tio sekunder
       door   became opened for/in ten seconds
       'The door was opened for/in ten seconds'.

This is not tantamount to saying that the Swedish be-passive is purely stative like the German sein-passive (cf. below). Note that the above examples are truncated passives and the preference for the stative interpretation in the be-passive is at least partially due to the superficial similarity of this construction to predicative adjective clauses. In addition, the fact that the be-passive in the present tense may occur with the adverb nyss 'just recently' which relates a time in the near past to the time of the utterance indicates that (6) refers

130

THE PERIPHRASTIC PASSIVE

both to the event and the resultant state.

(6) Dörren är nyss öppnad av Lars
door   is just opened by Lars
('The door is just recently opened by
Lars').

This adverb cannot be used in the stative predicative adjective clause.

(7) *Dörren ar nyss öppen
door   is just open
('The door is just open').

The Swedish be and become-passives cannot, therefore,
be viewed in terms of an absolute stative/actional
contrast, the distinction being rather one of emphasis. Similar facts hold for Icelandic (Einarsson
1945). The Icelandic become-passive displays an
additional difference in introducing an extra modal
meaning. Compare (8a,b) and (9a,b) from Einarsson
(ibid:150).

(8) a. Þu   ert doemdur
you are condem:p.part.
'You are condemned'.

b. Þu   verður doemdur
you become condem:p.part.
'You will be condemned'.

(9) a. Þeim var   ekki bjargað
they were not   save:p.part.
'They were not saved'.

b. Þein varð   ekki bjargað
they become not   save:p.part.
'It was not possible to save them'.

In contrast to Swedish and Icelandic the German
be-passive is purely stative, while the become-
passive, as in the other two languages, expresses
both the event and the resulting state with particular emphasis on the former.

(10) a. Der Tisch ist   gedeckt
the table is   lay:p.part
'The table is laid'.

THE PERIPHRASTIC PASSIVE

(10) b. Der Tisch wird   gedeckt
       the table become lay:p.part
       'The table is (being) laid'.

Although most linguists refer to (10a) as passive
(e.g. Curme 1960; Hammer 1971; Borget and Nyhan
1976; Beedham 1982), under the definition of the
passive which we have adopted, this is not a passive clause, but rather a copulative clause with an
adjectival attribute. German does possess passive
clauses with sein, but their use is very restricted.
In Middle High German, as in present day Dutch, the
be-passive was used only in perfective tenses. This
former usage still lingers on in the North German
dialects (Curme 1960:296). In the standard language
the become-passive is now used in all tenses. The
be-passive nowadays mainly occurs in imperatives
(11) and after modal verbs especially wollen (12)
(Curme 1960:297; Borgert and Nyhan 1976:140).

(11) Gelobt   sei unser Herr
     praise:p.part be our   lord
     'The Lord be praised!'

(12) Das will gelernt   sein
     that will learn:p.part   be
     'That requires to be learnt'.

In addition to werden and sein, the three verbs
bekommen, erhalten and kriegen may be used as passive auxiliaries (Curme 1960; Erben 1972; Stein 1979),
as in (13), (14) and (15).

(13) Die Kinder   bekamen vom   Grossvater eine
     the children got   by:the grandfather a
     Geschichte erzählt
     story   tell:p.part
     'The children got told a story by grand-
     father'.

(14) Jedermann erhielt 15 Patronen   zugezählt
     everyone got   15 cartridges deal out:p.
     part
     'Everyone got 15 cartridges dealt out'.

(15) Er kriegte seine Miete von der Firma
     he got   his   rent by the firm
     bezahlt
     pay:p.part
     'He got his rent paid by the firm'.

132

THE PERIPHRASTIC PASSIVE

The passive with bekommen, erhalten and kriegen
occurs mainly with ditransitive verbs which convey
the concrete or abstract meaning of 'give' (Stein
1979:70).[2] The three verbs are not freely interchangeable. Thus while it is possible to say (16a),
(16b) is ungrammatical.

(16) a. Der Schüler bekam die Aufgabe
       the student got   the exercise
       erklärt
       explain:p.part
       'The student was explained the exer-
       cise'.

     b.*Der Schüler erhielt die Aufgabe
       the student got   the exercise
       erklärt
       explain:p.part
       ('The student was explained the exer-
       cise').

These passive constructions also differ stylistically. The erhalten - passive is regarded as the
most formal (of the three), the kriegen - passive
as colloquial. Another passive auxiliary associated
with a colloquial style is gehören 'to belong, to
fit'. It expresses obligation or necessity and is
used as a substitute for müssen 'ought' (Curme
1960:297; Stein 1979:68).

(17) Er gehört eingesperrt
     he belong prison:p.part
     'He should be put into prison'.

The Finnish be and become-passives differ mainly in that the subject of the become-passive is perceived as having somehow induced or being partially
responsible for the situation expressed in the
clause (Östman, 1981:292).

(18) a. Tytöt   olivat poikien rakastamia
        girls:nom were   boys:gen love:pass:pl
        'The girls were loved by the boys'.

     b. Tytöt   tulivat poikien rakastami-
        girls:nom became boys:gen love-trans-
        ksi
        lative
        'The girls got loved by the boys'.

The be-passive carries no such implications.

133

THE PERIPHRASTIC PASSIVE

Italian also possesses a number of passive auxiliaries: essere 'to be', venire 'to come' and andare 'to go'. (Lepschy and Lepschy 1977:140; Stein 1979:71). Andare is used in a similar way to the German gehören (19) (Lepschy and Lepschy 1977: 142).

(19) Questo   va finito   per domani
     this:m:s go finish:p.part by tomorrow
     'This must be finished by tomorrow'.

It appears with only a restricted number of verbs. Essere is the basic Italian passive auxiliary. A clause with essere and a past participle in the present tense may be ambigious between a passive and an adjectival reading (Lo Cascio 1976).

(20) La   stanza è illuminata
     the:f:s room   is light:p.part
     'The room is lit (by someone)'; 'The room is lit'.

No such ambiguity arises with venire.

(21) La   barca viene affondata
     the:f:s boat come sink:p.part
     'The boat is (being) sunk (by someone).

Venire, like the Swedish and Icelandic bliv and verða respectively, adds a dynamic meaning to the passive. Essere and venire also differ in that venire may suggest that the action expressed is for someone's benefit. In addition, venire is much more restricted than essere. It cannot be used in compound tenses.

In English the use of be and get is largely governed by stylistic factors, get-passives being more characteristic of colloquial speech. The frequency of occurrence of the get-passive also depends on dialectal and sociolectal factors. Sussex (1982) states that this construction is considerably less frequent in British than Australian English and more common in North American English than in either of the other two varieties.

The be and get passives carry different conversational implicatures. According to Lakoff (1971) the get-passive is frequently used to reflect the attitude of the speaker towards the events described in the clause while the be-passive is far more neutral. She suggests that clauses like (22) and (23) would be uttered by someone directly in-

THE PERIPHRASTIC PASSIVE

volved and affected by the events expressed, while the equivalent clauses with be would be more appropriate for a person trying to present an objective account of an event.

> (22) My cache of marijuana got found by Fido, the police dog.
> (23) This department is going to hell. Six linguists got arrested for possession of marijuana.

Stein (1979:58) disagrees with Lakoff's interpretation and contends that passive get - clauses rather than conveying personal involvement reflect the speaker's opinion on the given event. Hatcher (1949), Shopen (1972:334) and Chappell (1980) express a view similar to Stein. Hatcher and Chappell claim that passive clauses with get may be used only to describe events which are perceived as having fortunate (24) or unfortunate (25) consequences for the subject.

> (24) Susan got three of her paintings accepted for an exhibition in Melbourne. (Good for her!)
>
> (25) Kevin got rejected by another firm. (How unfortunate for him)

According to Shopen (1972), the fact that the paintings were accepted in (24) is interpreted as positive achievement while (25) is viewed as a failure or negative achievement on the part of Kevin. He holds that all passive get - clauses must be interpreted in these terms. Shopen points out that the attitude of the speaker is most clearly expressed in interrogatives and wh-questions formed from get-passives. Compare (26a), (26b), (27a) and (27b).

> (26) a. How did you get rejected by another firm?
> b. Did you get rejected by another firm?
>
> (27) a. How did you get invited to give a concert in Sydney?
> b. Did you get invited to give a concert in Sydney?

Clauses which presuppose negative achievement with how convey the sympathy of the speaker. Interrogatives on the other hand may indicate disrespect or

THE PERIPHRASTIC PASSIVE

insolence. The opposite holds for clauses which presuppose positive achievement.[3]

Get-passives are not freely interchangeable with be-passives. The clauses (28a,b) are grammatical, but (28c,d) are awkward to say the least (Shopen 1972).[4]

(28) a. I got reminded of Jenny the other day.
b. Bill got seen with a member of the Cosa Nostra.
c. ?The problem got explained to us yesterday.
d. ?The electric light got invented in the XIX century.

However, judgements differ from speaker to speaker. The same holds for passive agents. (22) and (25) are unquestionably grammatical while (29a,b) are labeled by Hatcher (1949:435-6) as unacceptable. For us, though, they are fine.

(29) a. He got fired by the superintendent.
b. He got run over by the man next door.

Not all clauses with get and a past participle are compatible with the definition of the passive adopted herein.   Consider the following examples from Stein (1979:49,55).

(30) a. I blame him for ever getting involved in it.
b. I was surprised at his getting married at all.
c. Let's get started.
d. She got lost.

These clauses differ from the previous set not merely in that they do not allow the expression of an agent, but rather that in no instance is an agent even implied. In each case the overt or implied (30c) subject has brought about the situation expressed in the clause. These clauses cannot be analysed in terms of subject demotion of NP promotion for they are active not passive. Clauses containing become (31) and grow (32) are similar in this respect.

(31) a. Dialectic expressions sometimes become established in the literary language.
b. The whole world is rapidly becoming Americanized.

THE PERIPHRASTIC PASSIVE

(32) a. He grew increasingly frightened
b. Colin hasn't grown bored yet.

Jespersen (1927), Curme (1931), Svartvik (1966), Zandvoort (1969) and Stein (1979), who use the term *passive* for the above clauses, maintain that the passive in English consists of be (or auxiliaries commutable with be) and a past participle. Under such a definition of the passive, become and grow-clauses are passive. However, they cannot be regarded as such under any definition based on grammatical relations. Rather they should be treated as predicative adjective clauses identical to those in (33).

(33) a. The child ran wild.
b. The cream turned sour.
c. They stood perplexed.
d. Everyone seemed interested.

The active status of some become clauses is called into question by the grammaticality of clauses like (34) from Svartengren (1948) quoted in Stein (1979: 52).

(34) a. This phrase (...) became obscenely interpreted by Classical writers as a perverted passion by Pasiphoe.

b. She became paralyzed by two things.

The only possible active counterparts of (34) do not convey exactly the same meaning as the become - clauses. Nevertheless, this cannot be taken as an argument against the passive nature of (34a,b).
Bengali, in contrast to all the other languages mentioned, does not possess a be-passive, but a become (35a) and go (35b) passive (Klaiman 1981:74).

(35) a. Omukke   taaṛaano   hoyeche
so-and-so:acc driving-out has:become
'So-and-so has been driven out'.

b. Omukke   taaṛaano   jaabe   naa
so-and-so:acc driving-out will:go not
'So-and-so cannot be driven out'.

Klaiman (ibid:73-78) maintains that the two primary usages of the become-passive are in statements of fact and in aphorisms and in statements implying

137

THE PERIPHRASTIC PASSIVE

completion of an activity. When used in the latter way the passive may convey an additional sense of "manage to V". The major difference between the two passive clauses is that only the become-passive may co-occur with an overt agent (in the genitive). There is, furthermore, a semantic difference illustrated by the following examples:

(36) a. E   darjaaṭaa aeto   soru   aamaar or
        this door   so-much narrow my:gen its
        moddhe ḍhokoia habe   naa
        inside going-in will:become not
        'The door is so narrow that I won't be
        able to squeeze through it'.

    b. E   botolṭae khub soru,   khejur
        this bottle   very narrow dates
        ḍhokaano   jaabe   naa
        putting-in will-go not
        'This bottle is very narrow, dates can't
        be squeezed into it'.

The become-passive may express a capabilitative meaning, the activity referred to in the clause not being *a priori* impossible just impossible under the circumstances stated. The go-passive on the other hand may convey a possibility nuance; the activity cannot be performed under any conditions.

    The very existence of more than one passive construction within a given language leads one to anticipate differences between them. In the case of the languages discussed above the differences are not surprisingly perceived to be associated with the use of be as opposed to become or get or come etc. As the passives with the various verbs are not interchangeable, these constituents cannot just be empty grammatical markers. Do they thus carry a lexical meaning? It is evident from the preceding discussion that they do not. They do, nevertheless, contribute to the semantics of the clause. The nature of this contribution does not, however, appear to be connected with the type of constituent involved for neither aspectual differences, nor modal meanings or beneficial or adversative connotations are associated with any one verb cross-linguistically.

    The differences noted above are fully compatible with the traditional auxiliary analysis of the passive be, become, go etc. The particular semantic nuances observed cannot be attributed to the auxiliary verb alone, but rather to the combination of

138

THE PERIPHRASTIC PASSIVE

the auxiliary with the past participle or nomina-
lized verb (Finnish, Bengali). Why one auxiliary is
used as opposed to another will depend on language
internal factors.

4.2   The Be-Passive as a Stative Construction.

Be-passives in languages such as English, French,
Italian, Spanish, Swedish, Polish etc. are formally
similar to predicative adjective clauses. The following clauses are ambiguous between an adjectival
(a) and passive (b) reading.

> (37) a. The glass is broken.
>   b. The glass is (regularly) broken by
>   vandals.
>
> (38) a. His bills are paid.
>   b. His bills are paid by his mother.
>
> (39) a. Mike was frightened.
>   b. Mike was frightened by her indicisive-
>   ness.

This ambiguity is not manifested by all be-passives
being dependent on the homophony of adjective and
past participle. The examples below are open to
only a passive interpretation.

> (40) a. The door was opened.
>   b. The dingo was killed.
>   c. Agatha was helped.
>   d. Ken was given an ultimatum.

The potential ambiguity of (37a-39a) has led
numerous linguists to call these clauses *stative*
passives.[5] According to the definition of the passive adopted in this work, (37-39), under the adjectival reading, are not passive. In 2.3 we argued
that if the passive is not defined with reference to
the corresponding active it cannot be defined universally at all. *Stative* passives qualify as passive only if the passive is defined either in terms
of the semantic role of the subject (and then it
would be impossible to distinguish passive clauses
from certain actives) or if it is defined in terms
of the presence of an auxiliary verb and a deverbal
adjective as suggested by Svartvik (1966), Stein
(1979) or Beedham (1982). Since (37-39) under the
adjectival reading are active, they cannot be defined

THE PERIPHRASTIC PASSIVE

with reference to a non-existing active. They
depict a state the origin of which is not specified
by the structure of the clause. Passive clauses as
argued in the previous section, depict both an action and resulting state. Although most linguists
who portray the be-passive as expressing 'a state
resulting from a previous action' tend to explicate
the stative rather than the dynamic quality of the
passive, its integral dynamic component cannot be
denied. Irrespective of whether the agent is specified or not, clauses such as (41) clearly refer to
both the act of dispersing or discovery and the
resultant state of completion.

> (41) a. The crowd was dispersed by the Militia.
>   b. The Sex Pistols were discovered by
>   Malcolm McLaren.

The dynamic quality of the passive is particularly
evident in (40) where the possibility of confusing
the past participle with an adjective does not arise
due to the non-existence of a corresponding adjective or lack of homophony between the two. The fact
that passive clauses may occur in the progressive is
a further indication that the be-passive cannot be
regarded as a purely stative construction.[6] Nevertheless, two of the more recent proposals of dealing
with the be-passive, within the transformational
framework, namely the complex sentence analysis and
the adjectival analysis either implicitly or explicitly impose a stative interpretation on this construction.

4.2.1   The Complex Sentence Analysis

The complex sentence analysis of passive clauses was
induced primarily by factors internal to TG relating
to both the form and function of transformations and
the role attributed to underlying structure as a
reflection of logical form and input to semantic representation. In early TG (Chomsky 1957) actives
and passives were derived from a common underlying
structure, the latter by a passive transformation
which introduced the passive be and the preposition
by *ex nihilo* with no meaning assigned to them and no
justification for their presence (cf. p.6). After
it was realized that meaning changing transformations
would not enable an adequate semantic representation
to be carried out at the level of underlying structure, the meaning preserving requirement on transformations was introduced and with it arose the problem

140

THE PERIPHRASTIC PASSIVE

of providing distinct underlying representations for actives and passives.

In order to avoid inserting the passive be *ex nihilo* and simultaneously express the propositional synonymy of actives and passives Hasegawa (1968) and Lakoff (1971) proposed an underlying structure for passives in which the active sentences were embedded as complements of the verb be as in (42b) (Hasegawa) and (42c) (Lakoff).

(42) a. "Northern Muse" was written by Van Morrison

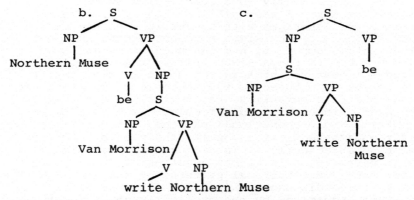

The passive transformation was abandoned and passive clauses were derived by subject-object inversion in the lower clause and Equi-NP deletion, under Hasegawa's analysis, and subject-raising under Lakoff's. A version of (42bc) is postulated as the underlying structure of the passive by all linguists who view the passive as underlyingly complex and advocate a transformational as opposed to a lexical analysis of passive clauses (e.g. Bouton 1973; Langacker and Munro 1975; Emonds 1976; Huddleston 1976; Radford 1977; Wasow 1977). Under lexical approaches to the passive the passive be as a main verb takes a verb phrase complement (e.g. Bresnan 1978, 1982b; Horn 1981; Hudson 1984) or an adjectival one (e.g. Friedin 1975a; Starosta 1978). In this second instance the passive clause is simplex.[7]

The above analyses obscure the dual nature of the passive for if be is the main verb, the passive can only receive a stative interpretation. Although not all advocates of the main verb analysis would concede that it necessarily imposes a stative interpretation on the passive, we fail to see how such

THE PERIPHRASTIC PASSIVE

a conclusion can be avoided.

If be is a main verb it must be a manifestation of either the copula or existential verb or constitute a separate third form of be. A purely existential analysis is implausible due to the different distribution of the two bes. Therefore, linguists who have addressed themselves to the problem of the status of the passive be typically equate it with the copula. The copula analysis is not without merit since the be in passive clauses, like the copula be, does not appear to have intrinsic semantic content. The copula is regarded by many linguists as 'semantically void functioning solely as a marker of a predicator' (Allan 1973:394). The existence of languages with synthetic passives, which similarly to be- passives possess both an actional and statal component, and languages such as Latin and Greek with be-passives only in the perfect, suggests that the stative component of the passive cannot be attributed to the presence of be alone and thus that its semantics are similarly indeterminate. However, since the copula combines with adjectives, nominals and prepositional phrases, but not verbs, if the passive be is a copula, the past participle must be an adjective. The adjectival analysis of past participles is highly questionable, due to the different distributional patterns of the two constituents to be discussed in 4.2.2. It's validity is further undermined by the explicit stative interpretation which it imposes on the passive. Although both adjectives and verbs may be partitioned into stative/non-stative sets, it is an undisputable fact 'that to be stative is normal for the class of adjectives, but abnormal for verbs' (Lyons 1968:325). A few non-stative adjectives cannot be used as an argument against the necessarily stative interpretation which the adjectival analysis involves.

The third possibility of treating the passive be as a separate main verb is implicit in the analyses of Hasegawa (1968), Lakoff (1971), Bouton (1973), Radford (1977), Horn (1981) and Bresnan (1979, 1982b) who combine a higher verb analysis of be with a verbal treatment of past participles. None of these linguists discuss the meaning of this new lexical verb and one can only assume that it is somehow distinct from both the copula and existential verb. Langacker and Munro (1975) suggest that it is a stative-existential predicate with real semantic content combining properties of both the copula and existential verb. Under their analysis, the copula

142

THE PERIPHRASTIC PASSIVE

properties are manifested by the basically stative nature of this construction, the existential by the non-agentive role of the subject. As argued above, the passive possesses both statal and actional components, which the stative analysis ignores. Langacker and Munro view the stative characteristics as definitive not only of the be-passive, but of all passive clauses, an analysis which cannot be substantiated. The second existential element similarly lacks justification. If the non-agentive role of the subject is taken as evidence for "existentiality" then the passive is indubitably existential, but so are many active clauses. In fact, Langacker and Munro posit an underlying existential predicate for both actives and passives, do and be respectively, thus detracting from their own argument. Timberlake (1977:234) sees the existential component of the passive in that it 'asserts that the condition in which the subject exists is the result of a preceding action'. His use of the term *existential* bears little resemblance to traditional usage hardly warranting an identification of the passive be with the existential verb. If the *existential* component of Langacker and Munro's interpretation of passive be is disregarded we are left with the stative part which *ipso facto* identifies the passive be again with the copula.

Beedham (1982:52-3) contends that the identification of the passive be with the copula is methodologically unsound for:

> the assumption that the be in passives can best be described by finding the constructions which passives are nearest to structurally and semantically and saying that be means in the passive whatever it means in the similar constructions (...) is surely misconceived, because the meaning of be wherever it appears is determined wholly by the items it links.

This is precisely the interpretation of be under the traditional auxiliary verb analysis, which accomodates both the stative and active components of the passive and avoids imposing an explicit stative or existential reading.

The problems arising from the identification of passive auxiliaries other than be with the homophonous main verbs considerably undermine the whole validity of this procedure. Consider, for example, the case of the English get. The main verb get may

143

THE PERIPHRASTIC PASSIVE

convey any of the following meanings (Luelsdorff 1978:54):

(43) a. Where did you get (obtain) that hat?
b. Did you get (receive) my telegram?
c. He got (caught) the measles.
d. She got (succeed in having) her way.
e. Get (procure) me a ticket.
f. When did you get (arrive) here?
g. I don't get (understand) it.
h. He's not getting anywhere (making progress).

The meaning of the passive get cannot be equated with any of the above, its semantics being typically analyzed as either incipient action or incipient state, neither of which accounts for the adversative or beneficial meanings associated with the get-passive in English. The semantics of the two gets are sufficiently remote for their relationship to be tenuous at best. The differences which exist between the be and get-passives may be seen as a function of the semantics of be and get respectively, but this does not necessitate an identification of these verbs with the homophonous main verbs. Similar discrepancies exist between the semantics of the passive go, come, become etc. and the corresponding main verbs in other languages. This problem will be resumed in the discussion of the passive in the South-East Asian languages in 4.3.

Linguists who consider the be-passive as a stative construction often quote the get-passive as the dynamic counterpart. Get-passives, unlike some be-passives, are not ambiguous between a stative (non-passive) and actional reading, but, nevertheless, the stative and kinetic elements are present in both constructions. (44a) as well as (44b) refers to an action and the resulting state.

(44) a. Jack was injured by a careless player.
b. Jack got injured by a careless player.

If *stative* passives are not passive there is little justification for a stative characterization of the be-passive and an actional one for the get-passive.

Passive clauses do differ in the degree to which they stress action vs state, but this is not necessarily related to the use of be as opposed to other auxiliaries or, in fact, the use of an auxiliary verb at all. As noted in ch.3, the emphasis on

144

THE PERIPHRASTIC PASSIVE

state vs action may correlate with the personal/
impersonal distinction unrelated to verbal forms.
Similar differences may be observed between reflexive and *plain* passives to be discussed in ch.5.
Frajzyngier (1978:138-9) contends that:

> if a language has only one form to indicate
> passive (periphrastic or synthetic) this form
> will be ambiguous with respect to the feature
> stative while if a language has two devices to
> indicate passive and one of them uses a form of
> be then the stative meaning of the passive will
> be realized by this form and not by the form
> that does not employ be.

Neither of Frajzyngier's observations hold cross-
linguistically. Even if this first statement is
reinterpreted to mean not ambiguous, but possessing
both statal and actional components as we believe it
must (stative passives not being passive), this
characteristic is not restricted to languages with
only one passive form, as evidenced by the English
be-passive and the German become-passive. The
become-passive in Polish indicates that the second
prediction is also false. Since become occurs only
with perfective verbs, it is the become-passive not
be-passive which is the more stative.

4.2.2   The Adjectival Analysis

That past participles may have certain adjectival
properties has long been recognized. Like adjectives
they can occur:

a) prenominally

    (45) A broken box lay on the table.

b) be conjoined with adjectives

    (46) The box was dirty and broken

c) as the complements of certain verbs like become,
look, remain, seem, sound etc

    (47) Celia seemed surprised.

d) with the degree modifiers very, extremely.

    (48) a. Her family was very respected.
          b. They were extremely frightened.

145

THE PERIPHRASTIC PASSIVE

e) with the negative un

    (49) The parcel was unopened.

Furthermore, in languages such as Polish or Russian past participles agree in number, gender and case with the nominal head. The above adjectival proper- ties of past participles have led a number of linguists to claim that past participles are adjec- tives. Linguists disagree on whether this adjectival analysis should apply to all passive clauses or only some. Friedin (1975a), Babby and Brecht (1975), Starosta (1976, 1978) and Platzack (1980) argue that all past participles in passive clauses can be analyzed as adjectives, while Wasow (1977) and Light- foot (1979) contend that only passive clauses in which the subject corresponds to an underlying di- rect object can be treated in this fashion. Wasow and Lightfoot claim that passive clauses have to be divided into those which contain adjectival past participles and those which contain verbal past ' participles since the participles formed from ditran- sitive verbs (50), certain idioms (51), raising verbs (e.g. believe), verbs that take NP complements (e.g. elect) and the verbs help and thank, don't possess the enumerated adjectival properties. All the clauses below are ungrammatical.

    (50) a. *The told story was very sad.
          b. *The beautiful and given dress was torn.
          c. *Mary seems given a reward.
          d. *The very shown picture was by Picasso.
          e. *The extremely awarded girl looked happy.
          f. *Sue was unsent the invitation.
          g. *The danced attendance on woman was
             very pleased.
          h. *The silly and found fault with boy was
             not invited.
          i. *Martha seems paid attention to.
          j. *The very made fun of teacher left the
             school.
          k. *The extremely set fire to house was the
             biggest in the neighbourhood.
          l. *Advantage was untaken of the offer.

In addition, passive participles of ditransitive verbs may be followed by a NP, while adjectives may not.[8]

    (51) a. The winner was given a prize.
          b. *The winner was happy a prize.

146

THE PERIPHRASTIC PASSIVE

The situation is not, however, as straightforward
as linguists like Wasow suggest. Although some of
the past participles which correspond to mono-
transitive verbs do possess the above adjectival
characteristics, others do not. Consider, for instance, the following clauses.

(52) a. *The chased man was from Sydney.
b. *The child was both spanked and noisy.
c. *The law seems obeyed.
d. *John was very pushed.
e. *Susan was extremely congratulated.
f. *Mary was unkilled.

Friden (1975a) argues that the inability of certain
past participles to occur with degree modifiers and
as complements to verbs like seem, look, sound etc.
can be accounted for on semantic grounds. He notes
that certain adjectives are restricted in a similar
fashion as in (53).

(53) a. *The theory seems unpublished.
b. *The lizard was very dead.
c. *You are extremely next.

Friedin claims that the complement of seem must
describe a quality or condition which is accessible
to direct observation. (52c) and (53a) are anomalous because it is impossible to tell from direct
observation whether something is obeyed or unpublished. (52d,e) and (53b,c) are ungrammatical
because it is impossible to speak of events or absolute states in terms of degree. Friedin does not,
however, comment on the ungrammaticality of (52a,b,
f). Nor does he mention the fact that past participles, but not adjectives, may occur in infinitive
clauses (54), be modified by adverbs like well,
often, and seldom (55) and may take an adjectival
complement (56).

(54) a. The book remains to be read.[9]
b. *The book remains to be red.

(55) a. This is a well (often, seldom) read
book.[10]
b. *This is a well (often, seldom) red book.

(56) The chair is painted red.[11]

Friedin also fails to point out that the past participles which display the greatest amount of adjec-

147

THE PERIPHRASTIC PASSIVE

tival properties come from *stative* passives, such as (37a-39a). Only when used statively can a past participle be coordinated with an adjective (57) or act as a complement to verbs like <u>seem</u>, <u>look</u>, <u>sound</u> etc. (58).

> (57) a. *The glass is dirty and broken by vandals.
> b. *The turkey was good and cooked by Tom.
> c. *Mike was annoyed and sad by them.

> (58) a. *The radio seems damaged by my daughter.
> b. *Everything looks packed by my father.
> c. *John sounded annoyed by Dorothy.

Clauses like (59) are not an exception because here reference is also made to a state.

> (59) a. Mary appeared convinced by that argument.
> b. John seemed excited by the news.
> c. Mike seemed annoyed by that suggestion.

If the main evidence for treating past participles in passive clauses as adjectives comes from *stative* passives, constructions which under the definition of the passive proposed here are not passive, little justification for such an analysis remains. The adjectival analysis of passive past participles has little to recommend itself for if such an analysis is adopted it is still necessary to distinguish between those adjectives which have the syntactic properties of adjectives and those that do not. Moreover, as this analysis identifies the passive <u>be</u> with the copula, how can clauses such as (37-39) be disambiguated if not by reference to the adjectival vs verbal status of the past participle?

That the past participles in (37-39) under one reading are adjectival is undeniable. However, contrary to Wasow's (1977) and Lightfoot's (1979) claim, adjectival past participles are not confined to those based on passivizable transitive verbs as evidenced by (60) (Bresnan 1978:8).

> (60) a. elapsed time (time that has elapsed)
> b. a fallen leaf (a leaf that has fallen)
> c. a widely travelled man (a man who has travelled widely)
> d. a lapsed catholic (a Catholic who has lapsed)
> e. a failed writer (a writer who has failed)

THE PERIPHRASTIC PASSIVE

Bresnan (1982b:29) argues that adjectival partici-
plesare formed not from transitive verbs, but from
intransitive participles of verbs by a rule of adjectival conversion applying to past participles with
theme subjects.[12] This process converts verbal predicates into adjectival predicates thus accounting
for the ambiguity of (37-39). A similar solution is
suggested by Horn (1981). Both Horn and Bresnan,
unlike Wasow and Lightfoot, advocate a lexical derivation of all passive clauses and show that this
analysis does not depend on an adjectival treatment
of passive past participles. If *stative* passives
are not passive, the arguments for the adjectival
analysis no longer obtain.

4.3 The Passive in South-East Asian Languages.

Vietnamese, Thai, Japanese and possibly Burmese
appear to possess two types of passive constructions:
a direct passive, the analog of the European passive and an *indirect* passive corresponding to the
English (1) repeated here as (61).

> (61) John had his books stolen by a thief

Both constructions have been claimed to be incompa-
tiblewith the relational approach to the passive.
The ensuing discussion of the two constructions will
reveal that only the *indirect* passive fails the test
for passivization, according to the criteria adopted
herein.

4.3.1 The *Direct* Passive

Thai (62), Vietnamese (63), Mandarin (64) and Burmese (65) all possess constructions which translate
into English as passive.

Thai

> (62) Suk thùuk[13] rót chon
> sook car collide
> 'Sook was hit by the car'.

Vietnamese

> (63) Nam bị Nga đánh
> Nam Nga beat
> 'Nam was beaten by Nga'.

149

THE PERIPHRASTIC PASSIVE

Mandarin

> (64) John bei ta da-le
> John   him beat-asp
> 'John was beaten by him'.

Burmese

> (65) Mɑ́u   khôi thyŷk khacàw khaâ
> friend I   they   kill
> 'My friend was killed by them'.

All of the above clauses communicate a definite
meaning of unpleasantness. This is not only due
to the presence of the verbs hit, beat, kill as
evidenced by (66) (Lekawatana 1970:128), (67) (Truitner 1972:369) and (68) (Teng 1975:14).

Thai

> (66) Daaŋ thùuk sùdda chə́ən
> Dang   Suda   invite
> 'Dang was invited by Suda (but he did not
> want to be invited)'.

Vietnamese

> (67) Kim bị John yêu
> Kim   John love
> 'Kim was loved by John (it was unfortunate
> for her)'.

Mandarin

> (68) Li Si bei Zhung San kan-jian-le
> Li Si   Zhung San look-see-asp
> 'Li Si was seen by Zhung San (to his
> embarrassment)'.

According to Lekawatana (1970), Filbeck (1973),
Chaiyaratana (1961), Warotamasikkhadit (1963) and
Wongbiasaj (1979), thùuk - clauses in Thai will
always be interpreted prejoratively by native speakers. This is also the case in Vietnamese (Shum
1965; Hou 1965; Du'ong 1971; Khai 1972; Truitner
1972). In Mandarin on the other hand bei - clauses
appear to be in the process of losing some of their
negative connotations (Li and Thompson 1975:179; Li
1971). Vietnamese in addition to these adversative
constructions possess clauses which convey a beneficial meaning such as (69).

150

THE PERIPHRASTIC PASSIVE

(69)   Kim   được John khen
       Kim   John compliment
       'Kim was complimented by John'.

Again the pleasant association is not due only to
the meaning of the verb since verbs which under normal circumstances express a distasteful situation
are in the được - clauses reinterpreted as beneficial (70).

(70)   John được Kim dánh
       John   Kim hit
       'John was hit by Kim (He liked it, it was
       good for him)'.

There is no equivalent construction in the other
languages. Kullavanijaya (1974:195) claims that in
Thai a neutral situation can be expressed by what
she calls the dooy - passive, as in (71b).

(71)   a. Nákkhǐan mii chîɨ khǐan rîaŋ nán
          writer   have name write story that
          'A famous writer wrote that story'.

       b. Rîaŋ nán khǐan dooy nákkhǐan mii chîɨ
          story that write by writer   have name
          'That story is written by a famous
          writer'.

This construction can only be found with factitive
verbs i.e. verbs which express the meaning of
"coming into being" e.g. do, make, write, cook,
build etc. Note also that unlike the được-clauses,
the dooy - passive differs structurally from the
adversative construction.
     Although the adversative and beneficial construc-
tions quoted above are translated as passive,
their passive status is open to question. Nevertheless, a considerable number of linguists contend
that they are indeed passive. They disagree only on
whether these clauses should be regarded as simplex
(e.g. Chaiyaratana 1961; Shum 1965; Hou 1965;
Du'ong 1971; Li 1971; Perlmutter and Postal 1977) or
complex with a structure such as that postulated by
Hasegawa (1968) for English (e.g. Warotamasikkhadit
1963; Hashimoto 1969; Lekawatana 1970; Chu 1973;
Kullavanijaya 1974; Wongbiasaj 1979).
     The arguments for the complex sentence analysis
concern the alleged equivalence of the passive
thùuk, bị, được with the homophonous main verbs of

151

THE PERIPHRASTIC PASSIVE

other constructions. The Mandarin <u>bei</u> can no longer function as a main verb and <u>this</u> fact alone, for the majority of linguists working on Mandarin, is adequate justification for the simplex approach. The converse argument is used for the main verb status of the Thai <u>thùuk</u> and Vietnamese <u>bị/được</u> in passive clauses. Truitner (1972) and Le (1976) quote the following examples as evidence that bị/được like stative verbs such as <u>chịu</u> 'be subjected to', 'submit to', <u>cun</u> 'need', <u>muốn</u> 'want', may:

a) function as main verbs in simplex clauses

(72) Kim ⎰muốn⎱ mốt trán đon
          ⎰bị ⎱ one clf beating
          ⎰được⎱

       Kim ⎰wanted ⎱ a storm of beating
              ⎰suffered⎱
              ⎰received⎱

b) be followed by an intransitive verb (73) or a verb which can be used both transitively and intransitively (74).

(73) Kim ⎰muốn⎱ đi
    Kim ⎰bị ⎱ go
          ⎰được⎱

       Kim ⎰wanted ⎱ to go
              ⎰was forced ⎱
              ⎰was permitted⎱

(74) Kim ⎰muốn⎱ yêu
    Kim ⎰bị ⎱ love
          ⎰được⎱

       Kim ⎰wanted   to love
             ⎰was forced to love
             ⎰received   love

c) take a sentential complement where the matrix subject is coreferential with the underlying subject (75) or P (76) of the embedded clause.

(75) Kim ⎰muốn⎱ dánh John
    Kim ⎰bị ⎱ hit John
          ⎰được⎱

152

THE PERIPHRASTIC PASSIVE

(75) Kim ⎡ wanted   ⎤ to hit John
      ⎢ was forced   ⎥
      ⎣ was permitted ⎦

(76) Kim ⎧ muốn ⎫ John đánh
      ⎨ bị   ⎬ John hit
      ⎩ được ⎭

      Kim ⎡ wanted to be hit by John
      ⎢ was   hit by John
      ⎢   (adversative)
      ⎣ was   hit by John
               (beneficial)

The above examples indicate that bị/được may function as verbs. This does not necessarily entail
that the bị/duoc in (72) are identical to the bị/
được in (76). The clauses in (72) are not passive.
The "passivity" of (73), (74) and (75) is due to the
translation of bị/được as be allowed, be permitted
and be forced respectively. Truitner argues that if
bị/được in (73), (74), (75) and (76) are treated as
main verbs, similarly to muốn, the identical surface
structure of these clauses would be accounted for.
Both the bị / được and the muốn - clauses
could be derived by Equi-NP-deletion which would
delete the underlying subject in (73), (74) and (75)
and the underlying object in (76) coreferential with
the matrix subject. According to Truitner, Equi-NP-
deletion for bị / được and muốn - type clauses is
optional. The clauses in (77) are grammatical surface structures in Vietnamese.

(77) a. Kim muốn   John đánh Kim
        Kim wanted John hit Kim
        'Kim wanted John to hit her'.

     b. Kim bị   John đánh Kim
        Kim   John hit Kim
        ??Kim suffered John hit her

     c. Kim được   John đánh Kim
        Kim   John hit Kim
        ??Kim received John hit her

However, we fail to see how (77b,c) can be regarded
as passive. (77b,c) are clearly complex sentences.
There is no evidence for deriving (76) from (77) as
opposed to (78).

153

THE PERIPHRASTIC PASSIVE

(78) John dańh Kim
      John hit Kim.

In (77b,c) bị/được have to have a lexical value,
while in (76) they only add an adversative or beneficial meaning. Bị/được similarly cannot have full
semantic content in the clauses below.

(79) Ngày tấn   công được quyết định hôm qua
      day attack   decide   day past
      'The day of the attack was decided upon
      yesterday'.

(80) Trật tự được văn   hồi
      order law   re-establish
      'Law and order was restored'.

Consider now the following example from Le (1976:
443-44).

(81) Hôm qua Mary được John thành thật hứa
      day past Mary   John sincerely promise
      giúp tuần tới
      help week come
      'Yesterday Mary was sincerely promised by
      John that he would help her next week'.

The sentence in (81) is modified by two time adverbials hômqua 'yesterday' and tuần tới 'next week'.
Le (1976) contends that as the two adverbs are incompatible, they cannot occur in the same simplex
clause and thus (81) must be a complex sentence. It
is difficult to imagine that anyone would want to
claim otherwise. What Le has shown is that hứa
'promise' and giúp 'help' belong to two different
clauses. He has not demonstrated that được and hứa
are not in the same simplex clause.
     The passive auxiliaries and the homophonous main
verbs in the well known European languages display
different distributional characteristics and diverge
semantically. Similar facts appear to hold for the
Vietnamese bị/được and Thai thùuk. The arguments
which Le (1976) and Truitner (1972) present do not
conclusively determine that we are not dealing with
homophonous verbs. If this is indeed the case the
discussed clauses may be assumed to be simplex.

4.3.2 The *Indirect* Passive

The Japanese *indirect* passive (82c) differs from the
direct passive (82b) in that it has no active count-

154

THE PERIPHRASTIC PASSIVE

erpart. (82a) is the corresponding active of (82b) not of (82c).

(82) a. Doroboo ga Taroo no zitensha o
       thief   nom Taroo gen bike   acc
       nusanda
       steal:past
       'A thief stole Taroo's bike'.

   b. Taroo no zitensha ga doroboo ni
      Taroo gen bike   nom thief   by
      nusum-are-ta
      steal-pass-past
      'Taroo's bike was stolen by a thief'.

   c. Taroo ga doroboo ni zitensha o
      Taroo nom thief   by bike   acc
      nusum-are-ta
      steal-pass-past
      'Taroo had his bike stolen by a thief'.

Keenan (1975) claims that (82c) has an underlying structure where Taroo is the topic and doroboo the subject. Under this analysis, the underlying sub-ject.is demoted by the passive and subsequently the topic is converted to subject. Shimizu (1975) makes a similar claim the only difference being that the topic Taroo is itself derived from a possessor NP. Thus according to Shimizu, (82c) is derived from (82a), but indirectly. Hasegawa (1964), Kuroda (1965), Howard (1968), Kuno (1971) and McCawley (1972, 1975) derive (82c) from a complex underlying structure, as in (42b), where rare or the abstract predicate affect are the main verbs.
    Vietnamese (83b) and Thai (85a) appear to pos-sess similar constructions.

Vietnamese

(83) a. Radô của   Nam bị cảnh sát tịch thâu
       radio belong Nam   police   confiscate
       'Nam's radio was confiscated by the
       police'.

   b. Nam bị cảnh sát tịch thâu   radô của
      Nam   police   confiscate radio belong
      nó
      he
      'Nam had his radio confiscated by the
      police'.

THE PERIPHRASTIC PASSIVE

Thai

> (84) a. Lûuk Sùdaa thùuk khrùu tii
> child Suda teacher beat
> 'Suda's child was beaten by the teacher'

> (85) a. Sudaa thùuk khəmooy khîn bâan
> Suda thief enter house
> 'Suda had his house entered into by a
> thief'.

The difference between (83b) in Vietnamese and (84a)
and (85a) in Thai parallels the difference between
the Japanese (82b) and (82c). The Thai (84a) could
be derived from (84b), but (85b), according to Lekawatana (1970), is not the active of (85a).

> (84) b. Khəmooy khîn bâan Sùdaa
> thief enter house Suda
> 'A thief broke into Suda's house'.

> (85) b. Khruu tii lûuk Sùdaa
> teacher beat child Suda
> 'The teacher beat Suda's child'.

Note also that both (84c) and (85c) are ungrammatical.

> (84) c. *Bâan Sùdda thùuk khəmooy khîn
> house Suda thief enter
> ('Suda's house was broken into').

> (85) c. *Sùdaa thùuk khruu tii lûuk
> Suda teacher beat child
> ('Suda has his child beaten by the
> teacher').

Le (1976) as one of the arguments for the complex
sentence analysis quotes the following example.

Vietnamese

> (86) a. John bị Paul không mời bạn gái
> John Paul not invite friend girl
> của nó
> belong he
> 'John suffered; Paul did not invite his
> girl friend'.

156

THE PERIPHRASTIC PASSIVE

(86) b. John không bị Paul mời bạn gái
John not   Paul invite friend girl
của nó
belong he
'John did not suffer Paul's inviting
his girl friend'.

The examples (86a) and (86b) appear to differ only
in the position of the negative particle không. Le
argues that if bị and mời belong to the same simplex,
the shifting of the position of không would not produce a change in meaning. But (86a) and (86b) are
not synonymous. (86a) means that John suffered in
that Paul did not invite his girl friend, while (86b)
means that John was not subjected to the embarrass-
ment, indignity etc. of Paul's inviting his girl
friend. This discrepancy in meaning, according to
Le, indicates that bị and mời belong to two different clauses. Since (86) are examples of the *indirect* passive, the scope of the negative kông supports
a complex sentence analysis of *indirect* passives
not the *direct* passive.

The *indirect* passive, unlike the *direct* passive,
does not appear to be compatible with the relational
approach to passivization. Neither Keenan's (1975)
nor Shimizu's (1975) analyses are particularly con-
vincing. Consider, for example, the Japanese (87a)
(McCawley 1975:131).

(87) a. Taroo ga niwaka-ame ni hur-are- te
Taroo nom sudden-rain   fall-pass in
komatte ita node
trouble as ...
'As it rained suddenly and Taro was in
trouble ...'

It is impossible to claim that (87a) is derived from
either (87b) or (87c) because both are ungrammatical.

(87) b.*Niwaka - ame ga Taroo ni o hut-ta
sudden   rain nom Taro   acc fall-past
('The sudden shower fell to Taro').

c.*Taroo no niwaka - ame ga hut-ta
Taro gen sudden - rain nom fall-past
('Taro's sudden shower fell').

In fact, the relevant active clause involved in (87a)
is (87d).

THE PERIPHRASTIC PASSIVE

    (87) d. Niwaka - ame ga hut-ta
         sudden - rain nom fall-past
         'The sudden shower fell'.

(87a) is clearly a complex sentence with <u>Taroo</u> as
both the underlying and surface subject.
   Clauses like (87a) can be treated as passive
only if either the passive is defined in structural
terms or abstract underlying structures which are
never realized on the surface are "permitted" in
grammar. The same applies to (82c), (83b), (85b)
and (86). If on the other hand it is assumed that
passive clauses must have a corresponding active
which actually may occur in the language, the enumerated examples are not passive. Note that the
lack of a corresponding active to (87a) cannot be
treated as an accidental gap or the result of a language specific constraint as in Nitinaht or Tiwa.
   If we have interpreted the Vietnamese and Thai
data correctly, both these languages, like Japanese,
have a *direct* passive and an *indirect* passive. Le
(1976) and Wongbiasaj (1979) argue that the Vietnamese and Thai passives invalidate the relational
characterization of passivization because no promotion or demotion or, in fact, any NP movement is
involved. Both linguists fail to differentiate
between the *direct* and *indirect* constructions. The
indirect passive does not meet the criteria for passivization, but the direct passive does. Even if
the *direct* passive were to be analyzed as a complex
sentence, how can (88b) under Le's analysis be accounted for by other than a rule of spontaneous demotion.

Vietnamese

    (88) a. Ông đó bị họ giết ở Sàigon
            Man that   they kill in Saigon
            'The man was killed in Saigon by them'.

         b. Ông đó bị giết ở Sàigon
            man that   kill in Saigon
            'That man was killed in Saigon'.

Le maintains that the subject of the embedded clause
họ does not lose any of its subject properties and
continues to function as a subject. The free deletability of họ argues for its oblique status as pre-
dicted under the relational view.
   If all passive clauses, just periphrastic passives or in fact only passive clauses in Vietnamese

158

THE PERIPHRASTIC PASSIVE

and Thai are treated as complex sentences, then
indirect passives have to be regarded as passive
too. This would not be a problem if it would not
entail abandoning the relational definition of the
passive. Unfortunately, it does. As the relational
definition of the passive is the only definition
which appears to be applicable to the majority of
clauses which have been called passive, if it is
abandoned a new definition has to be found. Truitner
(1972), and Clark (1974a,b) have suggested that
the passive in the South-East Asian languages should
be defined as a structure containing a complement
verb which requires that at least one NP of the
complement clause must be correferential to the
subject of the matrix clause. If the term *passive*
is used to describe complement verbs with the above
characteristics, then it cannot be used to describe
structures which do not display these properties.
Conversely, if the term *passive* is used in the sense
that it has been employed here and Truitner's (1972),
Clark's (1974a,b), Le's (1976) and Wongbiasaj's
(1979) analyses of the discussed structures in the
South-East Asian languages are correct, then these
structures are not passive.

NOTES

    1.   Wasow (1977) and Lightfoot (1979) contend
that only some passive past participles are adjectives. (cf.p.146).
    2.   Note that (13), (14), (15) and (16a) are
personal passives, not impersonal. Thus, with these
auxiliary verbs, German allows passivization of
certain recipients.
    3.   Sussex (1982) claims that get-passives may
also be used in neutral contexts and that the adver-
sative/beneficial dichotomy depends on various con-
tingent rather than inherent properties of the get-
passive.
    4.   For some speakers of English only the get-
passive is possible with be being as in (I).

      I.   John $\left\{ \begin{array}{l} \text{will be} \\ \text{would be} \\ \text{has been} \\ \text{had been} \\ \text{will have been} \\ \text{would have been} \end{array} \right\}$ getting killed.

    5.   The term *stative* passive is not a very
appropriate one for a large number of passive

THE PERIPHRASTIC PASSIVE

clauses such as (II), which do not fulfil the two characteristics mentioned below are also semantically stative.

II. a. He was known by all the people in the neighbourhood.
 b. The problem was understood by everyone.
 c. Mother was displeased by Mark's behaviour.
 d. The square is surrounded by a circle.
 e. The dinner was followed by a show.

We use the term here as it has been used by Curme (1931), Svartvik (1966), Huddleston (1971), Stein (1979) and Beedham (1982).
6. The inability of passive clauses to occur in the imperative (with few exceptions) reflects the stative component of the passive, which is not being questioned here.
7. Fiengo (1974) combines an adjectival treatment of past participles with a complex sentence analysis. Jackendoff (1977) also discusses such a proposal.
8. This is not the case in all languages. In Swedish and Polish, for example, both adjectives and past participles may take a nominal complement, as in (III).

Polish

III. Marek   był wierny   żonie
 Mark:nom was faithful wife:dat
 'Mark was faithful to his wife'.

9. They may of course occur with <u>seem</u>, <u>look</u>, <u>sound</u>, and <u>appear</u> etc.
10. Adjectives may be qualified by <u>often</u> and <u>seldom</u> if they occur in predicative position.

IV. He is $\begin{cases} \text{seldom} \\ \text{often} \end{cases}$ happy.

11. Only a restricted number of past participles may take an adjectival complement.

V. The dog was found dead
 They were buried alive.
 It was washed white.
 It is eaten raw.

12. The notion of *theme* is used in the Gruberian sense where it refers to the central participant

160

THE PERIPHRASTIC PASSIVE

in the proposition expressed by the clause. According to S. Anderson (1977:367), for example, with a motion verb it is the entity that moves; with a verb specifying location it is the entity whose location is thus defined; with many transitive verbs it is the patient or entity that undergoes the action described.

13.   We will not gloss any of these constituents because we have not been able to determine what the correct gloss should be. The Thai <u>thùuk</u> is typically glossed as 'to receive', 'come in contact with'; the Vietnamese <u>được</u> 'to receive', 'obtain', 'benefit' 'undergo' or 'experience something pleasant' and <u>bị</u> as 'to suffer, be victim of, undergo', or 'experience something unpleasant'. However, we are not at all sure whether these glosses are appropriate in all instances.

Chapter Five

REFLEXIVE PASSIVE

5.0   General Comments

Passive clauses such as the Russian (1c) which display similar morphological marking to reflexive
clauses have been called reflexive passives.

(1) a. Rebenok-∅ umy-l   -sja
       child-nom wash:perf-past -refl
       'The child washed himself'.

    b. Devock-a my-la   pol-∅
       girl-nom wash:imperf-past floor-acc
       'The girl was washing the floor'.

    c. Pol-∅   my-l   -sja[1] devock-oj
       floor-nom wash:imperf -refl   girl-inst
       'The floor was being washed by the girl'.

Reflexive passives are found mainly in the Slavic,
Germanic, and Romance branches of Indo-European, in
the Uto-Aztecan languages, in some Turkic languages
(Uigur, Tatar, Turkish), Ethiopian Semitic languages
(Tigre, Tigrinya, Amharic, Harai, Aggrobba, Gurage),
languages of the Australian continent (Lardil,
Ngarinjin, Guugu-Yimidhir, Dja:bugay) and in the
Dravidian language Dhangar-Kurux. According to
Tucker and Bryan (1966), the North East African
languages: Dongo, Mba, Ngunga, and Ma also use this
construction, but only with a restricted number of
verbs.
       The term *reflexive* passive is not often used in
the literature primarily because *reflexive* passives
are frequently confused with other constructions
containing a reflexive morpheme. This is not surprising for in many cases it is extremely difficult
to determine whether a given construction is passive

162

REFLEXIVE PASSIVES

or not. Some of the difficulties will be illustrated below.
   The use of a reflexive morpheme in Indo-European
passives is generally attributed to the original
active/middle voice system of Indo-European. In
Indo-European the active voice was used to portray
the subject as simply the doer of the action, while
the middle voice expressed actions or states which
immediately affected the subject or its interests.
The middle voice, according to Lyons (1968), Barber
(1975) and Klaiman (1982) (among others), embraced:

a) plain middle - results of action accrue to subject
b) reciprocal middle - referents of plural subject
   do action to one another
c) reflexive middle - subject performs action to
   self
d) nucleonic middle - object of action belongs to,
   moves into or moves from sphere of subject
e) deponent middle - action denotes physical/mental
   disposition of subject
f) passive - subject does nothing, is affected in
   consequence of action

In the course of time languages such as English
underwent a reanalysis due to which the middle category was lost. The first five functions of the
middle were subsumed by the active voice and the
passive function was singled out to constitute a
new separate passive voice. Russian, Greek, Hebrew
and German, for example, have partially retained
the Indo-European middle voice displayed by the formal similarity of reflexives and some passives while
simultaneously developing a separate passive, in the
case of Russian and Greek confined to the perfective.
The common denominator of reflexives and passives
under this interpretation is the "affectedness" of
the subject.
   Haiman (1976) and Langacker and Munro (1975)
have suggested two other explanations for the use
of reflexive morphology in passive clauses. Haiman
claims that the use of the same morpheme to mark
both reflexives and passives is not surprising since
the two constructions are similar in the sense that
the superficial subject of each is identical to the
underlying direct object. Langacker and Munro on
the other hand contend that the identical morphological marking is due to the fact that in both constructions the subject and the object are nondistinct.
They state that (ibid):

163

REFLEXIVE PASSIVES

in reflexives subject and direct object are
nondistinct by virtue of coreference and in
passives by virtue of the fact that the subject
is unspecified and hence cannot contrast with
the object in either reference or content.

Langacker and Munro do not consider the passive
agent to be an integral part of the passive. They
do not derive passive clauses from underlying active
ones, but rather from complex clauses with an unspecified agent embedded under the predicate be (cf.
p.143).
Both Haiman's and Langacker and Munro's analyses could potentially account for the reflexive
marking of personal passives, such as the Russian
(1c). However, by their own admission, they fail
to explain the presence of a reflexive morpheme in
impersonal passives formed from basic intransitive
verbs as, for instance, in Czech.

(2) W tomto městě se žija dobře
    in this town refl live:s well
    'People live well in this town'.

Langacker and Munro argue that although the notion
of non-distinctiveness in their opinion is not applicable to intransitive clauses, languages may extend
tend the reflexive morpheme to mark unspecified
subjects *per se* not just instances of non-distinctiveness. The whole argument rests on the assumption
that the underlying subject of all passive clauses
is unspecified. This is by no means an uncontroversial suggestion. Nevertheless, even if this analysis is not correct from a synchronic point of view,
it is a feasible diachronic interpretation. The
relationship between reflexives and passives is
indubitably an interesting problem. However, it
will not be pursued here.
    This chapter will be concerned with the problem
of synchronically distinguishing reflexive passives
from other constructions containing a reflexive
morpheme (5.1). The second section will briefly
deal with some of the differences observed between
plain and reflexive passives in European languages.

5.1   Reflexive Passives and Other Constructions

Reflexive passives like *plain* passives may be divided into personal and impersonal. The former are
superficially similar to regular reflexives and
anticausatives (cf.p.77), the latter to indefinite

REFLEXIVE PASSIVES

active clauses.

5.1.1   Personal Reflexive Passives

In some languages regular reflexives and reflexive passives can be distinguished quite easily. Thus, for instance, in Russian regular reflexives occur typically with animate subjects and obviously do not allow an agent in the instrumental case, while passive constructions are restricted to inanimate subjects and˅can co-occur with an agent. Compare (1c) with the ungrammatical (3) and (4).

> (3) *Kŏsk-a my-la   -s' devočk-oj
>   cat-nom wash:imperf -refl girl-inst
>   ('The cat was being washed by the girl'.)

> (4) *Rebonok-∅ umy-l   -sja devočk-oj
>   child-nom wash:perf-past -refl girl-inst
>   ('The child washed itself by the girl'.)

In most of the European languages personal reflexive passives also tend to occur with inanimate subjects. Clauses such as (5) from Spanish (Hadlich 1971:91), (6) from Italian (Costa:1975:115), and (7) from Serbo-Croatian (Spalatin 1973:119) are less typical.[2]

Spanish

> (5) Adán y Eva se   expulsaron   del
>   Adam and Eve refl. expel:past:3pl of:the
>   Edén
>   Eden
>   'Adam and Eve were thrown out of Eden'.

Italian

> (6) Nel   medio evo si   bruciavano
>   in:the middle age refl. burn:imperf:3pl
>   le   streghe
>   the:f:pl witches
>   'In the middle ages witches were burned'.

Serbo-Croatian

> (7) Zukupnici   su   se   silom
>   tenants:nom were refl. force:inst
>   istjerivali
>   throw out:past:3pl
>   'The tennants were forced off'.

165

REFLEXIVE PASSIVES

No animacy restriction on the subject of reflexive passives exists in other languages as evidenced by (8) from Greek (Warburton 1975:563), (9) from Shoshoni (Langacker 1976:22) and (10) from Lardil (Klokeid 1976a).

Greek

    (8) O Nickos skoto-θike   apo tus exθrus
        Nick kill-refl:3s:past by the enemy
    'Nick was killed by the enemy'.

Shoshoni

    (9) Haɨwañ ʔa-t ʔɨ-wuu   ʔab ʔamɉɨd   g
        cow:nom aux-perf refl rope there from art
        Huan
        John
    'The cow got roped by John'.

Lardil

    (10) Nyingki pe-yi   kun   ngawun
        you:abs bite-refl eventive dog:dat
      'You were bitten by the dog'.

The reflexive personal passive in the Romance languages is restricted to third person subjects. In addition, pronominal subjects referring to animate entities cannot be used. In Italian, for instance, when a NP like _le belle donne_ in (11a) is pronominalized it takes the form of an accusative (11c), not a nominative (11b) pronoun   (Napoli 1976:129).

    (11) a. Si   notano   subito   le
           refl note:pres:3pl immediately the:f:pl
           belle   donne
           beautiful women
        'Beautiful women are immediately noted'.

        b.*Loro   si   notano   subito
          they:f:nom refl note:pres:3pl immediately
          ('They are immediately noted'.)

        c. Le   si $\begin{Bmatrix}\text{notano}\\\text{nota}\end{Bmatrix}$ subito

          they:f:acc refl $\begin{Bmatrix}\text{note:pres:3pl}\\\text{note:pres:3s}\end{Bmatrix}$ immedia-
                                        tely

        'They are immediately noted'.

REFLEXIVE PASSIVES

The resulting construction is thus more like an impersonal reflexive passive than a personal one. However, when an inanimate NP is pronominalized, for example i libri gialli in (12a), it may take either the nominative pronoun (12c) or the accusative (12b).

(12) a. Si prendono   i   libri gialli
        refl take:pres:3pl the books mystery
        'The mystery books are taken'.

     b. Li   si   ⎰prendono⎱
                        ⎱prende ⎰

        they:m:acc refl ⎰take:pres:3pl⎱
                        ⎱take:pres:3s ⎰

        'They are taken'.

     c. Essi   si   prendono
        they:m:nom refl take:pres:3pl
        'They are taken'.

As indicated by (9) and (10), the reflexive passive in Shoshoni and Lardil is not restricted in a similar fashion.

The existence of a passive agent is not a sufficient criterion for distinguishing reflexive passives and regular reflexives as only in Lardil, Papago, Dhangar-Kurux, and Russian is an agent regularly permitted.[3] Examples such as (13) from Portuguese (Naro 1976) and (14) from Romanian (Vasiliu and Golopentia-Eretescu 1972) are far less frequent.

Portuguese

(13) Don Nuno examinou   se   pelos
     Don Nuno examine:past:3s refl by
     examinadores
     examiners
     'Don Nuno was examined by the examiners'.

Romanian

(14) Cartea se   citeşte de   către studenţi
     book   refl read:3s by   students
     'The book is read by the students'.

Consequently the Greek (15) (Warburton 1975:570) and Papago (16) (Langacker 1976:12) can be understood as either passive or reflexive.

167

REFLEXIVE PASSIVES

Greek

(15) dieike
dress:refl:3s
'He got dressed (himself)' // 'He was
dressed by someone'.

Papago

(16) Ta'mɨ   na-pui-ka
we:incl refl-see-resultative
'We are seen' // 'We see ourselves'.

In most cases this type of ambiguity would be resolved by context or the nature of the verb. The
Spanish (5), although similar to a reflexive, would
not be assigned a regular reflexive reading, for
according to tradition Adam and Eve did not leave
Eden voluntarily. The passive interpretation in
this case is the only likely one.

Whereas reflexive passives with animate subjects
can be interpreted either as passive or reflexive,
reflexive passives with inanimate subjects are often
ambiguous between a passive and an anticausative
reading. The similarity between reflexive passives
and anticausatives in Russian has already been discussed, (cf.2.3). In Russian the two constructions
can be disambiguated by reference to an agent which
can be expressed in the former but not the latter.
Similarly in Dhangar-Kurux the passive (17) can co-
occur with an agent but the anticausative (18) cannot (Gordon 1973:101).

(17) Xess   xooy-r-a   naraynas xekkh -ti
paddy reaped-refl Narayan's hand   by
'The paddy was reaped by Narayan'.

(18) DanDa es-r-a   (*naraynas xekkh-ti)
stick broke-refl Narayan's hand-by
'The stick broke (*by Narayan)'.

The same criterion cannot be used in Amharic.
Titov (1976:64) claims that each of the following
clauses can be interpreted either as passive or anticausative.

(19) Bɛr tə   - kəffətə
door refl - opened
'The door was opened' // 'The door opened'.

168

REFLEXIVE PASSIVES

(20) Ṭorənnət tə-fəssəmə
war   refl-ended
'The war was ended (stopped)' // 'The war
ended'.

(21) Jəbəna   tə-səbbərə
coffee pot refl-broken
'The coffee pot was broken' // 'The coffee
pot broke'.

He maintains that only the exact linguistic or extralinguistic context will resolve this ambiguity.
Many clauses which have been labeled *passive*
(Contreras 1974), (Donaldson 1970), (Green 1975),
notional passive (Wołczyńska-Sudół 1976), *middle*
(Kayne 1975), (Napoli 1976), (Valfells 1970), *pseudo-reflexive* (Schroṭen 1972), *quasi-reflexive* (Channon
1974) or *illogical reflexive* such as the following
examples from Icelandic (22), French (23), Polish
(24), Portuguese (25) and German (26) appear to be
in fact anticausatives.

Icelandic

(22) Glasið fyllti-st
glass filled-refl
'The glass filled'.

French

(23) Cette étoffe se   lave   bien
this cloth refl wash:pres:3s well
'This cloth washes well'.

Polish

(24) Brud ściera   się
dirt rub off:pres:3s refl
'The dirt rubs off'.

Portuguese

(25) O   papel se   enrugou
the paper refl wrinkle:past:3s
'The paper wrinkled'.

German

(26) Die Tür öffnet   sich
the door open:pres:3s refl
'The door opens'.

169

REFLEXIVE PASSIVES

All these clauses involve actions that logically require an outside agent. Yet in each case there is a feeling that the inanimate subject is by its nature affecting or initiating the action. As mentioned previously, a reflexive pronoun is somehow inherent. in these constructions. García (1975:33) states that Spanish children frequently add de solo 'on its own' to this type of clause. Horn (1977), Valfells (1970), Gordon (1973), and Wołczyńska-Sudół (1976) make similar claims for Italian, Icelandic, Dhangar-Kurux and Polish respectively. Passive clauses in these languages cannot co-occur with a reflexive agent.

In anticausative constructions the subject is understood as possessing some property which facilitates the action as, for example, in (27) from Italian.

Italian

(27) Il   libro si   è venduto
     the book refl is sell:p.part:m;s
     a causa della   copertina molto sexy[4]
     because of:the cover   very sexy
     'The book has sold because of its sexy
     cover'.

When passive clauses occur with manner adverbs e.g. well, easily, etc. the adverb is interpreted as qualifying an agent irrespective of whether the agent is specified or not. In clauses such as the German (28) and the French (22) the adverb qualifies the verb.

German

(28) Das Buch liest   sich leicht
     this book read:pres:3s refl easily
     'This book reads easily'.

(22) and (28) can be paraphrased as The cloth is washable and The book is readable. The canonical passives would mean Somebody washes the cloth well and Somebody does the reading well.

Although the subject NPs are viewed as partially responsible for the action, they are not fully agentive as evidenced by the ungrammaticality of these clauses with agentive adverbs such as celowo in Polish (29) and deliberadamente in Spanish (30).

170

REFLEXIVE PASSIVES

(29) *Drzwi-ó zamknęły   się celowo
     door-nom shut:past:3pl refl deliberately
     ('The door shut deliberately'.)

Spanish

(30) *Las ventanas se   rompieron
     the windows   refl break:past:3pl
     deliberadamente
     deliberately
     ('The windows broke deliberately'.)

Passive clauses freely occur with these adverbs.
      Are these clauses thus passive or anticausative?
As far as we have been able to determine the Polish,
Icelandic, and French examples can only be interpreted as anticausative. García (1975) argues that
both interpretations are possible in Spanish, but
not in all cases. A clause like (31), for instance,
depending on the context can be understood as a passive or anticausative.

(31) Se   quemó   el dulce
     refl burn:past:3s the jam
     'The jam was burnt' // 'The jam burnt.'

(32) on the other hand is only open to a passive
reading.

(32) Se   cumplieron   las promesas
     refl fulfil:past:3pl the promises
     'The promises were fulfilled'.

García suggests that the difference between the two
is related to the nature of the verbs. Jam left
unattended may burn by itself, whereas promises, at
least in one sense of the word, can only be fulfilled
by someone.   The clauses (33) and (34) (Hadlich
1971) could hardly be assigned an anticausative
reading.

(33) Esta novela se   escribió   en 1938
     this book   refl write:past:3s in 1938.
     'This book was written in 1938'.

(34) Las pirámides se   contruyeron   hace
     the pyramids refl build:past:3pl ago
     muchos anos
     many   years
     'The pyramids were built many years ago'.

171

REFLEXIVE PASSIVES

The situation in Italian is similar. With the verbs _apire_ 'open', _congelare_ 'freeze', _iniziare_ 'initiate, _chiudere_ 'close' etc. an anticausative inter-pretation is more probable, while (35) (Lo Cascio 1976a:57) and (36) (Costa 1975:113) can only be interpreted as passive.

(35) Le due proposte di legge domani si
     the two bills   of law   tomorrow refl
     discuteranno
     discuss:fut:3pl
     'The two bills will be discussed tomorrow'.

(36) I   fatti si   sanno   già
     the facts refl know:pres:3pl already
     'The facts are already known'.

In both Spanish and Italian, word order may help to disambiguate potentially ambiguous clauses. Costa (ibid) claims that a clause with a NP in preverbal position (37) will be interpreted as an anticausative, while (38) with the NP in postverbal position will be assigned a passive reading.

(37) Questa porta si   apre   in continuazione
     this   door   refl open:pres:3s continually
     'The door keeps on opening'.

(38) Si   apre   questa porta
     refl open:pres:3s this
     in continuazione
     continually
     'This door keeps on being opened'.

García (1975) notes the same facts for Spanish.

Curme (1960) and Hammer (1971) profess that German clauses with reflexive morphemes, like the Spanish and Italian ones, are also open to both a passive and an anticausative interpretation, but again not in all cases.

(39) So etwas   spricht   sich schnell
     so something speak:pres:3s refl quickly
     herum
     about
     'Such a thing is soon spread about' //
     'Such a thing soon spreads'.

REFLEXIVE PASSIVES

(40) Der Mut   verlernt   sich nicht, wie
     the courage acquire:pres:3s refl not   how
     er sich nicht lernt
     it refl not   learn:pres:3s
     'Courage is a natural gift that cannot be
     acquired or learnt'.

Reflexive passives, especially in the Romance languages, are structurally similar to indefinite active constructions. In fact, many of the enumerated clauses are usually considered as active with an unspecified or indefinite subject corresponding to the English one, German man, and French on. An active interpretation is also typically assigned to impersonal reflexive passives to which we now turn.

5.1.2 Impersonal Reflexive Passives

The literature on impersonal reflexive passives is confined to German, the Slavic and the Romance languages.[5] The German impersonal reflexive passive is rather infrequent and occurs only with intransitive verbs or verbs like read, write, smoke etc. which can be used both transitively or intransitively.

(41) Es tanzt   sich gut hier
     it dance:pres:3s refl well here
     'One dances well here'.

(42) Es liest   sich in der Dämmerung
     it read:pres:3s refl in the twilight
     schlecht
     badly
     'It's bad reading in the twilight'.

In Czech and Serbo-Croatian both basically intransitive (2) and transitive verbs (43) can be found in this construction.

Czech

(43) W tomto obchodě se   prodává   chleb
     in this store   refl sell:pres:3s bread
     'Bread is sold in this store'.

Similarly in the Romance languages as illustrated by the Romanian (44) (Vasilu and Golopentia-Eretescu 1972), Spanish (45) (Comrie 1977a), and Italian (46) (Costa 1975).

173

REFLEXIVE PASSIVES

Romanian

> (44) Se   citeşte   mult acolo
>   refl read:pres:3s much here
>   'One reads a lot here'.

Spanish

> (45) En Europa no   se   nos   conoce
>   in Europe not refl we:acc know:pres:3s
>   'In Europe we are not known'.

Italian

> (46) Non si   dice   queste cose
>   no   refl say:pres:3s these   things
>   'These things aren't said'.

No agent can be overtly expressed in any of these clauses.

Like *plain* impersonal passives, reflexive im - personal passives are often treated as active imper- sonal or indefinite constructions. Hadlich (1971:36) for example, states that the Spanish clauses (47) and (48) cannot be interpreted as passive because the verb vivir in (47) is intransitive and the noun relojes in (48) does not govern verbal agreement and, therefore, cannot be treated as the subject of the clause.

> (47) Se   vive   bien en América.
>   refl live:pres:3s well in America
>   'One lives well in America'.

> (48) Se   compra   relojes aquí
>   refl buy:pres:3s clocks   here
>   'Clocks are bought here'.

Wołczyńska-Sudół (1976:163) gives similar arguments against a passive treatment of the Polish (51) in ch.3.Napoli (1976:130) contends that the existence of clauses such as (46) and (49) proves that there are no reflexive passive clauses in Italian, but rather indefinite active constructions.

> (49) Dopo la   lezione, si   va   a casa
>   after the lesson   refl go:pres:3s to house
>   'After the lesson one goes home'.

She states:

REFLEXIVE PASSIVES

> If we are to analyze indefinite si-sentences as
> passive, where the deep accusative object
> becomes the surface subject, how do we account
> for indefinite sentences which have no accusa-
> tive object?

Apparently, the possibility of treating the above
clauses as impersonal passives has not occurred to
any of these linguists. Neither the intransitivity
of the verb nor the lack of nominative case marking
or verbal agreement necessarily precludes a passive
interpretation.

Although the above mentioned clauses cannot be
labeled as active on the basis of the arguments
given, their passive status, especially in Italian
and Spanish, is also quite controversial.[6] In most
works on Italian and Spanish si/se-clauses containing basically transitive verbs which display no verbal agreement are treated as active indefinite,
active impersonal or indeterminate subject clauses.
Many linguists do, nevertheless, admit that these
clauses are open to a passive interpretation. Si/
se-clauses with intransitive verbs on the other
hand are almost without exception regarded as active.
Whether at least some of these clauses should be
treated as active or passive, depends on the status
attributed to the morphemes si and se. Linguists
who contend that all the above mentioned clauses are
active regard si and se as indefinite subjects.
Those who allow for a passive interpretation view
these clauses as subjectless, (Green 1975; García
1975; Stefanini 1982).

Si/se do not display the distributional characteristics of subject pronouns, but rather that of
clitics. Since no subject clitics exist in either
Italian or Spanish, no ready criteria are available
to determine whether these constituents can be classified as subjects. Napoli (1976) argues that they
are indeed subjects. She contends that all si-
clauses in Italian are active not passive. Under
her analysis, the underlying subject of si-clauses
is an indefinite third person plural subject which
is labeled as Pro. Si is introduced by a rule of
si-insertion which obligatorily deletes Pro and
inserts si. Napoli points out that although she
prefers to call si a subject clitic, it may also be
treated as a marker for the loss of the underlying
subject. Under the definition of the passive adopted
herein, if si is a marker indicating the loss of
the underlying subject, then si-clauses qualify as

175

REFLEXIVE PASSIVES

passive. Assuming, however, that si- is an indefinite third person plural subject, then what is the
difference between si and the indefinite pronoun
uno? Napoli claims that si differs from uno in
that uno is not a clitic and also in that si, unlike
uno, can replace indefinite direct objects as well
as subjects, as in (50a) and (51a).

(50) a. Si è giudicati   dal re
        refl is judge p.part:m:pl by king
        'One is judged by the king'.

(51) a. Si è pagati   molto
        refl is pay p.part:m:pl much
        'One is paid much'.

In all the works consulted (50a) and (51a) are
labeled passive. As in canonical passive clauses,
the verb is in the past participle and is preceded
by the auxiliary essere 'to be'. Napoli argues
that the rule of si-insertion applies to an underlying
direct object Pro (indefinite third person plural
pronoun). However, there are no surface structures
like (50b) and (51b) in Italian where si can be
interpreted as an indefinite third person plural
direct object.

(50) b. *Il   re   si   giudica
         the:m:s king refl judge:pres:3s
         ('The king judges one'.)

(51) b. *Qualcuno si   paga   molto
         someone refl pay:pres:3s much
         ('Someone pays one very much'.)

Therefore, if Napoli's analysis is correct, passivization must be obligatory in these instances. Note
also that the past participle in (50a) and (51a) is
in the plural which is viewed by Napoli as evidence
that si is the subject of these clauses. There is
one major problem with Napoli's analysis, namely the
grammaticality of (52) and (53) (Lepschy and Lepschy 1977:213, 216).

(52). Questa   opera si   accoglie   con
      this:f:s opera refl acclaim:pres:3s with
      entusiasmo da tutti
      enthusiasm by all
      'This opera is enthusiastically acclaimed
      by all'.

176

REFLEXIVE PASSIVE

(53) Questo   giornale si   legge   ogni
     this:m:s paper   refl read:pres:3s every
     mattina da moltissima gente
     morning by lots   people
     'This paper is read every morning by lots
     of people'.

If si is a third person plural subject in these
clauses, how should da tutti and da moltissima gente
be treated? If conversely si is not a subject clitic,
but a third person plural marker of the demoted
subject, then only third person underlying subjects
should be allowed in si-clauses. This is not the
case because (54) (Costa 1975) with an underlying
first person plural subject is grammatical.

(54) Si   la   vita è sventura, perché da
     if   the:f:s life is tragedy why   by
     noi si   dura
     us refl bear:3s
     'If life is a tragedy why is it borne by us?

Interestingly enough, in (52), (53) and (54) the
verb is in the third person singular agreeing with
what appears to be the subject, namely questa opera,
questo giornale and la vita. Hence both of Napoli's
proposals fail to account for all the facts.
     What then are the alternatives? Linguists like
Hadlich (1971), Contreras (1974), Costa (1975),
Cinque (1976), Lo Cascio (1976a), Lepschy and Lepschy (1977) and Perlmutter and Postal (1978) claim
that some si-clauses in Italian are passive. Unfortunately, they cannot agree on when a clause is passive and when not or on the status of the si. Lepschy
and Lepschy (1977), for instance, state that (55) is
active, (56) passive and (57) can be interpreted as
either active or passive.

(55) Si   sono comprate   due penne
     refl are   buy p.part:f:pl   two pens
     'One has bought two pens'.

(56) Si   sono viste   due stelle
     refl are   see p.part:f:pl   two stars
     'Two stars have been seen'.

(57) La   verità non si   può sempre dire
     the:f:s truth not refl can always tell
     'One cannot always tell the truth'//'The
     truth cannot always be told'.

177

REFLEXIVE PASSIVE

Why (56), but not (55) should be treated as passive is a mystery. In both (55) and (56) the NPs due penne and due stelle govern agreement with the auxiliary in person and number and past participle in number and gender. Yet Lepschy and Lepschy regard due stelle in (56) as the subject and presumably si either as a passive marker or a pronominal copy left "behind" by the original P, while due penne in (55) is taken to be a P and si the subject. The fact that due penne in (55) governs verbal agreement argues that it is the subject of the clause. However, both Napoli (1976) and Lepschy and Lepschy (1977) state that although P NPs typically do not govern verbal agreement in Italian, they may do so. Costa (1975) contends that si is not synchronically related to the reflexive morpheme si and should be treated simply as a passive marker. This analysis also suffers from a number of deficiencies, the most important being that if si is taken to be a passive marker, (50a) and (51a) would have had to have undergone passivization twice. This does not appear to worry Costa (1975:124) who speaking about (58) states:

> The fact that the subordinate clause of (58), under my analysis, would have undergone passivization twice need not raise too many eyebrows, for the two rules perform quite different functions. The auxiliary passive says something about the result of an action or an event, while the agent postposing rule of si- constructions is a prominence reducing rule.

(58) Si   è   fieri   quando si   è
     refl is proud:m:pl when   refl is
     nominati   ambasciatori
     nominate:m:pl ambassador:pl.
     'One is proud when one is nominated ambassador'.

The difference between *plain* and reflexive passives which Costa is referring to will be commented on in 5.2. In any case, if si is a passive marker in (46), (50a), (51a), (52), (53) and (54) what is its function in (55), the active version of (57) and (59) and (60)?

(59) Si   è   capito
     refl is understand:p.part:m:s
     'One has understood'.

178

REFLEXIVE PASSIVE

(60) Si   è   lavorato
     refl is work p.part:m:s
     'One has worked'.

Lepschy and Lepschy (1977), who quote the above two examples, claim that (59) and (60) cannot be understood as passive. Note that the past participle is in the masculine singular and thus under Napoli's (1976) analysis would not agree with si.

The clauses (50) and (51) also pose a problem for RG. In RG the reflexive morphology of reflexive passives is attributed to the fact that when a "2" advances to "1" it retains "2"-hood in the stratum where it assumes "1"-hood i.e. it leaves behind a pronominal copy. (Klokeid 1976a, 1978). As one nominal bears simultaneously two relations to the verb, the lower ranking relation - the pronominal copy - is erased and the verb is marked with the reflexive morpheme. The derivation of (55), for example, is as in (61).

(61)

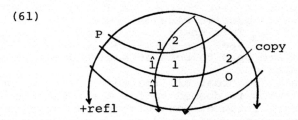

The above analysis of reflexive passives if applied to (50a) and (51a) violates the 1-*Advancement Exclusiveness Law* (1-AEX) which states: 'No clause can involve more than one advancement to "1". If it is assumed that si marks the fact that a nominal has advanced from "2" to "1" and that the passive morphology in (50a) and (51a) i.e. the auxiliary essere and the past participle also indicate that a nominal has advanced from "2" to "1", then the underlying "2" of (50a) and (51a), which according to Perlmutter and Postal (1978) is unspecified, must have advanced to "1" twice. The 1-AEX explicitly precludes such derivations. Nevertheless, (50a) and (51a) are perfectly grammatical. Perlmutter and Postal (1978: 75) have suggested that the 1-AEX should be weakened to account for the grammaticality of (50a) and (51a). The weaker version of the 1-AEX allows two advancements to "1" if the two constituents involved in advancement overlap. Although Perlmutter and Postal now can allow for (50a) and (51a), this does not,

REFLEXIVE PASSIVE

in fact, mean that the above analysis is correct.[7]
Perlmutter and Postal appear to assume that all instances of si should be accounted for in the same
terms. Under such an analysis, all si-clauses would
have to have an underlying "2" which, in fact,
advances to "1". In (46) and (62) the NPs queste
cose and due penne apparently cannot be interpreted
as subjects, while (49) and (63) possess no underlying "2".

(62) Si   compra   due penne
     refl buy:pres:3s two penne
     'One buys two pens'.

(63) Si   parte   alle dieci
     refl leave:pres:3s at   ten
     'One leaves at ten'.

Thus if Perlmutter and Postal assume that the si in
these clauses is also the result of a "2" advancing
to "1", they would have to posit a dummy, like for
other impersonal passive clauses, which advances
from "2" to "1". This sheds no light on the problem
of why some si-clauses are perceived to be active,
while others are open to both an active and a passive interpretation.

Any attempt to treat all instances of si or se
in the same terms is doomed to failure. Under a
demotional definition of passivization a large number of the si/se-clauses could be regarded as passive with si/se functioning as an invariant marker
for the demoted agent. However, si cannot be treated
as a passive marker in (50a) and (51a) or in
regular reflexives. Its status in (59) and (60) is
also a problem. Hopefully, future research will
throw some more light on this issue.

5.2 Reflexive vs *Plain* Passives

Lack of sufficient data on reflexive passives in
non-European languages such as: Lardil, Amharic,
Shoshoni, Tepecano, Northern Paiute etc. makes it
difficult to determine whether reflexive passives
differ from *plain* passives in any major respect.
The only regular feature observed is the underlying
human subject which may be merely coincidental.

In the European languages which possess reflexive passives the agent of a passive clause whether
specified or implied is also human. Russian constitutes the only notable exception in allowing both

REFLEXIVE PASSIVE

non-human agents (64) and inanimate ones (65)
(Beedham 1982:54).

    (64) Jagody   klievali-s pticami
          berries:nom picked-refl birds:inst
          'The berries were being picked by the birds'

    (65) Listja   vzmjetyvali-s vjetrom
          leaves:nom flung-refl   wind:inst
          'The leaves were being flung up by the wind'

Duškova (1972:106) gives the following example with
an inanimate agent from Czech:

    (66) Zivne   latky   se   poblcuji
          nutritive substances refl absorbe
          filtrem,   takze   filtrat byl borsim
          filter:inst so-that filtrate was worse
          mediem pro rust   bakteriï
          medium for growth bacteria
          'Nutritive substances were absorbed by the
          filter so that the filtrate was an inadequ-
          ate medium for the growth of bacteria'.

(66) is atypical since the Czech reflexive passive
does not tend to occur with an overt agent. Amastae
(1983) cites a reflexive passive with a non-human
agent (67) from the St. Thomas French dialect.

    (67) I se   fet tw̃e   par oẽ rétchẽ
          he refl make killed by a   shark
          'He was killed by a shark'.

It has been impossible to establish whether (67) is
similarly an exception or whether this creole freely
permits non-human agents.
    Costa (1975) and García (1975) argue that in
Italian and Spanish there is a significant difference
between reflexive and canonical passive clauses.
They contend that whereas the canonical passive is
a means of backgrounding the agent, the reflexive
passive implies that any specific agent is irrelevant.[8] Consequently in (68a) the agent is said to be
more strongly implied than in (68b) (García 1975:15).

    (68) a. Los   prisioneros fueron
             the:m:pl prisoners   were
             fusilados
             shoot:p.part:m:pl
             'The prisoners were shot'.

REFLEXIVE PASSIVE

(68) b. Se   fusiló   a los   prisioneros
       refl shoot:part:3s the:m:pl prisoners
       'The prisoners were shot'.

However, (68b) is not a personal reflexive passive,
but rather an impersonal one. Kirsner (1976) claims
that in impersonal passives the agent is always more
strongly backgrounded than in personal passives,
because the former, in contrast to the latter, do
not possess a subject. In impersonal passives, since
there is no subject and, therefore, no scale of comparison, no reference point, the backgrounding of
the agent is absolute. If Kirsner is correct, the
difference between (68a) and (68b) would be due
rather to the personal/impersonal distinction not
the *plain*/reflexive one. There does not appear to
be any difference in terms of agent backgrounding
between (69a) and (69b).

Spanish

(69) a. Las   paces fueron firmadas
       the:f:pl peace were   sign:p.part:f:pl
       (por los   embajadores)
        by   the:m:pl ambassadors
       'The peace was signed by the ambassadors'

     b. Se   firmaron   las   paces por
        refl sign:past:3:pl the:f:pl peace by
        los   embajadores
        the:m:pl ambassadors
        'The peace was signed by the ambassadors'

    García's, Costa's and Kirsner's observations
contrast with that of Frajzyngier (1982) (cf. 3.1.2)
who contends that all impersonal passives formed
from intransitive verbs are strongly agentive possessing an indefinite human subject overtly indicated
by the structure of the whole clause. The reflexive
passives quoted in this chapter reveal that a human
agent is not only characteristic of impersonal passives, but also of personal ones and hence invalidate
Frajzyngier's claim pertaining to the lack of restrictions on the agent of passives formed from transitive verbs. Since reflexive passives are typically confined to human agents, the properties of the
agent cannot be used as the defining characteristic
of intransitive impersonal passives.
    Reflexive passives in Italian and Spanish are
also claimed to differ from the corresponding periphrastic passives in relation to topicalization.

182

REFLEXIVE PASSIVE

Note, for example, that while in the periphrastic passive (69a) the patient occurs in initial topic position, in (69b) as well as (6), (12), (31), (32), (38), (46) and (48) it does not. Cinque (1976:26) contends that reflexive passives with patient topics are ungrammatical in Italian. A preference for post-verbal subjects in the reflexive passive is also noted by García (1975) and Costa (1975) (cf. p.172). However, although the patient need not necessarily appear in initial topic position in the reflexive passive, the Spanish (5), (33) and (34) and Italian (35), (36), (52), (53) and (57) quite clearly show that it may. It has already been pointed out (cf.p 41) that in Spanish and Italian the subject in the periphrastic passive need not be the clausal topic. In both languages, as well as in Slavic, which con- stituent is placed in initial position typically de- pends on its given/new status. This issue will be discussed in more detail in 7.1. For the present it is enough to note that, contrary to Cinque's claim, the reflexive passive, like the periphrastic passive, may be used to topicalize the patient.

Whereas *plain* passives are said to portray sim- ultaneously an event and the state arising from that event, reflexive passives in the European languages appear to be purely dynamic. The dynamic character of the reflexive passive is particularly evident in Russian and Greek where the construction is confined to imperfective verbs. In Czech, although there is no similar restriction, the language nevertheless displays a strong preference for using the reflexive passive in the imperfective. Platzack (1980:65) argues that the Swedish s-passive, diachronically related to the reflexive, is also more actional than the two periphrastic passives with be and become because in contrast to the periphrastic passive it:
a) may occur in the imperative

> (70) a. Bollen kastas   till Erik!
>   ball   throw:pass to   Eric
>   'The ball is thrown to Eric!'
>
>   b. Bollen är/blir   kastad till Erik!
>   ball   is/becomes thrown to   Eric
>   'The ball is thrown to Eric'.
>   (acceptable if not interpreted as a
>   command)

b) does not differ semantically from the active with modal auxiliaries.

183

REFLEXIVE PASSIVE

(71) a. Avfallet   kan förstöras
         waste products can destroy:pass
         'The waste products can be destroyed'.

   b. Avfallet   kan bli   förstört
         waste products can become destroyed
         'The waste products may be destroyed'.

c) may take both a stative and an actional adverbial
phrase as the active

(72) Dorren oppnades på/i   tio sekunder
      door   open:pass in/for ten seconds
      'The door was opened in/for ten seconds'.

Compare (72) with (5) in ch.4. The actional element
in the reflexive passive may be seen as a consequence of the reflexive morpheme which in the plain reflexive indicates agency on the part of the subject.
   All the personal reflexive passives cited in the
literature possess patient subjects. This again may
be merely coincidental. The fact that the Swedish
s-passive may take a recipient subject suggests
that reflexive morphology may also be extended to
other semantic roles. Platzack (ibid) regards this
characteristic of the s-passive as yet another indication of the dominating actional function of this
passive, setting it apart from the two periphrastic
constructions.
   The reflexive passive in Czech, Serbo-Croatian,
German and Romance is primarily associated with the
colloquial language. In German its use is fairly
restricted. In Slavic and Romance on the other hand
it is used very extensively in both speech and writing, being preferred to the periphrastic passive in
all but formal registers.
   It is impossible at this stage to determine
whether the differences between *plain* and reflexive
passives noted in the European languages will also
hold for other languages. Further research may enable a comprehensive comparison to be made.

NOTES

   1.   All the morphemes which are phonologically
identical to the reflexive morpheme will be glossed
as refl. This does not mean, however, that we are
dealing with the same morpheme from a synchronic
point of view.
   2.   Stefanini (1982) contends that word order
may influence a passive as opposed to a reflexive

184

REFLEXIVE PASSIVE

interpretation; clauses such as (Ia) being much
more likely to be assigned a passive reading, those
like (Ib) a reflexive one.

I. a. Si   loda   troppo   questo ragazzo
       refl praise:3s too much this   boy
       'The boy is praised too much'.

   b. Questo ragazzo si   loda   troppo
       this   boy   refl praise:3s too much
       'The boy praises himself too much'.

3.   The Greek passive is typically agentless.
The only agents permitted are plural rather than
singular or collective with general rather than
specific reference (Warburton 1975).
4.   The past participle in Italian agrees in
number and gender with the subject.
5.   Langacker and Munro (1975:801) claim that
in Aztec the prefix ne- originally used to indicate
coreference between an unspecified human subject and
direct object, is now also used in impersonal constructions. However, no examples are given.
6.   As mentioned in ch.3, many linguists question the passive status of impersonal passives formed
from intransitive verbs *per se*. We confine the discussion to Italian and Spanish, but similar problems
arise in Portuguese, Romanian, Czech and Serbo-
Croatian.
7.   Timberlake (1982) gives an example of an
impersonal passive formed from a personal passive in
Lithuanian as counterevidence for the promotional
treatment of the impersonal passive. Perlmutter and
Postal's revised I-AEX does not accommodate this
particular problem. More about the 1-AEX will be
said in the next chapter.
8.   The terms *background* and *foreground* as used
by Kirsner (1976) and others in reference to the
passive agent and subject/topic respectively are
slightly unfortunate because from the point of view
of the relative communicative importance of the constituents the subject typically represents background
information while the agent constitutes the focus
of the clause   (cf. ch.7).

Chapter Six

EXCEPTIONS TO THE PASSIVE

6.0   Introduction

Exceptions to the passive have received a considerable amount of attention in recent years, e.g. Bach
(1979), Beedham (1982), Bolinger (1977), Bresnan
(1978), Cureton (1979), Davison (1980), Perlmutter
(1978), Riddle et al. (1977), Sinha (1974, 1978),
Stein (1979) and Ziv and Sheintuch (1981). Nevertheless, the precise factors precluding passivization continue to elude linguists.

   The problem has been attacked from the angle of
syntax, semantics and pragmatics. Linguists who
maintain that the passive depends on the syntactic
relationship between NPs and the verb obviously make
a syntactic distinction between clauses which do and
those which do not passivize, e.g. Emonds (1972, 1976),
Perlmutter and Postal (1978, 1983b), Bresnan (1978) and
Bach (1979). Since for most linguists transitivity
is the defining characteristic of the passive, they
generally claim that clauses which do not have passive counterparts are intransitive. In the literature on the English passive this type of analysis has
been typically used for pseudo-passives, less so for
the passive of non-prepositional objects which has
been unsuccessfully dealt with in terms of strict
subcategorization (the famous Lees (1960) and Chomsky (1965) manner adverbial analysis), thematic relations[1] (e.g. Jackendoff 1972; S. Anderson 1977) or
case frames (e.g. Fillmore 1968, 1977; Starosta
1978). For the second group of linguists the passive is a semantically governed rule in the sense of
Green (1974). By definition a governed rule need
not apply whenever the structural description is met.
It's application is conditioned by semantically spe-
cifiable classes of lexical items. Although the
concept of *rule government* is fairly new, the princ-

EXCEPTIONS TO THE PASSIVE

iple behind it is not. Linguists such as Jespersen
(1933) Owen (1914) and Poutsma (1926) attempted to
handle exceptions to the passive precisely in semantic terms.

Unfortunately, neither transitivity nor semantic
criteria have been capable of dealing with certain
classes of exceptions. Analyses based on transitivity by definition ignore the problem of impersonal
passives and personal passives formed from other
than transitive verbs, while semantically based approaches fail to account for exceptions which do not
appear to have any semantic property in common.

The failure of both syntactic and semantic solutions to the problem has induced some linguists to
seek the answer in pragmatics. The analyses of
linguists such as Bolinger (1977), Davison (1980),
Palmer (1972), Tuyn (1970) and Ziv and Sheintuch
(1981) all suggest that passivization depends on considerations involving the notions: *activity, affect /
result* and *volition*.

The attempts at dealing with exceptions to the
passive in terms of these parameters will be discussed in 6.1. Since all the syntactic proposals of
handling passive exceptions, apart from that of Perlmutter and Postal, are confined only to personal
passives, 6.2 will be devoted to a brief appraisal
of Perlmutter and Postal's analysis. The problems
encountered by both the pragmatic analyses and Perlmutter and Postal's syntactic solution with respect
to the personal passive will be illustrated primarily on the basis of English. However, similar facts
obtain in other languages.

The felicity of passive clauses in any given
language is dependent on an array of not only clause
internal, but also contextual factors. This chapter
will be concerned primarily with the relationship
between the verb and its nominal arguments.

6.1 Exceptions to The Passive and Pragmatics

The factors precluding the personal passive are primarily connected with the relation between the verb
and the underlying direct object. Those affecting
the impersonal passive on the other hand involve the
underlying subject. The two constructions will be
discussed separately in 6.1.1 and 6.1.2 respectively.
Section 6.1.3 will deal briefly with exceptions
relating to coreference.

187

EXCEPTIONS TO THE PASSIVE

6.1.1   The Personal Passive

The significance attributed to the notions *activity*, *affect/result* and *volition* in determining the possibility of passivization differs from linguist to linguist. The ensuing discussion will reveal that no combination of these parameters is sufficient to handle the full range of recalcitrant data. Consider first the clauses below.

(1) a.   Tom weighed the gold.
    b.   The gold was weighed by Tom.
    c.   Grace weighed only 46 kg.
    d.   *46 kg were weighed by Grace.

(2) a.   The young man fitted the carpet.
    b.   The carpet was fitted by the young man.
    c.   That new suit fits him marvellously.
    d.   *He is marvellously fitted by that new suit.

(3) a.   The police held the thief.
    b.   The thief was held by the police.
    c.   The jar holds oil.
    d.   *Oil is held by the jar.

(4) a.   John turned the page.
    b.   The page was turned by John.
    c.   George turned the corner.
    d.   ?The corner was turned by George.

(5) a.   The surveyor paced the distance between the two points.
    b.   The distance between the two points was paced by the surveyor.
    c.   Mary paced the floor.
    d.   *The floor was paced by Mary.

(6) a.   The mightiest fleets in history have sailed the Pacific.
    b.   The Pacific has been sailed by the mightiest fleets in history.
    c.   My brother Joe sailed the Pacific.
    d.   *The Pacific was sailed by my brother Joe.

(7) a.   They approached the danger cautiously.
    b.   The danger was approached cautiously by them.
    c.   The train approached the station.
    d.   *The station was approached by the train.

EXCEPTIONS TO THE PASSIVE

(8) a. The thief entered the house.
 b. The house was entered by the thief.
 c. The gas entered the house.
 d. *The house was entered by the gas.

(9) a. The chairperson concluded the meeting.
 b. The meeting was concluded by the chairperson.
 c. A magnificent banquet concluded the
  festivities.
 d. *The festivities were concluded by a
  magnificent banquet.

The ungrammaticality of all the (d) examples can be attributed to the absence of one of the four properties. In (1-3), the (b) and (d) examples differ primarily in that the verbs in the former express an activity, while those in the latter a state. Each of the (a) and (b) clauses, but not the (c) and (d) clauses, can be used as answers to a question such as *What did X do?* or *What happened to Y?* In (4-6) the grammaticality of the passive appears to be determined by whether the verb is viewed as having some conceivable affect on its nominal argument. The page in (4a) has changed position due to the action carried out by John. The distance in (5a) has been measured by the fact that the surveyor paced it. The Pacific in (6a) is well known due to the numerous fleets which have sailed it. In (4d), (5c) and (6c) the corner, the floor and the Pacific can hardly be viewed as affected in the same manner. The grammaticality of the passives in (7-9) depends on whether the action expressed by the verb is volitional or not. Naturally, inanimate NPs cannot be regarded as volitionally involved. The same facts obtain in the majority of languages for all measure verbs (e.g. cost, last, number), verbs of equality and comparison (e.g. equal, mean, resemble), verbs of suiting (e.g. suit, become) and verbs of possession (e.g. have, belong, lack).

 Terms such as *activity, affect* or *volition* are very subjective. Stein (1979), who contends that only activity verbs can be used in the passive, views all the following as activity verbs.

(10) Jack is { liked / loved / adored / hated / despised / admired } by many people

EXCEPTIONS TO THE PASSIVE

(11) The results were $\left\{\begin{array}{l}\text{believed}\\\text{understood}\\\text{doubted}\\\text{suspected}\end{array}\right\}$ by everyone

Yet none of the passive clauses containing the above
verbs, nor the actives, can be used in answer to the
question, *What happened to Y? or What did X do?*
The clauses in (12a-15a), conversely, do appear to
involve an activity but the corresponding passives
(12b-15b) are ungrammatical.

(12) a.   The prisoner escaped the jailer.
     b. *The jailer was escaped by the prisoner.

(13) a.   John left the room.
     b. *The room was left by John.

German

(14) a.   Helmut traf Christina auf der Strasse
          Helmut met Christina on the street
          'Helmut met Christina on the street'.

     b. *Christina wurde von Helmut auf der
          Christina became by Helmut on the
          Strasse getroffen
          street meet:p.part.
          'Christina was met by Helmut on the
          street'.

Russian

(15) a.   Prepodavatel wybranil   studenta
          teacher   scold:past student
          'The teacher scolded the student'.

     b. *Student był wybranen   prepodavatelem
          student was scold.p.part teacher:instr.
          'The student was scolded by the teacher'

Stein (1979:90) maintains that activity verbs have
to produce a change in the extra-linguistic situation. The action which they express has to be directed and must lead to a result in the form that someone or something is affected or effected. Thus
presumably in (10) <u>Jack</u> is affected by being <u>loved</u>,
<u>hated</u>, etc., while <u>the jailer</u> in (12) is not <u>affected</u>
<u>by</u> the fact that the <u>prisoner escaped</u>. The oppo-
site case could hold equally well. Note also that
the event or action expressed by the verbs in (10)

190

EXCEPTIONS TO THE PASSIVE

does not necessarily have to be volitional, while that in (12-15) definitely is.

Bolinger (1977) points out that whether or not a NP is conceived as truly affected by the action of the verb may depend on factors such as size (6), relevant power (16) or even amount of usage (17).

(16) a. The army was deserted by its commander-in-chief.
b. *The army was deserted by Private Smith.

(17) a. The stairs have been run up so much that the carpet is threadbare.
b. *The stairs were run up by Jane.

As mentioned in 2.2.2, Bolinger argues that passivization is possible only when a NP is genuinely affected by the action of the verb. This is, in fact, his definition of semantic transitivity. Otherwise the relationship between the verb and the NP is purely spatial or existential. Under this analysis, all the ungrammatical passive clauses quoted contain NPs which denote 'things or persons that are merely located with reference to others or existence itself' (Bolinger 1977:68). The relevance of factors such as size and power is also noted by Cureton (1979) and Beedham (1982) particularly with respect to verbs such as: <u>judge</u>, <u>know</u>, <u>need</u>, <u>want</u>, <u>enjoy</u>, <u>deserve</u> etc. In some languages (e.g. <u>Welsh</u> <u>and Spanish)</u> these verbs cannot occur in the personal passive. In English many speakers regard them as more felicitous with plural, generic or quantified NPs than with single definite ones. Compare the examples below:

(18) a. War is wanted $\begin{cases} \text{by America} \\ \text{by no-one.} \end{cases}$

b. Help is needed $\begin{cases} \text{by John} \\ \text{by the elderly.} \end{cases}$

c. George is expected $\begin{cases} \text{by Bill} \\ \text{by everyone I know} \\ \text{by many experts} \end{cases}$ to win the election.

Huddleston (1971), Tuyn (1970) and Davison (1980) also stress the importance of the notions affect and result in determining whether passivization is possible. However, they confine their remarks only to

EXCEPTIONS TO THE PASSIVE

prepositional passives. Tuyn (1970:62) states:

> The only criterion that can be applied to sentences of this pattern (S Vintr A place) is the semantic one of observable result. If the result can be observed the noun in the adjunct of place can become the subject of a passive sentence, in spite of the fact that the verb may be classified as intransitive or used intransitively. If the result cannot be observed and we are not acting on our own or other people's previous knowledge [...] passive conversion is either impossible or very rare.

Tuyn distinguishes three different semantic types of prepositional passives:

a) Statements based on observation, direct evidence or previous knowledge as in (19).

> (19) a. The grass has been trodden on.
> b. Our swimming pool has not been swum in this year.

b) Statements based on hearsay

> (20) a. This room was lived and worked in a thousand years ago.
> b. This wall was most probably leant against by ancient Romans.

c) Statements having emotional, ironical, facetious or humorous overtones.

> (21) a. I can assure you that the North Sea has been swum in before.
> b. It may look unsafe, but it has been sat on before.

Although in statements based on hearsay the result may not be observable directly, the possibility that it may have been observable at one stage cannot be excluded. The passive of the third type, according to Tuyn, is a deliberate deviation from the syntactic norm and, therefore, can only be used in a specific linguistic context. Davison (1980) treats (21) and (22) as a separate sub-class of pseudo-passives indicating possibility.

> (22) a. The bridge has been flown under by Jack.

EXCEPTIONS TO THE PASSIVE

(22) b. The valley has been marched through in
two hours.

Although passive subjects do not necessarily
have to bear perceptible traces of the described
events, they indicate that the event is a possible
one.

The acceptability of passive clauses formed
from prepositional verbs, especially those of the
last type, depends to a large extent on the pragmatic
considerations involved in the interpretation of
these clauses. Bolinger (1977), Riddle et al.
(1977) and Davison (1980) point out that interpret-
ability may be facilitated by the context, individual experiences of the speaker/hearer, analogy,
predictability of the verb and preposition and noun
combination and repetition. Consider the following
examples from Bolinger (1977).

(23) a. He has been told lies about.
b. ?He has been written lies about.
c. *He has been published lies about.

(24) a. I don't like to be brought charges
against.
b. ?I don't like to be lodged charges
against.
c. *I don't like to be filed charges
against.

The relationship between the prepositional verbs and
the NPs, he and I is the same in each clause. One
could hardly suggest that someone would be more
affected by being told lies about than by being published lies about. If anything, then the latter
would be the more damaging. Nevertheless, the (a)
examples are undoubtedly acceptable; the (c) are not.
According to Bolinger, the difference in acceptability is due to the high frequency of the (a) clauses
in contrast to (b) and (c). Lies are more often
told than published. The phrase - to bring charges
against - is highly lexicalized, while to file
charges against is not. It thus appears that the
passive with the above type of verbs depends on the
speaker/hearer's ability to assign an interpretation
to the clause.

If the passive is indeed governed by features
such as activity, affect, volition, then it must be
assumed that these notions are not understood in the
same way in all languages. Consider the following
examples:

193

EXCEPTIONS TO THE PASSIVE

Polish

 (25) a. Ania wybaczyła Markowi
     Anne:nom forgive:past Mark:dat
     'Anne forgave Mark'.

    b.*Marek został wybaczony przez
     Mark:nom was forgive:p.part by
     Anię
     Anne
     ('Mark was forgiven by Anne').

German

 (26) a. Er dankte mir nicht.
     he thank:past I:dat not
     'He did not thank me'.

    b.*Ich wurde von ihm nicht gedankt
     I:nom become by him not thank:p.part.
     ('I was not thanked by him').

Romanian

 (27) a. Ion invaţa pe Petra chimia
     John teaches to Peter chemistry.
     'John teaches chemistry to Peter'.

    b.*Chimia este invătată de Ion lui
     chemistry is teach:p.part by John
     pe Petra
     to Peter
     ('Chemistry is taught by John to Peter').

Thai

 (28) a. Khǎw ʔàan còtmǎay chabáp nɨ́i lɛ́ɛw
     he read letter clf this already
     'He has already read this letter'.

    b.*Còtmǎay chabáp nɨ́i thùuk ʔàan lɛ́ɛw
     letter clf this   read already
     ('The letter has been read already').

Japanese

 (29) a. Hirosi wa sakana o takusan tot-ta
     Hirosi top fish acc lot catch-past
     'Hirosi caught a lot of fish'.

194

EXCEPTIONS TO THE PASSIVE

(29) b. *Sakana wa   takusan Hirosi ni
         fish   top lot   Hirosi by
         tor-rare-ta
         catch-pass-past
         ('A lot of fish were caught by Hirosi').

Indonesian

(30) a. Mereka taku semua restoran ini
         they   know all   resturant this
         'They are acquainted with all these
         resturants'.

     b. *Semua restoran   ini di-tahu   oleh
         all   restaurant this pass-know by
         mereka
         they
         ('All these restaurants are known by
         them').

Lardil

(31) a. Ngata wutha-kun pirngen-in wangal-kin
         I:nom give-inst woman-acc boomerang-acc
         'I gave the woman a boomerang'.

     b. *Wangal-ø   wu-yi   pirngen-in
         boomerang-nom give-pass woman-acc
         ngithun
         I:gen
         ('The boomerang was given to the woman
         by me').

Presumably the above active clauses, unlike their
English counterparts, fail to meet at least one of
the above mentioned criteria. Obviously, it does
not have to be the same criterion in each case. The
examples (25-31) reveal the difficulties involved
in attempting to account for exceptions to the passive universally on the basis of the notions activity,
affect/result and volition. Unfortunately, no ready
solution appears to be available.
    Linguists who have suggested other pragmatic
solutions to the problem of exceptions to the passive, such as Cureton (1979) and Wierzbicka (1980),
have met with little success. Cureton proposes to
deal with exceptions to the passive in English in
terms of what he calls the Implied Quality Predication Hypothesis (IQPH) which is:

EXCEPTIONS TO THE PASSIVE

An active sentence has a passive counterpart in English if and only if from the various propositions expressed by the active sentence a listener, in the normal case, can infer another pragmatically significant proposition which predicates a quality of the object NP of that sentence (Cureton ibid: 42-3).

The IQPH would exclude all the ungrammatical passive clauses quoted in this chapter by denying that the actives predicate a quality of the object. Cureton's IQPH is rendered vacuous by the unclarity of the term *"quality of the object"*, which he interprets as an aspect of the object's inherent nature, e.g. physical structure or behaviour rather than simply its relation to other things. Since this "definition" is so vague, Cureton can in principle dispose of any counter-example to his hypothesis by claiming that a particular characteristic or property does or does not fall under his definition of quality or is not pragmatically significant. Even if the term *quality of the object* were to be more precisely specified, it is difficult to imagine how characteristics such as <u>newness</u>, <u>dirtiness</u>, <u>wear</u> or <u>emptiness</u> in (32) can be <u>regarded</u> as <u>inherent in</u> <u>swimming pools</u>, <u>bowls</u>, <u>chairs</u> and <u>houses</u>, for instance.

(32) a. The swimming pool has never been swum in before.
b. The bowl has definitely been eaten out of.
c. That chair must have been frequently sat on.
d. The house has just been gone out of by the whole family.

The IQPH, as it stands, is not verifiable and hence devoid of empirical content. (cf. Siewierska (1985), for a more detailed discussion of Cureton's analysis). Wierzbicka's (1980:60) solution suffers from a similar deficiency. She contends that:

A passive is successful when it is clear <u>why</u> the speaker chooses to treat one participant (the subject of the corresponding active sentence) as peripheral and the other (the nonsubject of the corresponding active sentence) as central.

Wierzbicka holds that in passive clauses it is always the non-agentive constituent (in personal

EXCEPTIONS TO THE PASSIVE

passives, the subject) which is in the centre of the speaker's attention. Hence if the agent is mentioned at all it is in order to say something about the non-agent, not the agent. Thus, for example, (33a) is more felicitous than (33b) because:

> to say that convertibles are owned only by affluent young people is indeed to say something significant about convertibles; but it is not clear why to say that a convertible is owned by John (without identifying that convertible) should amount to saying something about a convertible, (rather than about John) (Wierzbicka ibid:61).

(33) a. A convertible is owned by John
b. Convertibles are owned only by affluent young people.

Wierzbicka's hypothesis accounts for the ungrammaticality of passive clauses such as (1-9), (13), (16), (17). It does not, however, shed any light on the degrees of felicity of (23) or (24). Nor does it explain why (1b) or (9b) are acceptable passive clauses while (12b) and (34) are not.

(34) a *Mary was eluded by the simple answer.
b *You are suited by that unusually pale green.
c *You are well fitted by those tight jeans.

Although it might be clear to some why the danger and the meeting in (7b) and (9b) respectively have been chosen as central participants, we cannot see what significant information can be deduced about either of these constituents. Conversely, from (12b). It is possible to say something significant about the jailer, namely that he is incompetent. We can also deduce significant information about the subjects in (34); that Mary is not very bright, that the person has an olive complexion and a good figure. Wierzbicka's proposal cannot, therefore, be regarded as superior to previous attempts at solving the problem of exceptions to the passive. None of the suggestions made account for all the data.

6.1.2   The Impersonal Passive

Both Perlmutter and Postal (1978) and Frajzyngier (1982) contend that the problem of exceptions to the

EXCEPTIONS TO THE PASSIVE

impersonal passive must be approached in terms of
the transitive/intransitive division, for whereas
the restrictions on impersonal passives of transitive verbs are language specific, those pertaining
to intransitive verbs centre on the semantic criterion of *true agency*. The above claim is immediately
invalidated by the impersonal passives of dative
object verbs in German (35) and Latin (36), for
example, where the underlying subject is an experiencer or a cognizer rather than a true agent.

German

    (35) Ihm   wurde von seinem Vater
         he:dat became by his   father
         geglaubt
         believe:p.part
         'He was believed by his father'.

Latin

    (36) Mihi ā rēginā ignotum   fuit
         I:dat by queen forgive:p.part has:been:3s
         'I was forgiven by the queen'.

Even if clauses with dative objects are treated as
transitive, the transitive/intransitive dichotomy
does not correlate with specific restrictions in
other languages.

In Hindi and Bengali (Klaiman 1980, 1981), for
example, the impersonal passive may be formed only
from verbs expressing volitional acts irrespective
of transitivity.

Bengali

    (37) Anek kaṣte   gaaṛi thaamaano
         many difficulty:loc car   stopping
         hoyeche
         has:become
         'The car was stopped with great difficulty'.

    (38)*Omuker   boi haaraano hoyeche
         so-and-so book losing   has:become
         ('His book was lost by so-and-so').

    (39) Aamerikaay inreji balaa   hay
         America:loc English speaking becomes
         'In America English is spoken'.

EXCEPTIONS TO THE PASSIVE

(40) *Omuker   ei   maatro marraa hoyeche
      so-and-so just now   dying has:become
      ('It has been died by so-and-so').

In Ute, according to Givón (1981), any verb may
appear in the impersonal passive provided that it
occurs with at least one argument be it only an
adverb.

(41) Siváatu-ci 'uwáy paxá-ta-xa
      goat-acc the:acc kïll-pass-ant
      'The goat was killed'.

(42) Púka-wúúka-ta-xa
      hard-work-pass-ant
      'Someone worked hard'.

Volition is not so much the relevant criterion, but
rather human agency.
    As mentioned in ch.3, the impersonal passive of
both transitive and intransitive verbs in the vast
majority of languages is confined to clauses denoting human agents the only exceptions being
Russian (Whalen 1978),[2] Lithuanian (Timberlake 1982)
and Welsh (Comrie 1977a).

Russian

(43) Moln-iej   svali-lo   višnj-u
      lightning-inst fell-part:n tree-acc
      'The cherry tree was felled by lightning'.

(44) Vod-oj   bylo zali-to
      water-inst was flood-part:n.
      'There was flooding by water'.

Lithuanian

(45) Giriu   čia snausta
      forests:gen here drowse:p.part:n:s
      '(One can observe) forests (used to)
      drowse here'.

(46) Atzályno   šiurenta
      saplings:gen rustle:p.part:n:s
      'Saplings must have rustled here'.

Welsh

(47) Fe'i lladdwyd (ef) gan ddraig
      him was:killed (him) by dragon
      'He was killed by a dragon'.

EXCEPTIONS TO THE PASSIVE

In Russian, if the underlying subject is semantically an agent and not an instrument or a natural cause, it cannot be expressed in the impersonal passive. Without an expressed instrument the impersonal passive is always understood as referring to an underlying human agent. The Lithuanian and Welsh passives freely allow the overt expression of a human agent, but in Welsh only with transitive verbs. Although Awbery (1976:142) states that the selectional restrictions on the NPs in the Welsh impersonal passive are identical to those on the active, no examples of other than human agents are given.

Perlmutter (1978a) and Perlmutter and Postal (1978) argue that the following predicates may not occur in the impersonal passives of one-participant verbs:

a) predicates describing: sizes, shapes, colours, smells, weights.
b) predicates whose subject is semantically a patient: burn, fall, drop, trip, dry, shake, gush, etc., including inchoatives like melt, evaporate, reduce, grow, etc.
c) predicates of existing and happening: occur, place, end up, vanish, happen, etc.
d) predicates expressing non-voluntary emission of stimuli that impinge on the senses (light, noise, smell) shine, sparkle, glisten, glow.
e) aspectual predicates: begin, start, continue, end.
f) duratives: last, remain, stay, etc.

Their claim is supported by the following examples from German, Turkish and Hindi.

German

(48) a. Es wurde gelacht
it became laugh:p.part
'There was laughing'.

b. Es wird gegangen
it become walk:p.part
'There is walking'.

c. *An etwas wird erkrankt
at something become sick:p.part
('There is getting sick').

EXCEPTIONS TO THE PASSIVE

(48) d. *Es wird   geschmeckt
         it became taste:p.part
         ('There is tasting').

Turkish

(49) a. Burada çalïş-ïl-ïr
        here   work-pass-aor
        'Here it is worked'.

     b. Burada mizikç-il-ik   edilmez
        here   cheat-pass-aor not
        'Here it is not cheated'.

     c. *Yazin burada bŏg-ul-un-ur
        summer here   drown-pass-aor
        ('In the summer here it is often
        drowned').

     d. *Bu   gibi durumlarda öl-ün-ür
        in/at such situations die-pass-aor
        ('In such situations it is died').

Hindi

(50) a. Rām se cala gayā
        Ram by left went
        'It was left by Ram'.

     b. Larkŏ se soyā nahĩ gayā
        boys by slept not went
        'It was not slept by the boys'

     c. *Phūl   se khilā jātā hɛ
        flower by bloomed goes aux
        ('It is bloomed by the flower').

     d. *Pānī   se ublā jātā hɛ
        water by boil goes aux
        ('It is boiled by the water').

All the (c), (d) examples above contain a predicate
which belongs to one of the classes distinguished by
Perlmutter and Postal. The grammatical (a), (b)
clauses on the other hand are formed from predicates
which denote willed or volitional acts or certain
involuntary bodily processes. Some of the above
verbs may be used to describe both voluntary and
involuntary actions. As evidenced by the Dutch (51)
(Perlmutter 1978a), the Hindi (52) (Pandharipande
1978) and the German (53) (Perlmutter and Postal

201

EXCEPTIONS TO THE PASSIVE

1978) these verbs may be passivized only when used
in a volitional sense.

Dutch

    (51) a. De edelen buigen   voor   de koning
           the nobles bend:past before the king
           'The nobles bend (bow) before the king'.

        b. Er   wordt door de edelen voor   de
           there become by the nobles before the
           koning gebogen
           king   bend:p.part
           'There is bowing before the king'.

        c. De bloemen buigen   in de wind
           the flowers bend:past in the wind
           'The flowers bend in the wind'.

        d. *Er   wordt door de bloemen in de
           there become by   the flowers in the
           wind gebogen
           wind bend:p.part
           ('There is bending in the wind by the
           flowers').

Hindi

    (52) a. Laṛkī andar ātī   hε
           girl   in   comes aux
           'The girl comes in'.

        b. Laṛkī se andar āyā jātā hε
           girl by in   came goes aux
           'It is come in by the girl'.

        c. Havā andar ātī   hε
           air   in   comes aux
           'The air comes in'.

        d. *Havā se andar āyā jātā hε
           air by in   came goes aux
           ('It is come in by the air').

German

    (53) a. Die Leute tun alles   für den lieben
           the people do everything for the beloved
           König und Herrn; treulich   kämpfen,
           king and lord; faithfully battle,

EXCEPTIONS TO THE PASSIVE

(53) a. willig   bluten, freudig in den Tod
willingly bleed, happily in the death
gehen Mehr als für ihn sterben.
go   more than for him die
'For the beloved king and lord people do
everything (they) faithfully battle,
willingly bleed, happily go to the death
and even more than die'.

b. Für den lieben König und Herrn wird
for the beloved king and lord become
alles   getan wird   treulich
everything done become faithfully
gekämpft, wird   willig   gebluten,
battled, become willingly bled,
wird   freudig in den Tod   gegangen für
become happily in the death gone   for
ihn wird   mehr als gestorben
him become more than died
'For the beloved king and lord everything
is done, it is faithfully battled, willingly bled, happily to the death gone,
and for him even more than died'.

c. Leute   sterben oft   in diesem
people die   often in this
Krankenhaus
hospital
'People often die in this hospital'.

d.*In diesem Krankenhaus wird   oft
in this   hospital   become often
gestorben
die:p.part
('In this hospital it is often died').

e. Die Leute bluten fast   niemals bei
the people bleed almost never   by
solchen Krankheiten
such   diseases
'People almost never bleed in such
diseases'.

f.*Bei solchen Krankheiten wird   fast
by such   diseases   become almost
nie   geblutet
never bleed:p.part
('In case of such diseases it is almost
never bled').

EXCEPTIONS TO THE PASSIVE

Perlmutter and Postal claim that although in most languages the passive agent must be both truly agentive and human, this may not be a universal constraint since Dutch permits the following:

(54) Er   word   geblaft,   gehinnikt,
     there become bark:p.part, while:p.part
     gekrast
     crow:p.part
     'It is being barked, whined, crowed'.

Frajzyngier (1982) contests the grammaticality of (54) under the non-human reading and argues that all verbs denoting sounds emitted by animals, as well as other typically animal activities (e.g. gnawing), in the impersonal passive will always be interpreted as referring to humans. This is definitely the case in the Romance languages and German. We have not been able to determine conclusively whether the same holds for Dutch, Turkish, Hindi and Bengali.
The universal restriction to volitional underlying subjects in the impersonal passive formed from basically one-participant verbs is invalidated by the Lithuanian examples (45) and (46) and Turkish (Ozkaragoz 1980), the very language which Perlmutter and Postal had used in support of their hypothesis.

Turkish

(55) Burada düş-ül-ür
     here   fall-pass-aor
     'Here it is fallen'.

(56) Bu   yetimhane-de çabuk   büyü-n-ür
     this orphanage-loc quickly grow-pass-aor
     'In this orphanage it is grown quickly'.

Ozkaragoz anticipates Frajzyngier in suggesting that the impersonal passive in Turkish is confined not to volitional activities, but human agents. Lithuanian can thus be regarded as highly exceptional.
It must also be noted that even in a language such as German in which Perlmutter and Postal's division of predicates appears to hold, certain verbs which describe willed or volitional acts, such as <u>kommen</u> 'to come', <u>nahen</u> 'to come closer', <u>gehen</u> 'to go' cannot appear in the impersonal passive. These verbs have to be viewed as irregular exceptions.

204

EXCEPTIONS TO THE PASSIVE

6.1.3   Coreferentiality

Passive clauses with reflexive, reciprocal or possessive pronominal subjects, as in the following
Polish, Welsh (Awbery 1976:131-135) and English examples are ungrammatical.[3]

Polish

> (57) *Siebie była widziana   w   lustrze
>   herself was   see:p.part in mirror
>   ('Herself was seen in the mirror').

Welsh

> (58) *Cafodd ei   gilydd eu   rhybuddio gan
>   get   each other their warning   by
>   Wyn ac Ifor
>   Wyn and Ifor
>   ('Each other were warned by Wyn and Ifor').

English

> (59) *His$_i$ foot was chopped off by the little boy$_i$.

In English, but not in the other languages, a reflexive pronoun may function as a passive agent if
stressed.

> (60) a. He was surprised by <u>himself</u>.
>   b. He is praised by <u>himself</u>.

Stein (1979:104) claims that the contrastive passive
with a reflexive agent is restricted only to those
verbs which can have reflexive or non-reflexive
objects, but where the reflexive object - if it is
used - is obligatory. These verbs have to be distinguished from verbs which always have obligatory
reflexive objects (61) and verbs which take an optional object even when used reflexively (62).

> (61) a. He prided himself on his cleverness.
>   b. *He was prided by himself on his clever-
>   ness.
>   c. He absented himself from the meeting.
>   d. *He was absented by himself from the
>   meeting.

> (62) a. He dressed (himself).
>   b. *He was dressed by himself.
>   c. He shaved (himself).

EXCEPTIONS TO THE PASSIVE

(62) d. *He was shaved by himself.

Passive clauses containing reciprocal pronouns, although uncommon, can also be found in English (Poutsma 1926:108).

(63) a. They betrayed each other.
     b. Each was betrayed by the other.
     c. They hated each other.
     d. Each was hated by the other.

These type of passive clauses are grammatical only when the two members of which the reciprocal pronoun is composed are separated, i.e. each occurs in initial position and other as the passive agent. If the active subject is plural, the plural has to be changed into the singular when used in a passive clause (Stein 1979:105).

(64) a. The children hated each other.
     b. Each child was hated by the other.

No passive clauses can be formed when the underlying subject consists of a co-ordinated NP.

(65) a. The boy and the girl hated each other.
     b. *Each boy and girl was hated by the other.

Note also the close similarity of the above passive clauses to active clauses such as (66).

(66) a. Each betrayed the other.
     b. Each child hated the other.

English again appears to be exceptional in allowing passive clauses with reciprocal pronouns.
   According to Huddleston (1971:94), passives with possessive NPs in subject position coreferential with the passive agent are marginally grammatical in English if the agent is stressed.

(67) a. Mary's briefcase was lost by her.
     b. John's sister was saved by him.

This does not appear to hold if the possessed NP is a body part as in (59) and (68).

(68) *His face was washed by him

In French (69) (Burston 1979:155) and Polish (70) parts of the body do not have to be qualified by a

206

EXCEPTIONS TO THE PASSIVE

possessive pronoun. Nevertheless, passive clauses
with body parts as subjects are ungrammatical.

French

(69) a. Jean a levé la main
John has raised the hand
'John has raised (the) hand'.

b. *La main a été levé par Jean
the hand has been raised by John
('(His) hand has been raised by John').

Polish

(70) a. Jola złamała nogę
Jola:nom break:past leg:acc
'Jola broke (her) leg'.

b. *Noga została złamana przez Jolę
leg:nom was break:p.part by Jola
('(Her) leg was broken by Jola').

It is not thus simply the presence of a possessive
pronoun which "disallows" the passive, but rather
coreference in general. In the words of Stein (1979:
106)

the passive is excluded whenever the activity
performed by the subject does not go beyond the
sphere of the subject itself.

Clauses containing what is generally regarded as
a cognate object constitute yet another set of exceptions to the passive. None of the following
English (71), German (72) (Curme 1960), Icelandic
(73) (Einarsson 1945:105) or Mandarin (74) (Teng
1975:34) clauses can, under normal circumstances, be
put into the passive.

English

(71) a. She smiled a kind smile.
b. *A kind smile was smiled by her.

German

(72) a. Er starb den Tod fürs Vaterland
he died the death for/the fatherland
'He died the death for the Fatherland'.

207

EXCEPTIONS TO THE PASSIVE

(72) b. *Der Tod   wurde von ihm fürs
the death became by him for/the
Vaterland   gestorben
fatherland die:p.part
('The death for the fatherland was
died by him').

Icelandic

(73) a. Mig   dreymdi draum
I:acc dreamt dream:acc
'I dreamt a dream'.

b. *Draum var dreymid   af min
dream was dream:p.part by me
('The dream was dreamt by me').

Mandarin

(74) a. Ta zhu-le   guo tang
he cook-asp pot soup
'He cooked a pot of soup'.

b. *Guo tang bei ta zhu-le
pot soup   he cook-asp
('The pot of soup was cooked by him').

A cognate object repeats and in a way explains more
fully the idea expressed by the verb. Whether a NP
is viewed as a cognate object depends largely on the
set of possible objects which can occur with a given
verb (Stein 1979:107). Thus, for instance, the verb
to smile implies only a smile, to dream only a dream,
to cook only food, but to write can occur with any
of the following: a letter, a book, an article, a
poem, a story, an opera, a paragraph, an insult, a
compliment, etc. Languages may vary in how they
treat a given NP. As evidenced by the Mandarin
example, Mandarin appears to be more restrictive
than English. The only language that we have come
across which allows passive clauses with cognate
objects is Kinyarwanda (Kimenyi 1980: cf. ch.2 (27).
   The above discussion of exceptions to the passive has revealed that it is impossible to deal with
all exceptions to the passive in terms of notions
such as *activity, affect, volition*. These notions
appear to play a very important role. However, they
can only be used to differentiate grammatical and
ungrammatical passive clauses if these notions are
interpreted in a very loose manner.

208

EXCEPTIONS TO THE PASSIVE

6.2 Exceptions to the Passive in Relational Grammar

Perlmutter and Postal maintain that a number of exceptions to both the personal and impersonal passive can be dealt with in terms of the 1-*Advancement Exclusiveness Law* (1-AEX) (cf.p. 179) which we repeat for convenience;

'No clause can involve more than one advancement to "1"'

Since in RG the passive is viewed as an advancement to "1" rule, the 1-AEX "predicts" that if the passive is applied to clauses derived via previous advancement to "1" an ungrammatical sentence will be produced.
Three types of clauses are said to be derived by advancement to "1":

a) Clauses involving sporadic advancement to "1".
b) Inversion clauses.
c) Unaccusative clauses.

The following clauses belong to the first group (Perlmutter and Postal, 1978:21):

(75) a. $5 bought a lot of heroin in 1827.
b. 1939 found the U.S. on the brink of disaster.
c. This cabin sleeps twenty people.

The NPs $5, 1939 and this cabin are considered as being advanced from an underlying oblique relation to subject. Since (75a,b,c) already involve advancement to "1", the 1-AEX correctly predicts that they cannot be passivized.

(76) a. *A lot of heroin was bought in 1877 by $5.
b. *The U.S. was found on the brink of disaster by 1939.
c. *Twenty people are slept by this cabin.

Although the 1-AEX makes a correct prediction as far as passivization is concerned, there is no evidence that (75abc) involve advancement to "1". Perlmutter and Postal argue that (75a) is related to (77).

EXCEPTIONS TO THE PASSIVE

(77) a. Melvin bought a lot of heroin for $5.

But (75a) is generally regarded as corresponding to (77b), not (77a).

(77) b. One could buy a lot of heroin for $5 in 1827.

There is no justification for treating (75a,b,c) as derived and not basic clauses. Naturally, if the clauses in (75) are not derived, then their inability to passivize has to be accounted for. Perlmutter and Postal (1978:22) claim that 'no other explanation of such cases of ill-formedness has ever been given'. However, these clauses do not comply with any of the parameters discussed in 6.1.1. They are definitely not volitional, nor do they affect the object. It would be difficult to argue that they involve an activity in the traditional sense of the word either. Hence they could be excluded from passivization due to the lack of all of these properties.

The next group of clauses which are excluded from passivization by the 1-AEX are inversion clauses such as (78).

(78) a. That girl mattered to me.
b. That belongs to Susan.
c. The idea occurred to him quite suddenly.
d. It finally dawned on me.
e. It also happened to me.
f. Harry seems to me to be wrong.
g. Lisa appears to me to be stupid.

According to Perlmutter (1978a) and Perlmutter and Postal (1978), the above clauses are derived as follows:

(77)

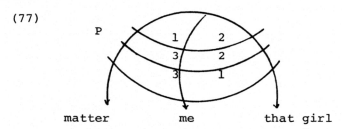

They are thus treated as derived intransitive clauses (see definition of transitivity in RG in ch.1) where the initial "1" functions as a final "3". The same

210

analysis has been proposed for dative subject clauses
in Italian, Japanese and Quechua (Perlmutter 1979),
Russian (Perlmutter 1978b), Kannada (Dryer 1982) and
Bengali (Klaiman 1981). Perlmutter and Postal argue
that the passive cannot apply because this would
involve two advancements to "1" as in (80).

(80)
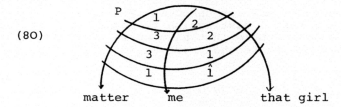
      matter   me   that girl

Perlmutter and Postal admit that there is one problem with this analysis, namely that although the
inability of (78) to passivize lends support to the
advancement of, for example, the girl in (78a) from
"2" to "1", there is no evidence in English that me,
the "3", was ever a "1". Perlmutter (1979) presents
a number of arguments from Italian for the underlying
"1"-hood of final "3s" with predicates such as
piacere 'like', rincrescere 'regret, secare 'bother',
mancare 'lack' etc. Dryer (1982) similarly argues
for the validity of this analysis in Kannada. Nevertheless, arguments based on other languages cannot
be seen as compelling evidence for extending the
same analysis to English.
    The inversion analysis is also suggested for
clauses such as (12a) which we repeat here as (81a).

    (81) a. The thief escaped the jailer.
         b. The answer eluded me.
         c. John pleased me.
         d. It will benefit all of us.

These clauses differ from the previous set only in
that the initial "1", the jailer, me, all of us, is
a final "2" not a final "3". The derivation of (81)
is shown in (82).

(82)
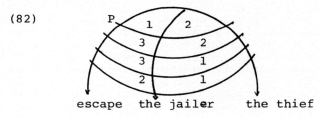
    escape   the jailer   the thief

EXCEPTIONS TO THE PASSIVE

Perlmutter and Postal again claim that no other explanation for the ungrammaticality of passive clauses corresponding to (81) has ever been given, ignoring the fact that both (78) and (81), with the exception of (81a),could be prevented from passivizing by reference to the notion activity.

The last type of clauses prevented from passivizing by the 1-AEX are unaccusative clauses. Perlmutter and Postal distinguish two types of intransitive clauses; those that have an initial "1" such as (83a), and those that have an initial "2" as in (83b).

(83) a. John laughed.
b. John collapsed.

The former are called *unergative* the latter *unaccusative*. The division into unergative and unaccusative clauses is carried out on the basis of the meaning of the predicates. Generally predicates occurring with NPs which can be regarded as agents, experiencers or cognizers belong to the unergative group, while those listed on (p.200), which typically take a patient subject, are unaccusative. Since the derivation of unaccusative clauses involves an advancement of "2" to "1", the 1-AEX predicts that all passives formed from unaccusative clauses will be ungrammatical.

The German (48), (53), Hindi (50), (52) and Dutch (51), quoted in 6.1.2, appear to bear out this prediction, but the Lithuanian (45), (46) and Turkish (55), (56) do not. The verbs in the above Lithuanian and Turkish clauses qualify as unaccusative on semantic grounds, but nevertheless the passive clauses are grammatical.

The Turkish and Lithuanian data can be interpreted as evidence against the unaccusative hypothesis, the 1-AEX or the advancement analysis of impersonal passives. Timberlake (1982) argues that the conditions on Equi-structures of bi-clausal passives in Lithuanian provide independent justification for the 1-AEX, while the distinct behaviour of S nominals with unaccusative predicates under sentence negation suggests that the unaccusative/unergative dichotomy is similarly valid. Ozkaragoz (1980) presents an argument for the unaccusative hypothesis in Turkish based on the gerund construction with the verbal suffix -<u>arak</u>. Thus it is the advancement analysis of impersonal passives that appears to be inapplicable for both languages.

212

EXCEPTIONS TO THE PASSIVE

Perlmutter and Postal's derivation of impersonal passives of basically one-argument verbs is based on two assumptions;

a) that the underlying subject is originally a "2"
b) that the derivation of impersonal passives involves advancement of a dummy nominal to "1".

Both of these claims must be correct for the analysis to hold, because if either one or the other is false, the 1-AEX is simply inapplicable. The derivation of the ungrammatical Hindi (50) is shown in (84).

(84)
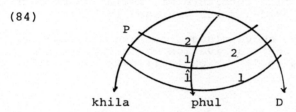

It has been impossible to determine whether there is any evidence for the "2"-hood of the underlying subject in languages other than Turkish and Lithuanian. Perlmutter and Postal definitely do not provide any. Since the only argument which supports the unaccusative hypothesis comes from passivization, the status of the underlying subject is largely a matter of interpretation. Assuming that the subject of unaccusative predicates is an underlying "2", does the second claim hold?

There is no evidence of the existence of a dummy nominal in the Turkish, Lithuanian, Hindi, Bengali, Kannada, Welsh or Russian impersonal passives. The presence of _es_ in the German impersonal passive is due to a language specific requirement. There remains the case of Dutch, Swedish, Danish and possibly French. In these four languages the dummy constituents of impersonal passives display some distributional subject properties. Perlmutter and Postal regard this as sufficient evidence for postulating hypothetical dummies cross-linguistically. In view of the above facts their analysis can hardly be seen as justified. If impersonal passives do not involve advancement to "1", but rather spontaneous demotion, as advocated by Keenan (1975) and Comrie (1977a), the exceptions to the impersonal passive, contrary to Perlmutter and Postal's claim, cannot be attributed to the 1-AEX.

EXCEPTIONS TO THE PASSIVE

The interaction of the 1-AEX and unaccusative hypothesis is also said to account for the ungrammaticality of English pseudo-passives such as (85).

(85) a. *The column was collapsed under by Bill.
b. *The room was burst in by the bubble.
c. *The field was grown in by flowers.
d. *The verandah was continued on by the argument.
e. *The bridge was existed under by the trolls.
f. *Germany was died in by John.
g. *The furniture was fallen on by dust.
h. *Mid-air was vanished in by it.

Since all the above clauses contain unaccusative predicates, their derivation would involve two advancements to "1" which is illustrated in (86).

(86)
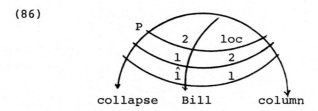

The semantic basis for the unaccusative/unergative distinction is undermined by the ungrammaticality of the following:

(87) a. *The ladder was stepped up by John.
b. *The house has just been gone out of.
c. *The day was slept during.
d. *The new stadium was arrived at.

All the above examples can be precluded from passivization in terms of the notions activity, affect/result and volition.

Clauses such as (4d) and (5d) repeated here as (88a,b) pose further problems for Perlmutter and Postal's analysis.

(88) a. *The corner was turned by George.
b. *The floor was paced by Mary.
c. *The room was left by Paul.
d. *Tables are waited by Susan.

Perlmutter and Postal have not to our knowledge suggested any explanation for the ungrammaticality

EXCEPTIONS TO THE PASSIVE

of (88). If these clauses are treated as underlyingly intransitive, they must be classified as
either unaccusative or unergative. Perlmutter and
Postal's semantic criteria suggest an unergative
analysis, since the underlying subjects qualify as
agents. The unergative analysis again entails
abandoning the generalization concerning the relation
between unergativity and passivization. An unaccusative solution on the other hand creates the
problem of establishing a new basis for assigning
unaccusativity. Perlmutter and Postal could view
(88) as transitive. However, as they state that
passives formed from transitive verbs are not governed in the sense of Green (1974), they would have
no way of accounting for the ungrammaticality of (88)
(Perlmutter 1978a:173)

It is evident from the above that the 1-AEX
leaves many exceptions to the passive unaccounted
for. Furthermore, Perlmutter and Postal's division
into unaccusative and unergative predicates does not
correlate with their behaviour under passivization.

Perlmutter and Postal's explanation for exceptions to the passive, like the pragmatic solutions
discussed in 6.1, is based on the notions *activity*,
affect/result and *volition*. The only real difference
between the two approaches is that Perlmutter and
Postal contend that the above notions determine the
syntactic status of the verbal arguments, while
under the pragmatic approach this is not necessarily
the case. The two solutions suffer from the same
deficiency namely that whether a NP is interpreted
as agentive or affected and the action volitional
depends on whether the clause in question has or does
not have a passive counterpart.

NOTES

1.   The term *thematic relations* as used by Gruber
(1976), Jackendoff (1972) and S. Anderson (1977)
covers relations such as: agent, source, goal, theme,
i.e. what others call semantic relations. However,
the notion of theme itself is regarded as central,
a theme being present in every clause (cf. ch.4,
fn.12 for one definition of theme).
2.   Note that the impersonal passive in (43)
lacks the passive auxiliary <u>byt</u>. Whalen (1978)
treats only (44) as passive and (43) as active impersonal. We follow Krakovsky (1973) and Babby and
Brecht (1975:37) and regard both constructions as
passive.

215

EXCEPTIONS TO THE PASSIVE

3. This is not the case, for instance, in Tagalog if Tagalog is viewed as having passive clauses (cf. 2.4).

Chapter Seven

THE PRAGMATICS OF THE PASSIVE

7.0   Introduction

Throughout the preceding chapters various functions
of the passive have been mentioned, which according
to Givón (1981), can be grouped under one of the
following functional domains: topic identification,
impersonalization and detransitivization. The topicalization function of the passive is manifested
by the assignment of subject/topic or just topic
function to a non-agent, the impersonalization
function by the removal of the underlying agent and
the detransitivization by agent demotion concomitantly with direct object promotion resulting in a
decrease of the 10 semantic high transitivity
features proposed by Hopper and Thompson (cf. p.15-18).
    As discussed in ch.2, the cross-linguistic
realizations of the passive differ in terms of the
number of functions displayed and the extent to which
these functions are displayed. Thus, for example,
while the Indo-European personal passive qualifies
as intransitive according to both syntactic and
semantic criteria, the passive in some Austronesian
languages, (e.g. Tagalog, Palauan, cf. ch.2) retains the majority of high transitivity features.
The Bantu passive formed from ditransitive verbs
with recipient and benefactive subjects on the other
hand can be regarded as syntactically transitive due
to the lack of direct object demotion.
    The fact that the passive may fulfil one, all or
any combination of the above functions does not in
itself explain why this construction is used as
opposed to other topicalizing, impersonalizing and
detransitivizing constructions. The conditions
determining the use of the passive differ from
language to language being dependent both on the
language internal characteristics of the passive and

217

THE PRAGMATICS OF THE PASSIVE

the number of strategies available for expressing
the above functions. The status of the passive
within the grammar of individual languages is by no
means uniform.

Since a cross-linguistic comparison of the pragmatics of the passive would require a book in its
own right, this chapter will be devoted again primarily to the English passive. An attempt will be
made to determine the most important differences in
the use of the English passive as compared to the
Slavic, Romance and other Germanic languages. We
will concentrate on the topicalization (7.1) and
impersonalization (7.2) functions of the passive
because it is the lack of alternative topicalizing
and impersonalizing strategies in English which
results in the frequent use of the English passive
and distinguishes it from its counterparts in other
European languages. Only the periphrastic personal
passive will be considered.

7.1 Topicalization

All discussions of information structure heavily
rely on the notion of *markedness*. An unmarked
phenomenon is usually taken to reflect a norm, a
standard, an expected or natural state of affairs,
a marked phenomenon a departure from this norm. Our
perception of what is normal or natural depends on
frequency of occurrence i.e. on what prevails. The
notion of markedness is therefore based primarily on
statistical frequency. In the literature an unmarked
construction in addition to being statistically more
common than a marked construction is also assumed
to be:

a) the most semantically neutral of a number of
possible alternatives not requiring various linguistic
or situational specifications for its occurrence,
b) comprised of fewer morphological elements than a
corresponding marked construction,
c) prosodically neutral i.e. lacking additional
suprasegmental features (as a consequence of a).

It has been found that in the overwhelming
majority of languages in constructions which according to the above criteria qualify as unmarked, given
information precedes new information. The term
given information refers to information which the
speaker assumes to be currently in the consciousness
of his interlocutor. *New* information on the other

218

THE PRAGMATICS OF THE PASSIVE

hand, even if not absolutely new in the sense that no prior knowledge of it existed, is assumed not to be in the consciousness of the interlocutor at the time of the utterance. Hence clauses such as (1b), from the point of view of information structure, are regarded as unmarked, while those like (2b) are considered to be marked.

(1) a. Who did Sue hit?
    b. She hit Larry.

(2) a. Who hit Larry?
    b. Sue hit him.

In unmarked structures given information tends to be conveyed in a weaker and more attenuated manner than new information, the former being uttered with lower pitch and weaker stress, the latter taking what is commonly referred to as tonic stress.[1] Given and new information are primarily associated with two distinct pragmatic functions, namely that of topic and focus respectively.
The term *topic* has been defined as:

a) the first propositional constituent in the clause (e.g. in TG and RG).
b) the constituent which sets the individual framework within which the sentence holds (e.g. Chafe 1976; Li and Thompson 1976).
c) the entity which sets the stage or is the point of departure for the clause (e.g. Halliday 1968; Hutchins 1975; Hinds 1975).[2]
d) the entity about which the predication predicates something in a given setting, or more informally, the constituent which states what the clause is primarily about   (e.g. Lyons 1968; Dahl 1974; Dik 1978, 1980).

The first three definitions of topic are virtually synonymous and equate the topic with the sentence initial constituent irrespective of its given/new status. Hence all the underlined constituents qualify as topics in this sense.[3]

(3) a. John saw the play
    b. The play John saw yesterday.
    c. The play, John saw it yesterday.

The last definition of topic is typically supplemented by a statement identifying the topic with given information. Some linguists who use this definition

219

THE PRAGMATICS OF THE PASSIVE

of topic take all the given constituents within the sentence to be the topic, while others single out only one of the given items as the topic, in the unmarked case the first propositional constituent. However, it is by no means always evident which constituent among the given entities represents what the sentence is primarily about. For example, (4b) could be about <u>Jane</u>, <u>the book</u>, or <u>the giving of the book to someone by Jane</u> depending on the following utterances.

> (4) a. Who did Jane give the book to?
> b. She gave it to Tim.

The term *topic* when equated with given information or the first propositional constituent is a clearly defined notion; when used strictly in the sense of *what the clause is primarily about* it is not. We will therefore speak of topic only in the sense of the initial constituent and given respectively.

Although the two senses of the term topic often coincide as in (1b) and potentially in (4b), they need not. For instance, in (2b) <u>Sue</u> qualifies as topic in the first sense and <u>him</u> in the second. In languages in which the unmarked distribution of information is new/given and not given/new such as Ojibwa and Hixkaryana the two notions of topic will obviously identify quite distinct NPs as topics.[4] We have already seen in our discussion of clause structure in the Philippine-type languages (2.4) that the two notions of topic have produced a certain amount of confusion; what some linguists have called topic being referred to by others as the focus. The topic may be simultaneously the focus of the clause only under the first sense of the term, not when the term *topic* is used in reference to given information. Therefore the two senses of the term topic must not be assumed to be synonymous.

The term *focus* is used to refer to the constituent which conveys the relatively most important information with respect to the pragmatic information between the speaker and addressee. It thus represents the information which constitutes the *raison de'être* for the utterance. Since given information by definition is known to both interlocutors, the motivation for an utterance is typically the imparting of some new information. Consequently the focus of the clause generally represents new information. Given information is focused upon only if there is something new to be said about it e.g. for purposes of

220

THE PRAGMATICS OF THE PASSIVE

contrast or emphasis. In speech focal constituents
are always prosodically salient. In unmarked constructions they take tonic stress;[5] in marked constructions they may be accompanied by additional
prosodic features such as higher pitch, a disjuncture and also morphological marking. The unmarked
position of the focus by virtue of it conveying new
information in the majority of languages is clause
final or in languages in which the verb tends to be
placed finally immediately before the verb. English
does not exemplify the preference for placing focal
material in final position well due to its fairly
rigid word order. Therefore (2b) is pragmatically
marked because the focus - Sue - is placed in clause
initial position and not in typical focal position;
but it is syntactically unmarked since the unmarked
location of subjects in English is pre- and not
postverbal.

In theory any NP may function as the topic or
the focus of the clause.[6] However, it has been
observed that some NPs are much more likely to be
singled out as topics than others. Cross-language
and intra-language investigations have shown that
human discourse exhibits a strong egocentric bias.
Human beings tend to talk primarily about themselves,
their interlocutors and other humans. Events and
situations are more likely to be interpreted from
the point of view of the persons involved rather
than in terms of the events themselves or non-human,
inanimate entities affected by the events. Hence not
all NPs possess the same inherent potential for
functioning as the topic of a clause. In fact,
linguists have noted the existence of two parallel
topicality hierarchies, an animacy hierarchy and a
semantic one.

The Animacy Hierarchy

> human > nonhuman

> 1st pers > 2nd pers > 3rd pers   animate > inanimate

The Semantic Hierarchy

> agent > recipient > patient > oblique
>   benefactive

In general, the higher a constituent ranks on the
two hierarchies the greater likelihood of functioning as the topic of the clause. Human, agentive NPs

THE PRAGMATICS OF THE PASSIVE

are therefore the most likely candidates for topic. Universal investigations of word order tendencies reveal that most languages favour a merger of topic and subject functions. As topics are typically given and consequently definite, clauses with definite, human agentive subject/topics are from the point of view of information structure and syntax the prototypical unmarked constructions. Experimental data indicate that sentences containing such subject/topics are both produced and comprehended more readily than those with other types of subjects (e.g. Bever 1970; Clark and Clark 1977; Bock 1982). Additional support for the unmarked nature of clauses with agentive human subjects comes from clauses which convey all given or all new information. In these instances it is again typically the agent which appears in subject/topic position.

The passive is seen as a topicalizing construction for it places a non-agentive NP in unmarked subject/topic position. The agentive passive simultaneously locates the agent in the focal position of the clause. The agentive passive thus fulfils two functions, a topicalizing and a focusing one. The primary motivation for the agentive passive in the majority of languages can be attributed to the relative higher topicality of the patient *vis-à-vis* the agent in terms of both inherent topicality and discourse topicality. As noted in ch.2, in languages such as Nitinaht and Tiwa it is the inherent topicality of agent and patient which plays the major role. Any event involving an agent lower on the animacy hierarchy than the patient is rendered via the passive. In European languages on the other hand discourse topicality is generally viewed as the decisive factor. Thus linguists such as Halliday (1968), Chafe (1970), Hutchins (1975), Hinds (1975) and Dik (1978), just to name a few, see the primary motivation for the passive as maintaining an unmarked given/new distribution of information i.e. as enabling a given patient to function as the unmarked topic or theme, a new agent as the information focus.

Since in the majority of the world's languages the subject/topic in the unmarked case occurs in clause initial position (cf. fn.2), the passive is considered to be a topicalizing strategy also under the first sense of topic presented above. In languages such as English, where this situation obtains, the use of the passive must be compared to other fronting strategies such as those in (3), irrespective of the given/new status of the initial

222

THE PRAGMATICS OF THE PASSIVE

constituent. Only a discussion of the passive in relation to topicalization under both interpretations of the term can reveal the full pragmatic potential of this complex construction. In order to facilitate discussion, the relation of passivization to topicalization in these two divergent senses will be analyzed in turn.

7.1.1   The Passive and Given/New order

Although the primary motivation for the agentive passive in English is attributed to the maintaining of a given/new distribution of information, the **givenness** of a patient and the newness of the agent do not always constitute sufficient justification for the passive, as evidenced by the unlikelihood of (5b) as a response to (5a).

    (5) a. Who bought the book?
        b. The book was bought by John.

Additional factors, such as a discrepancy in definiteness and animacy, must be involved for the passive to be preferred. In English, the passive is most likely to occur when a definite patient is higher on the animacy hierarchy than an indefinite agent, as in (6).

    (6) a. Charles was bitten by a snake.
        b. I was woken up by a knock at the door.
        c. My dog was run over by a car.

When the patient is either definite or animate and the agent indefinite or inanimate, as in (7), the passive is still highly probable.

    (7) a. Anne was deafened by the noise.
        b. The exhibition was opened by a woman.
        c. A horse was struck by lightning.

However, the likelihood of passive occurrence is noticeably reduced when no discrepancy in animacy or definiteness exists. According to Ransom (1977) and Krauthamer (1981), clauses such as (8) are much more likely to be rendered in the active irrespective of the given new status of the constituents.

    (8) a. German was deposed by English as the
           language of diplomacy.
        b. A cat was chased by a dog.
        c. Mary was found by John.

223

THE PRAGMATICS OF THE PASSIVE

When the agent exhibits inherent higher topicality than the patient, a preference for the active is generally shown. Hence the rarity of passive clauses with pronominal agents, particularly first person agents, which for many speakers of English are acceptable only under a contrastive interpretation. Similar facts obtain for German (Zubin 1979), Italian (Cinque 1976a), Polish, and the Bantu languages (Trithart 1979); while in Japanese (Howard and Niyekawa-Howard 1976) the subjectivization of an inanimate patient via the passive is not only less likely, but typically ungrammatical. Conversely in languages such as Hindi and Bengali, it is the passive agent and not the patient topic which must be animate due to the volitionality constraint on the passive in the two languages (cf. p.198).

Passivization is not the only strategy available for maintaining an unmarked given/new distribution of information in German (Kirkwood 1969), Norwegian (Faarlund 1981) or Dutch (Dik 1981) as evidenced by the following examples.

German

> (9) Diese   Ansicht vetritt   Hans
>   this:acc view   hold:pres:3s Hans
>   'Hans holds this view'.

Norwegian

> (10) Denne fisken fanga   Ola
>   this fish   catch:past:3s Ola
>   'Ola caught this fish'.

Dutch

> (11) Dit boek heeft Jan   gistern   gekocht
>   this book has   John yesterday buy:p.part
>   'John has bought this book yesterday'.

In all three languages a direct object may occur in initial topic position without subjectivization. The three languages are verb second languages i.e. the finite verb in main declarative clauses may be preceded by one and only one constituent. Topicalization of a non-agent involves the movement of the agent/subject after the finite verb. Although the topic in clauses such as the above may be used for purposes of contrast, it typically conveys given information and does not display prosodic characteristics distinct from subject/topics. The agent/

THE PRAGMATICS OF THE PASSIVE

subject may be given or new. When it is new, as it could be in (9-11), topicalization fulfils an identical function to the agentive passive.

Patient topicalization and agent focusing cannot be regarded as the sole motivation for passive occurrence particularly in languages which exhibit considerable freedom in major sentence constituent order such as the Slavic languages. The unmarked order of major sentence constituents in the Slavic languages reflects the distribution of given/new information irrespective of the grammatical functions of the constituents involved. SVO order is compulsory only when the subject and object display syncretism of nominative and accusative case forms and identical feature specifications for animacy and concretness as in the Polish (12):

> (12) a. Prosi-ę   widzi   ciel-ę
> piglet-nom/acc see:pres:3s calf-nom/acc
> 'The piglet sees the calf'.
>
> b. Samochód-ø wyprzedził   tramwaj-ø
> car-nom/acc overtake:past:3s tram-nom/acc
> 'The car overtook the tram'.

Any constituent other than a clitic may occur in initial topic position. In the unmarked case it will be given and unstressed (13), in the marked case new and with increased stress (14).

Polish

> (13) a. A   gdzie jest adapter?
> but where is   record player
> 'Where is the record player?'
>
> b. Adapter   zabrał   Marek
> record player take:past:3s   Mark
> 'Mark took the record player'.
>
> (14) a. Co   Marek zabrał?
> what Mark take:past:3s
> 'What did Mark take?'
>
> b. Adapter   zabrał
> record player take:past:3s
> 'He took the record player'.

Overt given subjects occur preverbally (14a), new ones postverbally (13b). Hence if the subject is

THE PRAGMATICS OF THE PASSIVE

postverbal, unlike in German, Norwegian or Dutch,
it will tend to be interpreted as new. This applies
to active (13b) and passive clauses alike (15).

(15) Wajda szczególnie faworyzował   młodych.
Wajda particularly favour:past:3s young
Przez Wajdę zostali wylansowani
by   Wajda became launch:p.part:pl
Olbrychski, Kolberger i   Sęp
Olbrychski, Kolberger and Sęp
'Wajda particularly favoured the young.
Olbrychski, Kolberger and Sęp were launched
by Wajda'.

In (15) although an unmarked given/new distribution
of information is maintained, it is the passive
agent which is the topic; the subject/patient the
focus. Clauses such as (15) are not common in
Polish. Final passive subjects are much more likely
to occur in agentless passives (16).

(16) Dyskusja   była długa i zażarta. W końcu o
discussion was long and heated in end at
10 została powzięta   ostateczna decyzja.
10 became reach:p.part final   decision
'The discussion was long and heated. In
the end the final decision was reached at
10 o'clock.

Passive clauses with subjects in postverbal focal
position can be found also in Russian, Czech, German
(Stein 1979), Spanish and Italian (Cinque 1976) (cf.
p.41 for examples from Polish and Spanish).

German

(17) Dem   Jungen wurde von dem Nachbarn
the:dat boy   became by the neighbour
der   Ball gegeben
the:nom ball give:p.part
'The boy was given the ball by the neighbour'.

Italian

(18) Il X Convegano della API si
the X convention of   API refl
concluderà   in serata
conclude:fut:3s in evening
'The tenth Convention of the API ends this
evening'.

226

THE PRAGMATICS OF THE PASSIVE

(18) Dai   congressisti sono stati
by:the participants have been
particolarmente trattati   i   problemi
particularly   treat:p.part the problems
economici e finanziari del momento
economic and financial of moment
'The current economic and financial problems
have been discussed by the participants'.

In English the passive agent may be placed in rare
instances in initial position as in (19) (Paterson
1983:61), but the subject cannot occur postverbally.

(19) By its many migrant residents Mona Vale
is called "Monna Wile".

In all these instances the motivation for the passive
cannot be the placing of a non-agent in initial topic
position. Although an unmarked g iven/new distribution of information is retained, the same effect
could have been achieved by the corresponding active.
Passivization in languages such as Maithili,
Quiche, Cakchiquel, Tzotzil and Kannada, (cf. 2.1.3)
similarly either does not or need not involve the
placing of a patient subject in the position of
primary topic. Due to lack of information on the
pragmatics of the passive in these languages, one
can only hypothesize that either the grammatical
subject is taken to be the topic irrespective of its
position in the clause, or that the passive agent
does not lose its topic status despite the oblique
morphological marking. If the latter situation
obtains, then topicalization is not the motivation
for the passive in these languages.
Since in all the languages mentioned either the
retention of given/new constituent order can be
achieved by means other than the passive and/or
passivization need not involve the placing of the
patient in unmarked topic position, why is this
construction used?
The use of the agentive personal passive may be
partially motivated by the functional role of the
subject. It is often stated that the passive is a
means of presenting the situation or event from the
point of view of the patient as opposed to the agent.
This shift in perspective is typically attributed to
the functional role of the subject which is seen to
represent the vantage point for the interpretation
of the sentence. However, as the functional role of
subjects has been discussed only in the context of
subject/topics, there is no evidence as yet suggest-

227

THE PRAGMATICS OF THE PASSIVE

ing that point of view is a function of subjects as opposed to topics. In fact since the topic by definition constitutes the point of departure for the clause (i.e. in the majority of languages), it is unlikely that topicalization of the patient without subjectivization would maintain the perspective of the subject. Nevertheless, it must be noted that it is the subject, not the topic, which governs verbal agreement. The passive subject/topic thus exhibits a closer semantic bond with the verb than a non-subjectivized topic. The distinction between the Polish active (20a) and the passive (20b), for example, is a subtle one.

(20) a. Problem-ø   ten   omawia
        problem-acc this discuss:pres:3s
        Klemensiewicz
        Klemensiewicz
        'Klemensiewicz discusses this problem'.

     b. Problem-ø   ten   jest omawiany
        problem-nom this is   discuss:p.part
        przez Klemensiewicza
        by   Klemensiewicz
        'This problem is discussed by
        Klemensiewicz'.

Although separately the two clauses would be interpreted in an identical fashion, when they are contrasted it is felt that the passive clause, but not so much the active carries the implication that the problem is discussed extensively or thoroughly.
   The subject apart from determining the vantage point in terms of which the speaker/writer wishes the situation to be viewed is also said to indirectly reveal the speaker/writer's attitude to the described event. According to Kuno (1976), Kuno and Kaburaki (1977) and Ertel (1977) the referent of the subject is "closer" to the speaker's cognitive field than any other NP in the sentence. Consequently the more the speaker identifies with a particular referent the greater likelihood of it being chosen as the subject of the sentence. This identification may reflect the animacy hierarchy and/or the speaker's familarity with one entity rather than another. *Familarity* is by definition a relative notion dependent on variables internal to the speaker. It undoubtedly correlates with givenness and referentiality, but may also involve individual factors such as emotional preferences, personal expertise etc. Again both

228

THE PRAGMATICS OF THE PASSIVE

Kuno's observations and Ertel's psycho-linguistic experiments are based on topicalized subjects. Therefore, whether or not speaker identification is a property of subjects and not topics remains to be determined. The possibility that it is indeed the subject irrespective of topicalization or that topicalized subjects more so than topicalized non-subjects reflect the speaker's attitude to the described situation cannot, however, be excluded. These factors may contribute to the choice of the passive over topicalization without subjectivization.

Another influencial factor determining the use of the passive as opposed to other topicalizing strategies is the register. The periphrastic passive in Indo-European languages has acquired the status of a sophisticated stylistic device. This may in part be due to the relative morphological complexity of the passive *vis-à-vis* the active, in part to the influence of Latin poetry and prose on the whole European literary tradition. Whatever the origins of the literary flavour associated with the passive it is unquestionable that such associations exist and, what is more, are continually perpetuated by the use of the passive particularly in academic, bureaucratic, literary and journalistic texts on the one hand and the lack of passive clauses in spontaneous speech on the other.

The lack of the passive in live discourse can be attributed to the extensive use of ellipsis. Although most discussions of the passive are based on question answer sequences such as (5), neither a passive nor an active clause is likely to occur in such instances, but rather an elliptical John did or John. Speakers do not tend to repeat anaphoric information unless propelled to do so by, for instance, the desire for emphasis, clarification or for purposes of contrast. When given information is restated it is not typically integrated into a clausal structure, but presented in the form of a separate proposition. Strategies such as those to be discussed in 7.1.2 are much more likely to occur than the passive.

The requirements imposed on the written language arising from the absence of common knowledge between writer and addressee as well as the impossibility of utilizing repair mechanisms rule out the wide - spread use of ellipsis. Since anaphoric information is much less likely to be omitted, the writer is induced to make decisions with respect to the sequencing of information which the speaker can quite

THE PRAGMATICS OF THE PASSIVE

happily avoid. The written language is to a higher degree than the spoken a planned mode of communication. As such it is expected to be more elaborate and varied both in terms of the lexical items and the constructions used. The passive may, therefore, be employed to achieve structural variation in compliance with the expectations for stylistic diversity. It may in alternation with active constructions produce a more rhetorically balanced text as in (21), for example.

> (21) The distinction between design and fashion
>   was further blurred in 1982. Design was
>   dominated by fickel fashion. And fashion
>   made free with the word design.
>   ("Fashionable is not enough" Time, Jan 3,
>   1983)

It may be chosen to facilitate the linking of successive clauses. This function of the passive is particularly characteristic of the agentless passive. Nevertheless, even the agentive may be used for such a purpose as illustrated in (22).

> (22) He paints a street singer, but she is his
>   favourite model, Victorine Meurent and
>   her taupe dress is far too fashionable to
>   have ever been worn by a musical beggar,
>   while her hat is of the type that was
>   worn by a male student in Paris. ("The most
>   Parisian of them all" Time, September 19,
>   1983)

The rigid word order of English, together with the possibility of passivizing not only direct, but also indirect and prepositional objects, has led to the relatively frequent use of the passive in English as compared to the other languages mentioned. However, although the passive in English occurs in colloquial speech and not practically exclusively in the written language as, for example, in Polish, it is similarly associated with more formal planned discourse or written texts.

Yet another factor determining passive occurrence is connected not directly with the passive itself, but with the characteristics displayed by the other topicalizing strategies available, which in contrast to the passive feature primarily in the oral mode, particularly in unplanned speech.

230

THE PRAGMATICS OF THE PASSIVE

7.1.2   Topicalization and Initial Position

Linguists who maintain that the passive is a means
of placing a given patient in unmarked topic
position contrast the passive with structures such
(23) and (24).

(23) Sometimes I find it difficult to talk to
people. Even with Reis. Now Reis, I really
like.

(24) I'm always overhearing stupid conversations.
This guy, I heard him say ...

Constructions such as (23) are referred to as
Y-movement or topicalizations, those in (24) as
left-dislocations. Topicalizations in English,
Italian and Portuguese differ from topicalizations
in Slavic and Germanic in both function and
register. They are used primarily in colloquial
speech and for many speakers are acceptable only if
the topic is a focus of contrast as in (25) (Napoli
1976:89).

Italian

(25) Il   cane sento   (non il   gatto)
the dog hear:pres:1s not the cat
'The dog, I hear (not the cat)'.

Topicalization in English when used non-contrastive-
ly differs from both topicalizations in Slavic and
Germanic, and the passive, in that the topic more
often than not is new as opposed to given which is
illustrated in (26) from Prince (1981:253).[7]

(26) [I graduated from high school as] an
average student. My initiative didn't
carry me any further than average. History
I found to be dry. Math courses I was
never good at. [...] Football was my bag.

In Italian the topic is typically indefinite (Napoli
1976:97).

(27) Libri non voglio!   Ne   ho
books not want:pres:1s of them have:pres:1s
già   troppi!
already too many
'Books, I don't want. I already have too
many'.

231

THE PRAGMATICS OF THE PASSIVE

In addition, the topic displays prosodic characteristics namely falling intonation, stress and often
a following short disjuncture which makes it informationally salient. Furthermore, the agent,
unlike in the agentive passive, is typically given
and occurs not in final focal position with tonic
stress, but in unmarked subject position.[8] Thus
whereas the focus in the agentive passive and topicalized clauses in Slavic and Germanic is typically
on the agent, in English, Italian and Portuguese
topicalized constructions it is on the patient/topic
and whatever new constituent if any occurs in the
remainder of the predication.

Left-dislocations differ from topicalizations in
that the topic in the former is resumed in the main
predication by an anaphoric pronoun (24) or a clitic
as in the Portuguese (28) (Dik 1981:170).[9]

> (28) Esse filme, o   João viu-o   ontem
>   this film   the John saw-it yesterday
>   'This film, John saw it yesterday'.

Hence the ensuing predication, constitutes a clause
in its own right. The left-dislocated topic in
English, Polish, Russian and Portuguese is followed
by a short disjuncture and is uttered with falling
or rising intonation. In Italian, Spanish, French
and German[10] it need not necessarily display such
prosodic characteristics.

The left-dislocated topic is often (in English
mainly) used to express new information. This information is generally deemed to be somehow pertinent
to the current discourse topic[11] as either a further
illustration of a point being made (24) or an alternative (not necessarily previously considered) to
information already specified (Keenan and Schieffelin
1976). In this second use the topic, like in topicalized clauses, may be a focus of contrast as in
(29).

French

> (29) J' ai   ouvert   la   porte; les fenêtres,
>   I have open:p.part the door   the windows
>   Henri les a   ouvertes
>   Henry them has open:p.part
>   'I opened the door; the windows, Henry
>   opened them'.

Alternatively, the left-dislocated topic may represent an entity which although previously evoked,

232

THE PRAGMATICS OF THE PASSIVE

is taken to have fallen into the background of the
hearer's consciousness. In many languages as in
Polish (29) and English such topics often occur with
expressions like as for, concerning, etc.

Polish

> (30) Jeśli chodzi   o   dzieci,   to
> if   concerns about children, (this)
> wysłaliśmy je   na   kolonie
> send:1pl them for   camp
> 'As for the children, we sent them to a
> camp'.

The topics in topicalized clauses and left-
dislocations which convey new information or re-
introduce information fulfil quite a distinct
function to that commonly attributed to the passive.
They are used as topic-shifting devices, for contrastive purposes or as strategies for seeking,
occupying and holding the floor (Duranti and Ochs
1979). The only point of convergence with the
passive is the initial sentence position of a non-
agentive constituent.[12]
The topic in English topicalized clauses, as
mentioned above, may convey given information. The
left-dislocated topic in all the enumerated languages
may also represent given information as in the
following examples from Italian (Cinque 1976) and
French (Galambos 1980).

Italian

> (31) a. Chi ha mangiato   la torta
> who has eat:p.part:m:s the cake
> 'Who has eaten the cake?'
>
> b. La torta, l'ha   mangiata   Piero
> the cake it-has eat:p.part:f:s Piero
> 'The cake, Piero has eaten it'.

French

> (32) a. Qu'est-ce   qui est arrivé
> what is-this which is happen:p.part
> à   Jean?
> to Jean
> 'What happened to Jean?'
>
> b. Jean, Pierre l'a   battu
> Jean Pierre him has beat:p.part
> 'Jean, Pierre beat him'.

THE PRAGMATICS OF THE PASSIVE

It is only in these instances that topicalizations and left-dislocations bear a closer similarity to the corresponding agentive passives (31c) and (32c) because not only is the topic non-agentive, but also given.

Italian

(31) c. La torta e stata mangiata da
the cake is been eat:p.part:f:s by
Piero
Piero
'The cake has been eaten by Piero'.

French

(32) c. Jean a été battu par Pierre
Jean has been beat:p.part by Pierre
'Jean was beaten by Pierre'.

In English, left-dislocations with given topics are said to be rare (Keenan and Schieffelin 1976). The Romance languages on the other hand are claimed to use left-dislocations as substitutes for the passive. Duranti and Ochs (1979) and Noonan (1977) contend that in Italian and Spanish they are, in fact, the discourse equivalents of the passive, while Galambos (1980) states that in popular spoken French they have completely ousted the passive. Nevertheless, the two constructions are not informationally identical. While the passive presents the patient topic as background information, left-dislocations forcibly draw attention to this constituent. This is due to the prosodic characteristics of left-dislocated topics and their resumption within the main predication. More importantly, however, it is the simultaneous presence of another topic - the subject/agent - which highlights the uncharacteristic topic choice.
Analyses of live discourse have revealed that the subject/agent in left-dislocations, unlike in passive clauses, in the overwhelming majority of instances is not new, but given and moreover human and pronominal. We have found only two examples in the literature of non-human subject/agents with transitive verbs namely from Italian (Lepschy and Lepschy 1977:155) and Spanish (Noonan 1977:378).

THE PRAGMATICS OF THE PASSIVE

Italian

(33) La carne, l'ha   mangiata   il gatto
the meat   it-has eat:p.part:f:s the cat
'The meat, the cat ate it'.

Spanish

(34) A   los peros los atropelló   el
acc the dogs them run over:past:3s the
camion
truck
'The dogs, the truck ran over them'.

Although as evidenced by the English translations
non-human subject/agents are also possible in
English, neither in English nor in the other languages are such subjects typical. Keenan and
Schieffelin (1976) and Duranti and Ochs (1979) have
noted that in English and Italian the dominant
subjects in left-dislocations are first and second
person pronouns. Our investigations reveal that
similar facts obtain for English topicalizations.
In a corpus consisting of 20 10-15 minute interviews
with Melbourne speakers conducted by students of the
Linguistic Dept. at Monash in 1980 we found 40 topicalizations and 39 left-dislocations all but two
of which contained human subjects and only one nominal as opposed to pronominal subject. The non-
human subjects occurred with left-dislocated topics
coreferential with the subject and not with non-
agentive topics which could be potentially substitutable by the passive. Left-dislocations, and
in English also topicalizations, thus tend to occur
with the very agents that are not generally overtly
expressed in the passive.
We noted above that pronominal human agents are
the most likely candidates for both topic and
subject functions. In left-dislocations and English
topicalization such constituents are typically
present, but while retaining their subject status
are not assigned the position of primary topics.
The unmarked topic position is usurped by another
less inherently topical, but contextually salient
constituent. The resulting construction possess
two topics. The less inherently topical one is made
prominent by virtue of placing it, and not the expected human pronominal constituent, in initial position. The subjectivization and topicalization of
a non-agent in passive clauses also constitutes a

THE PRAGMATICS OF THE PASSIVE

departure from the linguistic norm. However, as in passive clauses the agent tends to be both new and generally less inherently topical than the patient, it is the agent and not the subject/topic which constitutes the information focus. Thus left-dislocations and English topicalizations differ from the passive not only in the informational status of the patient, but also in the relative saliency of the agent. Since left-dislocations in all the languages mentioned are characteristic of unplanned discourse and topicalizations in English occur also practically exclusively in speech, in view of the egocentric bias of human verbal inter-action this is not altogether surprising.

We have seen that, in the Slavic and Germanic languages other than English, topicalized clauses may fulfil a function similar to the agentive passive. Left-dislocations in these languages are used infrequently, exclusively in unplanned dis-course and under conditions quite distinct from that which characterize either the passive or topicali-zations. In the Romance languages topicalizations are restricted to contrastive contexts and/or fronting of indefinite constituents. Left-dislocations although used primarily in speech, may perform a function similar to the passive. Note that in Italian and Spanish the subject in left-dislocations may occur in final focal position. This fact alone indubitably contributes to the potential substitutability of left-dislocations and the passive. Hence all the above languages possess a means of patient topicalization which, while not equivalent to the passive, is a possible alternative to the passive at least as a strategy for main-taining given/new constituent order.

The passive is found practically exclusively in the written language since it is contrasted with the other two topicalization devices which reflect the cross-linguistic preference for conflating subject and agent functions. In English, however, although topicalizations and left-dislocations may be used to front a given constituent, this is not perceived to be the primary function of either construction. Both show a strong preference for contrastive or new topics and given pronominal agents. Hence these constructions tend to occur under conditions dia-metrically opposed to those which facilitate the passive. The relative frequency of the passive in English is a direct result of the above. The passive, like the passive in the other

THE PRAGMATICS OF THE PASSIVE

languages, is not commonly used in unplanned speech; being associated with more formal modes of expression. Nevertheless, due to the characteristics of topicalized and left-dislocated structures even in speech it may be the preferred choice, particularly in instances where the patient displays not only discourse topicality but also inherent higher topicality.

7.2   The Passive and Impersonalization

The term *impersonal* in ch.3 was used in relation to clauses with no overt subject. The same term is also used to refer to constructions lacking a specified human agent. The agentless passive is an impersonalizing strategy in this second sense.

The agent may be suppressed because it is irrelevant, unknown or conversely known, but the speaker/writer does not wish to reveal its identity. The immediate rationale for agent omission in the latter case may be tact, deliberate vagueness, deception or desire to avoid implicating oneself or others.

Not all agentless passives are strictly impersonal. In (35), for example, a definite agent is involved directly retrievable from the sentential context, while in (36) the definite agent - the Australian electorate - is deducible on the basis of the knowledge of the world.

> (35) Manet's firmly built structures of light and dark were mostly done indoors. ("The most Parisian of them all" Time, Sept. 19, 1983)
> (36) On March 6, the day after Prime Minister Bob Hawke and the Labor Party were swept into office ... ("Spy trouble" Time, May 23, 1983)

The passive can only be regarded as impersonal if the implied agent is the general body of humans (36) or an incompletely specified set of individuals (38).

> (37) Individualism is prized, egotism is not.
> (38) In most of the rest of the world, private violence is not considered a high priority social problem. ("Private violence" Time, Sept. 5, 1983)

The passive is by no means the only impersonalization strategy available in English or in other

THE PRAGMATICS OF THE PASSIVE

European languages. However, as will be shown
below all of the impersonalization strategies differ
from the passive either in relation to the potential
inclusion of the speaker and addressee within the
set of possible agents or in terms of register or
information structure.

Below we will briefly compare the impersonalization strategies used in English with those
occurring in Romance, Slavic and Germanic.[13] The
discussion will reveal yet another set of factors
contributing to the relative frequency of the
passive in English

7.2.1 Indefinite Human Agents and the Passive

An indefinite human agent in English may be expressed not only via the passive but also through
the use of the active with an indefinite subject
such as someone,[14] everyone, people or the impersonal use of the pronouns one, we, you or they as in
(39), (40) and (41).

> (39) a. Such things are not done anymore in the
>   West.
>   b. One does not do such things anymore in
>   the West.
>   c. You do not do such things anymore in
>   the West.
>   d. People do not do such things any more
>   in the West.
>
> (40) a. It is said that time heals all pain.
>   b. They say that time heals all pain.
>   c. People say that time heals all pain.
>   d. Everyone says that time heals all pain.
>
> (41) a. This species is found in South America.
>   b. We find this species in South America.
>   c. One finds this species in South America.
>   d. You find this species in South America.

Similar indefinite subjects are used in the Romance
languages; the French on (42), tu (43) (Laberge and
Sankoff 1969:426), nous, ils, vous, les gens,
le monde, Italian and Spanish uno (44), Portuguese
gente (45) and in Germanic man/men (46), en/einer,
wir, jemand (47).

238

THE PRAGMATICS OF THE PASSIVE

French

    (42) Ici on parle   français
         here one speak:pres:3s French
         'French is spoken here'

    (43) C'est pas avec des guerres que tu
         this is not with the wars   that you
         réussis   à faire un pays
         succeed:pres:3s to make a country
         'You don't build a country with wars'.

Spanish

    (44) Uno desea   la felicidad
         one desire:pres:3s the happiness
         'One desires happiness'.

Portuguese

    (45) A gente trocou   saudações
         the people exchange:past:3s greeting
         'People exchanged greetings'.

Swedish

    (46) I Frankrike dricker   man mer
         in France   drink:pres:3s one more
         kaffe än te
         coffee than tea
         'In France they drink more coffee than
         tea'.

German

    (47) Jemand bemerkte   den Fehler
         someone notice:past:3s the mistake
         'Someone noticed the mistake'.

In languages which do not require the overt expression of a subject pronoun such as Italian (Lo Cascio 1976a:55), Spanish, Czech or Polish the second person singular and the first and third person plural forms of the verb function impersonally.

Italian

    (48) Diciamo   la veritá, lui aveva ragione
         tell:pres:1pl the truth he was   right
         'Let us tell the truth, he was right'.

THE PRAGMATICS OF THE PASSIVE

Czech

> (49) Mně řikaji   Karel
>   I:gen call:pres:3pl Charles
>   'They call me Charles'

Polish

> (50) Najgorsze to   że   nikomu nie możesz
>   the worst this that no-one   can:2s
>   wierzyć
>   believe
>   'The worst thing is that you can't believe
>   anyone'.

Polish also possesses an impersonal construction with the participle ending in no/to (51), in the past tense, and in the present tense with the third person singular form of the verb and the reflexive się (52) the controversial active/passive status of which was discussed in ch.3.

> (51) Wyniki konkursu   podano
>   results competition:gen give:part.imp
>   w   prasie
>   in press
>   'The results of the competition were issued
>   in the press'.

> (52) Takich decyzji   nie podejmuje   się
>   such   decisions:gen not make:pres:3s refl
>   pochopnie
>   rashly
>   'Such decisions should not be made rashly'.

The third person singular form of the verb with the reflexive se/si in Romance and se in Czech is also cited as an impersonal active construction by those who do not regard these clauses as passive (cf. ch.5).

Italian

> (53) A loro si   è   detta   la verità
>   to them refl. has tell:p.part the truth
>   'To them the truth has been told'.

Czech

> (54) Za to se   platí,   Jene
>   for this refl pay:pres:3s Jene
>   'That must be paid for John'.

240

THE PRAGMATICS OF THE PASSIVE

The reflexive passive in these languages is the most frequent substitute for the periphrastic passive.

The agent of impersonal constructions, like that of the agentless passive, need not be just anybody or everybody, but an incompletely specified collective or a generic NP determined by the linguistic or extra-linguistic context e.g. westeners in (39), Frenchmen in (46) editors in (51). It cannot, however, be a definite individual or group of individuals (but cf. p.246).

Although the agentless passive is not the only means of impersonalization in all the above languages, the impersonalization strategies mentioned do not always constitute viable alternatives to the passive. The implied indefinite agent of the agentless passive is ambiguous as to the inclusion of the speaker/writer and also addressee. Hence it is an ideal construction if the speaker/writer does not wish to directly implicate himself or his interlocutor, but simultaneously does not want to exclude either one or the other from the range of possible agents. Consider (55) and (56), for example.

(55) It may be argued that adoption is a cleaner and less cumbersome method than surrogate parenthood. ("Baby in the factory" Time, Feb. 14, 1983)

(56) The unwanted, the unusually brilliant or retarded and the physically handicapped children are often abused. ("The ultimate betrayal" Time, Sept. 5, 1983)

Both statements concern controversial issues in relation to which one would be unlikely to want to commit oneself or one's addressee. The probability of either of the interlocutors being potential agents in (55) is quite strong while in (56) although such an identification is not explicitly denied, the assumption is that the writer and addressee are not included. The interpretation, however, in both instances is left up to the addressee. An outright denial of the possible agenthood of the addressee in (56) would immediately alienate a potential child abuser, which is to be avoided since articles on child abuse are not only meant to inform, but also help those involved.

Indefinite subjects on the other hand are less ambiguous. The indefinite people, they and someone typically exclude both speaker and addressee.

THE PRAGMATICS OF THE PASSIVE

Compare the passive (38) with the corresponding
(57) in the context of a discussion on private
violence in the U.S.

(57) In most of the rest of the world they/
people do not consider private violence
a high priority social problem.

The agent in (38) and (57) is people in most of the
rest of the world. However, whereas the agentless
passive is ambiguous as to the affiliation of the
speaker and addressee with respect to the U.S. or
the rest of the world and hence can be interpreted
as either incorporating or excluding the interlocutors from the set of potential agents, the
indefinite subject sentences explicitly disassociate
speaker and addressee. Note also the incongruity of
(58) as a response to (40b,c).

(58) Maybe you're right, but I don't believe it.

We, you and one conversely include speaker and
addressee although in various degrees. Thus, for
example, while all three could be used as substitutes for the passive in the first clause of
(59), the agent of the second clause, which is
perceived to be distinct from the first, can only
be rendered by the indefinite someone or possibly
people.

(59) A child cannot be helped unless his or
her plight is reported. ("The ultimate
betrayal" Time, Sept. 5, 1983)

The indefinite we is used in order to involve
the addressee in the situation or event described,
to create a sense of mutual participation, commitment (60) and often responsibility (61).

(60) We routinely call Velasquez's pictures of
dwarfs "compassionate" not because we know
what Velasquez felt about dwarfs, but
because we believe we ought to feel sorry
for the deformed. ("Dramas of self presentation" Time, Jan. 10, 1983)

(61) The offence against them (animals), if
there is one, is not essentially the pain
we inflict upon them, but the fact that we
deprive them of life. ("Thinking animal
thought" Time, Oct. 3, 1983)

242

THE PRAGMATICS OF THE PASSIVE

The indefinite we is similar, but not identical
to the editorial we employed by speakers and
writers to turn attention away from themselves by
representing the reader/hearer as accompanying them
in thought. It occurs particularly often in intro-
ductory text books or popularized versions of
scientific works where the aim is to capture both
the interest and participation of the addressee.
The following passage from Radford (1981:34) illustrates this usage.

> (62) Before we look at how we might go about
> tackling (2) let's look more closely at
> (2i), the question of what we mean by
> saying that sentences have identical
> structure and how we can represent this
> structure.

The distinction between the two wes is a subtle
one, but whereas the editorial we refers to the
speaker/writer and addressee and often the authori-
ties which the speaker/writer represents, the
indefinite we encompassess everyone irrespective
of whether they have or have not addressed themselves to the problem at hand or see themselves as
involved.
    One is slightly more vague as to the inclusion
of the addressee than we and consequently its
function is more comparable to that of the agentless
passive. Nevertheless, one while not directly
implicating the interlocutors conveys a stronger
sense of involvement on the part of both than the
agentless passive. Thus while it can quite happily
be used as a substitute for the passive when the
situation or event carries favourable or at least no
pejorative overtones it would be totally inappropriate in (56), child abuse being an abhorent
practice, or (63c).

> (63) a. One can concoct mock academic theories
> about "Casablanca".
> b. One can lay the sweet thing down on a
> stainless-steel lab table and dissect
> it with instruments Freudian or an-
> thropological.
> c. A doctoral thesis might be written on
> the astonishing consumption of alcohol
> and cigarettes in the movie.
> ("We'll always have Casablanca" Time,
> Dec. 22, 1982)

THE PRAGMATICS OF THE PASSIVE

The writer does not hesitate to include himself or his addressee among those who like to play intellectual games the practice of which, at least in some circles, is highly valued. But to suggest that he or his addressee could be guilty of such a ridiculous endeavour as that of writing a doctoral thesis on such a ludicrous topic would be highly offensive. Thus the switch to the agentless passive.

The English one features primarily in written tests and formal registers. Most speakers regard the use of one in colloquial speech as pretentious preferring the indefinite you.[15] You unlike one explicitly involves the addressee in the described situation or event. The addressee is presented as a potential protagonist and his participation is not offset by the overt concomitant participation of the speaker as with we. Although the speaker is included among the set of possible agents, the emphasis is on the addressee. The use of you in written texts or formal registers is avoided precisely because it is too forceful. The writer is in no position to ascertain to what extent his addressee sees himself as a potential agent. If the addressee does not immediately identify with the statement being made, the use of you runs the risk of alienating him. One is much safer for while soliciting the involvement of the addressee it does not take his commitment for granted. Thus although you can be used instead of one in all instances apart from situations where it could be mistaken as referring exclusively to the addressee (68), it does not tend to be used in the written language particularly when a delicate or controversial subject is involved such as rape, for examples in (64).

(64) a. One thinks of lynch mobs before rape mobs.
b. You think of lynch mobs before rape mobs.

In speech you is preferred for the very reasons that may determine the choice of one in writing. The direct contact of the speaker and addressee obviates the need for excessive caution on part of the speaker because any potential misunderstandings can be immediately resolved. Moreover, the principles of successful human verbal interaction require that the addressee be at least superficially given the option of denying his involvement or acquiescence. As the addressee is directly included among the potential agents, he is in a position to deny his

244

THE PRAGMATICS OF THE PASSIVE

participation. The speaker conversely exposes himself to the possibility of such a denial. Hence you creates a bond between speaker and addressee while one a quite evidently greater distancing effect. Since the speaker has the option of using the expected you, the choice of one in speech due to its literary associations may be interpreted not as an attempt to solicit the involvement of the addressee, but to create a sense of social distance.

The third person plural pronouns or the third person plural forms of the verb, the indefinite people and someone in the Germanic, Slavic and Romance languages similarly to English exclude both speaker and addressee.[16] The implied agent of the Polish no/to participle construction cannot embrace the interlocutors either. The Romance and Czech reflexive passive and the Polish impersonal reflexive can be used similarly to the English one/ you (52-54) or may refer to an agent among which speaker and addressee are not included (65).

Polish

> (65) W Gdańsku buduje   się nowe
> in Gdansk build:pres:3s refl new
> osiedle
> housing estate
> 'A new housing estate is being built in Gdansk'.

The same applies to the Germanic man. Compare (46) with (66).

Swedish

> (66) Man kan se slott-et härifrån
> one can see castle-the from here
> 'You can see the castle from here'.

The indefinite we and you in all the languages mentioned appear to function as in English. In Polish and Czech (Duškova 1973), however, the second person singular and first person plural forms of the verb are not used as often as in English the third person plural and the reflexive constructions being preferred.

The referent of the French on although once restricted to an unspecified human including speaker and addressee, nowadays, according to Laberge and Sankoff (1979), may also be used as an

245

THE PRAGMATICS OF THE PASSIVE

alternative to <u>ils</u>, <u>les gens</u> and <u>la monde</u> or a specific <u>nous</u> or even <u>je</u>. The English <u>one/you</u> and the impersonalizing strategies in the other languages apart from those which exclude the speaker can also be used in the sense of <u>I</u> as exemplified in (67).

> (67) How did you know that?
> One simply knows such things.
> You simply know such things.

Such usage is particularly characteristic when the information conveyed carries unpleasant overtones be it for the addressee (the implication in (67) being, but you didn't) or the speaker as in (68).

> (68) Well, how do you think you'll cope?
> I don't know. One will have to grin and bear it.

Although it is quite evident that the agent is solely the speaker, the impersonalization creates a sense of distance, ameliorating the unpleasant affect of the statement being made.
Third and second person indefinite subjects, as in English, are generally perceived to be inelegant and consequently rarely feature in formal registers or written texts. The Spanish and Italian <u>uno</u>, according to Napoli (1976:171), is seen to be basically colloquial too. In the written language typically the periphrastic passive and nowadays also the reflexive passive is preferred. The Germanic <u>man</u>, the French <u>on</u>, the reflexive passive in Czech <u>and</u> both the impersonal participial and reflexive constructions in Polish are used in speech as well as writing often alternating with the periphrastic passive as in the following example from Polish (Rospond 1973:138).

Polish

> (69) a. Słowotworstwu gwarowemu poświęcono
> word formation dialectal devote:part.imp
> tu mało miejsca
> here little space
> 'Very little space has been devoted
> to dialectal word formation'.

246

THE PRAGMATICS OF THE PASSIVE

(69) b. Słowotworstwo nazewnicze jest również
word formation place names is also
uwzględnione
consider:p.part
'The composition of place names is
also taken into consideration'.

The Polish impersonal participial and reflexive
constructions are always preferred to the periphrastic passive in speech as are the reflexive
passives in Romance and Czech, but they are not
strictly colloquial, no such overtones being present
in (69). In German the indefinite man is favoured
particularly when in English we would have a passive
perception verb or a verb of "believing", "knowing"
or "understanding" followed by an infinitive as in
(70) (Curme 1960:299).

(70) a. Man glaubt, dass er in
one believe:pres:3s that he in
Brasilien ist
Brasil is
'He is believed to be in Brasil'.

b. Man sah, dass es zu spät war
one see:past:3s that it too late was
'It was seen that it was too late'.

Although clauses with indefinite subjects, like
the passive, may be used in order to omit specifying
an agent, they differ from the passive in terms of
pragmatic function. While in the agentless passive
the patient is placed in unmarked topic position,
the verb in focal position, in indefinite subject
clauses it is the patient which constitutes the
information focus. The passive, as noted above,
tends to occur with given as opposed to new patients. Clauses with indefinite one, we, on, man,
uno conversely favour new patients. Indefinite
subject clauses tend to be particularly preferred
to the passive when the patient is not only new,
but long or complex as in the following examples.

(71) One hears in his prose the happy sigh of
a man sinking into a hot bath.
(72) One imagines the snorting contempt with
which Truman would have regarded the
$1000 cowboy boots and the Adolfo gowns.
("A good snob is nowadays hard to find"
Time, Sept. 19, 1983)

247

THE PRAGMATICS OF THE PASSIVE

The corresponding passive would be stylistically
inept and informationally incongruous for it is the
direct object and not the verb which is informationally salient. Conversely when the verb constitutes the centre of interest as in (37) or (73)
the placing of the verb in non-focal position
before the direct object in an indefinite subject
clause would detract from the verb's communicative
force and consequently from the communicative
intent.[17]

> (73) Such execrable behaviour cannot be
> forgotten or forgiven.

In such instances the passive is typically preferred.
In colloquial speech the general predilection for
agentive human subjects even indefinite ones together with the possibility of utilizing supra-
segmentals to focus on the verb may override the
apparent incongruity of such a rendition of information and an indefinite subject clause may be
chosen instead of the passive. If the direct object
is a that-clause in English the passive with the
dummy it (40), (55) can be used as an alternative
to an indefinite subject clause. The German es,
Dutch er and French il can be used in a similar way.
The choice between an indefinite subject construction and the passive with a dummy subject may then
depend on to what extent the speaker/writer wishes
to involve himself and/or his addressee.
   Thus while the periphrastic passive in English
and the other Germanic languages[18] is not the only
means of impersonalization, it is the only construction which enables topicalization with con-
comitent impersonalization. In Romance the reflexive passive may be used as an alternative
topicalization and impersonalization device, while
in Slavic the patient may also be fronted in clauses
with the second person singular and first and third
person plural forms of the verb as evidenced by (50)
and (74) (Duškova 1973:17).

Czech

> (74) Záveského zavezli   do nemocnice
>   Zavesky   drive:past:3pl to hospital
>   'They have taken Zavesky to hospital'.

Note that the corresponding clauses in Romance do
not involve the movement of a direct object to

THE PRAGMATICS OF THE PASSIVE

clause initial position. Hence Polish and Czech not only possess an alternative passive construction, like the Romance languages, which may be used as an impersonalizing and topicalizing strategy, but also active constructions fulfilling a similar role. It is not therefore surprising that the periphrastic passive is not often used in these languages.

The alternative impersonalizing strategies do not always carry the same conversational implicatures as the corresponding periphrastic passives and hence the choice of construction may also depend on the type of implicature that the speaker/writer wishes to convey. This is particularly apparent with clauses expressing general statements either relating to the overall human condition or to the state of affairs at a specified time or place. Compare (39a) with (39b,c) and (39d), for example. While the passive will tend to be interpreted as a statement about what doesn't happen to such things in the West, the indefinite one/you clauses are more likely to be used as offers of advice about how anyone including the speaker and hearer should behave in the West. The same difference can be observed between the corresponding periphrastic passives and the Spanish and Italian uno or the Polish and Czech reflexive constructions. The alternatives with people, they or the third person plural form of the verb on the other hand comment on the type of people who live in the West.

Clauses with general indefinite human subjects by virtue of the type of referent that they evoke can also be used as endorsements. Consider the following examples.

> (75) a. Children are spanked when they are naughty.
> b. One spanks children when they are naughty.
> c. You spank children when they are naughty.

(75b,c) are open to a number of interpretations. If uttered by a grandparent to a parent they could be interpreted as advice on how to treat children. The passive is more likely to be addressed to a child as a warning. (75b,c) could also be produced in order to console a parent who has against his or her principles stooped to hitting a child. In such a context they are not open to an "advice"

THE PRAGMATICS OF THE PASSIVE

reading, but rather imply that the slapping of
children happens regularly and although perhaps a
practice not to be encouraged is nothing to be
ashamed of or make a fuss about. The passive
carries no such implications. The endorsement
reading of one/you clauses is not restricted to
situations with potential negative connotations.
A similar difference can be seen in (76).

> (76) a. Beautiful women are immediately noticed.
> b. One immediately notices beautiful women.
> c. You immediately notice beautiful women.

Although there is no reason to suppose that the
above behaviour could be regarded as reprehensible,
(76b,c) affirm the normality of such a reaction
despersing any potential doubts that anyone including the addressee might have had. The passive
merely makes a statement about beautiful women. The
indefinite subject clauses are therefore unlikely
to occur in the same context as the passive.

In 7.1 we noted that the relative frequency of
the passive in English can be attributed to the
lack of parallel strategies for patient topicalization with simultaneous agent focusing. We now come
to a similar conclusion with respect to alternative
impersonalizing strategies. Someone, people and
they exclude speaker and addressee and are generally
seen as inappropriate in more formal registers.
You strongly implicates the addressee and is
similarly colloquial. We while a possible substitute for the agentless passive in both speech and
writing entails a commitment on part of both
speaker and addressee which may not be desirable.
One although less explicitly inclusive than we or
you, may be not vague enough. Hence whereas the
Germanic man, the French on, the Romance and Czech
reflexive passive and the Polish impersonal reflexive constructions may be substitutable for the
agentless passive when the agent either includes or
excludes the speaker and addressee in both formal
and informal registers, none of the English impersonalization strategies exhibit similar versatility.
The agentless passive is the only impersonalizing
construction in English which enables the speaker/
writer to achieve similar ambiguity. Moreover, it
is the only means of impersonalization which permits
the retaining of an unmarked given new distribution
of information.

All three factors contribute to the wide spread
use of the passive in English. Which factor

250

THE PRAGMATICS OF THE PASSIVE

prevails in any individual instance can only be determined within the particular context. Although linguists typically focus on the topicalizing function of the passive, the degree of involvement which the speaker/writer wishes to impart to himself or his addressee cannot be ignored. Admittedly, as English does not possess alternative topicalization strategies, the inclusion or exclusion of the interlocutors may play a secondary role in the choice of the passive over other impersonalizing constructions. However, in the Romance and Slavic languages where such alternative means of topicalization with concomitant impersonalization are available and the patient in the periphrastic passive need not necessarily be given and consequently clause initial, the choice of the passive as opposed to other impersonalization strategies may well depend on the identity of the implied agent.

NOTES

1.   According to Chafe (1976) in English, nouns which convey new information are more consistently given stronger stress than verbs, (cf. Chafe (1974: 114-116) for details.)
2.   Halliday (1968), Hutchins (1975) and Hinds (1975) actually use the term *theme*, not topic. The notion of theme was first introduced by the Prague School linguist, Mathesius (cf. e.g. Mathesius 1975; Daneš 1964; Firbas 1964, 1966) who defined it in terms of the concept of communicative dynamism, a notion referring to the relative contribution that a particular constituent makes towards forwarding the communicative function of the whole discourse. The theme is defined as the entity with the lowest degree of communicative dynamism. Halliday as well as most other Anglo-Saxon linguists use the term theme with reference to the sentence initial constituent irrespective of its communicative dynamism.
3.   The topic or theme in the unmarked case is, however, assumed to represent given information. Halliday, for example, thus speaks of unmarked and marked themes.
4.   Creider (1979) among others has noted the very close relationship between a language's basic syntactic order and its positional strategy for topic and focus constituents, the subject position in all instances being the unmarked topic position,

251

THE PRAGMATICS OF THE PASSIVE

the direct object position the characteristic location of the focus. The preference for topics in
initial position follows from the fact that the
majority of the world's languages are subject initial i.e. SVO or SOV. (cf. Greenberg 1963;
Pullum 1977; Mallinson and Blake 1980). In VOS
languages e.g. Malagasy (Keenan 1976b) or Ojibwa
(Tomlin and Rhodes 1979) or in OVS e.g. Hixkaryana
(Derbyshire 1981) or OSV e.g. Apurinǎ (Derbyshire
and Pullum 1981) the unmarked position of given
constituents is not, however, clause initial.
Consequently for such languages the two definitions
of topic, as given information and as the sentence
initial constituent unlike in the majority of
languages would identify quite distinct constituents
as topic.
     5.   Some linguists regard all constituents
which take full stress as focal. Since in speech
all new items of information tend to be fully
stressed, there may be a number of foci in a single
sentence. In written texts the focus or foci will
be determined by the context. Under this analysis
focus is understood as 'being a matter of establishing the significant points of development in a
theme (or topic) of discourse'. (Allan to appear,
ch.7).
     6.   In order to simplify discussion we will
concentrate on nominal topics. Note, however,
that any propositional constituent may be the topic,
whether verb, adjective, adverb etc.
     7.   Prince (1981) claims that the topic in
English topicalizations is typically given not new,
where by given is meant not necessarily stated in
the preceding utterance or directly retrievable
from the situational context, but also information
which is inferentially related to some evoked
entity or in a salient set relation to such an
entity. Hence Prince regards the underlined topics
in (23) as given. We cannot see the validity of
extending the notion of given in this fashion for
one would have to assume that anything relating to
the educational system in (23) including the black-
board duster is given. As far as we have been able
to determine Prince's given means simply contextually relevant.
     8.   In Italian and Spanish, however, the
subject in left-dislocations may occur in final
position as in (I) (Cinque 1976a:14).

THE PRAGMATICS OF THE PASSIVE

Italian

    I. La   torta se l'e mangiata   Giorgio
       the cake it has eat:p.part:f:s Giorgio
       'The cake, Giorgio has eaten it'.

    9.   The left-dislocated topic may be restated in the main predication also by an anaphoric NP as in (II).

    II. John, I hate the bastard.

Cinque (1977) claims that it is necessary to distinguish two types of left-dislocations, those which involve a coreferential clitic and those in which a pronoun or other anaphoric element appears in the ensuing predication which are named constructions with "hanging topics". Cinque maintains that the two constructions exhibit a number of distinct characteristics one of which is that while in left-dislocated sentences of the first type prepositional objects are accompanied by the preposition and case marked NPs retain the case marking which they would have had if they had occurred in the main predication, in the latter the topic occurs in the neutral typically nominative form. Hence the English left-dislocated topics under this analysis qualify as "hanging topics" as evidenced by the ungrammaticality of (III).

    III. a. This job, I can't concentrate on it.
        b.*On this job, I can't concentrate it.

The distinction between the two types of left-dislocations is not always as clear as Cinque suggests even in Italian, French and Romanian the three languages which according to Cinque display both constructions. For a critique of Cinque's approach see Napoli (1981).
    10.   McCray (1982) claims that left-dislocations such as (IV) in German are of marginal acceptability. Left-dislocations with a coreferential diectic are preferred. The same applies to Dutch.

    IV. Den Professor, sie lobten   ihn
       the professor they praise:past:3pl him
       'The Professor, they praised him'.

    11.   The topic of discourse as opposed to the sentential topic is the general area of discussion over a wider stretch of communicative exchanges.

THE PRAGMATICS OF THE PASSIVE

(cf. e.g. van Dijk (1977).

12.　The left-dislocated topic may, of course, be coreferential with the subject.　Such left-dislocated constituents are not considered for we are interested in a comparison of left-dislocations with the passive.

13.　Infinitival constructions such as (V) will not be considered for they cannot be regarded as substitutes for the passive.

> V. To imagine any general reduction in human secrecy is intriguing, but oddly difficult. ("The public life of secrecy" Time, Jan.17, 1983)

14.　Someone differs from the other indefinite agents in that only a single individual is involved. Someone may be specific or non-specific.　Here only the non-specific someone is considered.

15.　Dušková (1973) claims that one is the least common of the devices used to denote general human agents.　Her 10 samples of scientific writing yielded only 11 instances of the impersonal one. One is indubitably the most stylistically marked of the impersonalizing strategies in English including the agentless passive.　According to general consensus it is either highly literary or "snobby". Nevertheless it occurs frequently in journalistic prose and also quite regularly in academic text books.　If Time magazine is to be taken as an indicator of American journalistic usage it is by no means rare.　One also appears to be used consistently as a substitute for you in some higher lects.

16.　According to Narro (1976) the Portuguese a gente typically includes the speaker.

17.　Similar observations were made independently by Dušková (1971, 1973).

18.　Swedish, Danish, and Norwegian also possess the s-passive which is typically used for customary or repeated actions or processes.　It is therefore the s-passive and not the periphrastic one with which some of the man-clauses alternate.

254

Chapter Eight

SUMMARY

The preceding chapters have been concerned with two major issues, the definition of the passive and the relation of the passive to transitivity.

Due to the fact that some of the characteristics associated with the European canonical passive (periphrastic personal passive) i.e. the non-agentive subject, the change in constituent order and/or nominal morphology and the specific verbal morphology are also to be found in other construc-tions both in European and non-European languages, the term *passive* has been extended to cover a wide range of structures. Although when each of these passives is compared to the canonical passive the label passive seems to be justified, there being at least one property which unites the two, as a group the whole body of so called passives does not have a single property in common.

A large number of passives possess a non-agentive subject. This property of the passive does not, however, suffice to distinguish the passive from clauses such as (1).

(1) a. John received a present.
    b. That suit fits you well.
    c. John resembles Fred.
    d. Mary is old.
    e. John died.

In addition it excludes from the domain of the passive constructions known as impersonal passives which do not possess an overt subject. Hence the passive, if it is to encompass impersonal passives cannot be defined in terms of the semantic role of the passive subject.

The characteristic which unites personal and impersonal passives and sets them apart from the

SUMMARY

clauses in (1) is the existence of a potential corresponding active, the subject of which functions as
the overt or implied agent of the passive. The
implied or overt agent in turn distinguishes passives
from anticausatives as in (2).

(2) a. The shirt irons well.
b. The shop opens at ten o'clock.

The passive may therefore be characterized as a
construction:

a) which has a corresponding active the subject
of which does not function as the passive
subject
b) the event or action expressed in the passive
is brought about by some person or thing
which is not the passive subject, but the
subject of the corresponding active
c) the person or thing if not overt is at least
strongly implied.

This characterization of the passive is not particularly illuminating. It says nothing about the
morpho-syntactic properties of the passive or the
various functions that the passive may fulfil. Such
an uninformative characterization is inevitable if
personal and impersonal passives are considered, the
latter of both transitive and intransitive verbs, as
well as the various less typical passives, with an
obligatory agent, for example (cf. 2.1.2) or with
the agent in topic position (cf. 2.1.3) be it only
in European languages.
The above characterization of the passive raises
the question of what qualifies as a corresponding
active. *Stative* passives have been claimed not to
be passive due to the lack of a corresponding active.
Nevertheless, the situations or states that they express have been brought about by an outside agent.
Consequently it could be argued that postulating an
active counterpart for these constructions does not
differ in essence from postulating an active counterpart for truncated passives. We believe that there
is a difference; whereas the agent in the truncated
passive is communicatively significant being
responsible for the situation or action expressed in
the clause, in the *stative* passive any agent is irrelevant since the focus of attention is on the
resultant state.

SUMMARY

The exclusion of the *indirect* passive may also be regarded as quite controversial. (3a) and (3b) are indubitably related in terms of propositional content.

(3) a. Daniela cut John's hair.
    b. John had his hair cut by Daniela.
    c. John's hair was cut by Daniela.

But the passive of (3a) is (3c) not (3b). The *indirect* passive may differ from both the active and the *direct* passive in terms of conversational implicature. For instance John in (3b) may be seen as having somehow initiated or being somehow responsible for the described state of affairs. However, as similar differences may also exist between the active and the *direct* passive such differences can hardly be taken as an argument against the passive nature of the *indirect* passive. In (3) the *direct* passive (3c) differs from the *indirect* passive in (3b), in that the latter is clearly a complex sentence with his hair functioning as the subject of the complement clause not the matrix clause as John's hair in (3c). John is not an argument of the verb in either (3a) or (3c), while in (3b) it definitely is. If the passive is assumed to change the grammatical function of verbal arguments, then (3a) cannot be treated as the corresponding active of (3b).

The non-synonymy of active and passive clauses containing quantifiers, negatives, pronouns and modal auxiliaries may also be treated as counterevidence to the claim that all passive clauses possess active counterparts. Since (4a), for example, is ambiguous due to the potential coreferentiality of everyone and his, while (4b) is not, (4a) may not be considered by some linguists to be the active counterpart of (4b).

(4) a. Everyone pleases his wife.
    b. His wife is pleased by everyone.

The same applies to (5a) and (5b).

(5) a. John cannot do it.
    b. It cannot be done by John.

The active (5a) is normally interpreted as expressing ability while the modal auxiliary in the passive

SUMMARY

(5b) is normally interpreted as indicating possibility (Quirk et al. 1972:807). Similar discrepancies
are to be found between actives and passives even
without quantifiers or modals (cf. the discussion of
the Bengali passive p.144 or Davison's (1981) analysis
of the Hindi passive). In English, differences in
conversational implicature are particularly apparent
between the active and pseudo-passives (cf. p.201-4),
and get-passives (cf. p.142-4). Truncated be-
passives may also convey different implicatures than
the corresponding active. Compare (6a) and (6b)
from Sinha (1973:621), for example.

(6) a. Doctors often diagnose tumors as
malignant even when they are benign.
b. Tumors are often diagnosed as malignant
even when they are benign.

According to Sinha (6b) implies that little is known
about tumors and therefore it is difficult to
diagnose them correctly while (6a) implies that
doctors are incompetent and cannot make a correct
diagnosis. We do not consider that the above discrepancies between passives and actives warrant
abandoning characterizing the passive in relation to
a potential corresponding active because only such
a comparison reveals the differences in grammatical
relations and enables the specification of the
functions of the passive. This is, however, basically
a matter of interpretation.

Under definitions of the passive not based on
the existence of a corresponding active *stative* and
indirect passives qualify as passive. Sinha (1978),
for example, defines the passive in terms of the
following two characteristics:

a) the argument toward which the verb is
directed (which may or may not be the
patient or object) has been affected
in some manner
b) the state which the affected argument
is in has been brought about by an overt
or implied cause (which may or may not be
the agent).

This characterization of the passive entails extending the label passive to anticausatives and
arguably even to reflexives. In a clause such as
(2a) there is also an implied cause. Possibly

258

SUMMARY

the <u>quality of the material</u> makes the <u>ironing easy</u>.
It is rather an implied agent which distinguishes
passives and anticausatives and not an implied
cause. Moreover, the agent must be distinct from
the passive subject to exclude reflexives.

Anticausatives also qualify as passive under
Keenan's (1982) definition of the passive. Keenan
approaches the passive not from the sentential
level as here, but from the predicate level. Consequently the passive is seen as a derivational
relation between predicates, not sentences. The
passive is defined as a means of deriving n-place
predicates from $n+1$-place predicates or in other
words, a means of reducing the argument structure
of the predicate by one. Although such a conception of the passive rules out the instances of obligatory agent retention, it does cater for personal
and impersonal passives of transitive, ditransitive
and intransitive verbs. However, Keenan (ibid:18)
himself admits that 'we cannot yet distinguish
passives from other detransitivising processes
such as reflexive, reciprocal, antipassive, unspecified object deletion etc.' (And we add anticausatives.) Hence this definition of the passive
is similarly deficient.

The term *passive* can only be valid and useful
for purposes of language description if it refers
to the same type of structure in all languages in
which this construction is said to be displayed.
The discussion here has shown that the constructions
called passive have very little in common. They
differ in:

a) verbal morphology
b) case marking
c) word order
d) the overt presence of a passive agent
e) the marking of the passive agent
f) the presence of a surface subject
g) the requirements made on the passive subject
   connected with semantic roles, hierarchies of
   person, definiteness, specificity etc.
h) transitivity restrictions
i) restrictions on tense, aspect, mood and verbal
   class
j) frequency of occurrence
k) discourse conditions and pragmatic functions

Whether the three properties that they share warrant
a common passive label is debatable. It could well

259

SUMMARY

be argued that the differences far outweigh the similarities.

The analysis of personal passives has led us to the conclusion that unless one makes the *a priori* assumption that passivization is dependent on transitivity and transitivity is determined by passivization, it cannot be argued that there is a one to one relationship between the passive and transitivity. If transitivity is defined in terms of a cluster of morphological, syntactic and semantic properties displayed by the nominal arguments of the verb then:

a) not all active transitive clauses have passive counterparts
b) not all passive clauses have corresponding actives which are transitive
c) not all passive clauses can be viewed as intransitive

The first point can be illustrated by the English clauses (7a).

(7) a. The soil grows good tomatoes.
    b. *Good tomatoes are grown by the soil.

Under a morpho-syntactico-semantic definition of transitivity (7a) is transitive; the NP following the verb has both the morphological and syntactic properties (other than the ability to function as the subject of a passive clause) associated with P NPs in English. However the passive of (7a) is ungrammatical. The clause (8a) from Olutsooto (Dalgish 1976a:61) demonstrates that not all passive clauses have transitive active counterparts.

(8) a. Xu -mu   -saala xu -pulush-il-uungwa   -
       loc-cl.3 -tree loc-fly-appl-pass t/asp -
       xwo neende lii - ñoñi
       loc by   cl.5   bird
       'On to the tree is flown by the bird'.

    b. Lii - ñoñi li - pulush - il - aanga
       cl.5 - bird cl.5 - fly   - appl-t/asp
       xu - mu   - saala
       loc - cl.3 - tree
       'The bird flies on to the tree'.

As discussed in 2.2.2, the locative NP in (8b) does not display all the typical P properties. Under

260

SUMMARY

most orthodox definitions of transitivity (8b) has
to be therefore regarded as intransitive. That the
passive cannot be restricted to P NPs is also indicated by (9a) from Kinyarwanda (Gary and Keenan
1977).

    (9). a. Maria y - ∅ - oher - er -
          Mary 3s -past - send - appl -
          ej - w - e ibaruwa na Yohani
          asp-pass-asp letter by John
          'Mary was sent a letter by John'.

       b. Yohani y - ∅ - oher -er - eje Maria
          John 3s-past - send -appl - asp Mary
          ibaruwa
          letter
          'John sent a letter to Mary'.

The reasons why <u>Maria</u> in (9b) cannot be treated as
a P NP were given in 2.2.1. The Kinyarwanda example
(9a) simultaneously illustrates that some passive
clauses appear to be syntactically transitive.
Although the NP <u>Maria</u> does not have the semantic
properties typical of active A NPs, it displays the
syntactic characteristics associated with subjects
in Kinyarwanda. The NP <u>ibaruwa</u> on the other hand
possesses both the semantic and syntactic features
of P NPs.
    The above discrepancies between transitivity and
passivization provide enough evidence for abandoning
the claim that passivization is definitive of transitivity in a universal sense. This does not mean
that the ability to function as the subject of a
passive clause cannot be treated as one of the criteria which identifies P NPs, but rather that this
ability has to be contrasted with the behaviour of
a NP under other syntactic rules and its morphological and semantic characteristics. Unfortunately,
which of the morphological, syntactic or semantic
properties that a NP displays determines whether it
is or is not a P appears to depend on the linguist. No
syntactic, morphological or semantic characteristic
is common to all NPs which have been treated as Ps.
Therefore the decisions made have to be based on
some other grounds. Usually they depend on the theoretical framework which a given linguist adopts and
on the importance assigned to syntactic rules,
morphological marking and semantic properties. The
outcome is therefore not uniform. The only way out
of this undesirable situation is, in fact, to assume

261

SUMMARY

that passivization is definitive of transitivity and
vice versa (only the personal passive). As not all
languages appear to possess passive constructions
this would simultaneously entail abandoning the
claim that transitivity is a linguistic universal.
Most linguists would regard this as very undesirable.
Of course there is no *a priori* reason why transitivity should not be defined language specifically.
Similarly there is no *a priori* reason why verbs have
to be classified in terms of the transitive/intran-
sitive distinction. It is quite conceivable that
verbs could be conveniently analyzed in terms of the
notion of *valency* and case frames.

The conclusions which we have arrived at are
basically of a negative nature. However, they do
not differ greatly from any of the conclusions
reached by linguists who have attempted to deal with
language universals. Languages are not uniform and
do not lend themselves to uniform analyses.

BIBLIOGRAPHY

Abbreviations Used

AS	African Studies
BLS	Proceedings of the nth Annual Meeting of the Berkeley Linguistic Society
CLS	Papers from the nth Regional Meeting of the Chicago Linguistic Society
FL	Foundations of Language
IULC	Indiana University Linguistic Club
JL	Journal of Linguistics
JCL	Journal of Chinese Linguistics
Lg	Language
LA	Linguistic Analysis
LI	Linguistic Inquiry
OL	Oceanic Linguistics
Ph.P	Philologica Pragensia
PSiCL	Papers and Studies in Contrastive Linguistics
SAL	Studies in African Linguistics
SL	Studies in Language
SLS	Studies in the Linguistic Sciences
TLP	Travaux Linguistiques de Prague.

Abraham, W. (ed.), (1978), *Valence, Semantic Case and Grammatical Relations,* (Studies in Language Comparison Series 1), Amsterdam, John Benjamins.

Adams, D.Q, (1971), 'Passives and problems in Classical Greek and Modern English', *Working Papers in Linguistics 10,* Colombus, Ohio, 1-7.

Agesthialingom, S, (1969), 'Passive in Dravidian' in S. Agesthialingom & N. Kumaraswami Raja (eds), *Dravidian Linguistics Seminar Papers,* Annamalainager, Annamahai University, 1-23.

263

BIBLIOGRAPHY

Alisova, T.B. (1968), 'Semantiko-kommunikativnyj
     substrat bezličnych predloženii' in the
     collective *Invariantnye Sintaksičeskie
     Zančenija i Structura Predloženija*, Moskva,
     Nauka.
Allan, K, (1973), 'Complement noun phrases and
     prepositional phrases, adjectives and verbs',
     FL 10, 337-397.
_____ (to appear) *Linguistic Meaning*, London,
     Routledge & Kegan Paul.
Allen, B.J. & D.G. Frantz, (1978), 'Verb agreement
     in Southern Tiwa', *BLS 4*, 11-17.
Amastae, J. (1983), 'Agentless constructions in
     Dominican Creole', *Lingua 59.1*, 47-76.
Amrilavalli, R, (1979), 'The representation of tran-
     sitivity in the lexicon', *LA 5.1*, 71-92.
Anderson, J, (1968) 'Ergative and nominative in
     English', *JL 4.1*, 1-32.
_____ (1977) *On Case Grammar*, London, Croom Helm.
Anderson, S.R, (1974), 'On the syntax of ergative
     languages' in L. Heilman (ed.), *Proceedings of
     the Eleventh International Congress of Linguis-
     tics II*, Bologna, il Mulino, 73-77.
_____ (1976), 'On the notion of subject in ergative
     languages' in C. Li (ed.), 1-23.
_____ (1977a), 'On mechanisms by which languages
     become ergative' in C. Li (ed.), 317-363.
_____ (1977b), 'Comments on Wasow' in P. Culicover
     et al. (eds), 361-377.
Andrews, A, (1982), 'The representation of case in
     Modern Icelandic' in J. Bresnan (ed.), 427-503.
Andrews, R, (1975), *Introduction to Classical
     Nahuatl*, Austin, University of Texas Press.
Andronov, M.S, (1969), *The Kannada Language*, Moscow,
     Nauka.
Apresjan, J.D, (1974), *Leksičeskaja Semantika:
     Synonimičeskie Sredstva Jazyka*, Moskva, Nauka.
Ariste, P, (1968), *A Grammar of the Votic Language*,
     The Hague, Mouton.
Atkinson, J, (1969), *A Finnish Grammar*, Helsinki,
     Suomalaisen Kirjallisuuden Seura.
Awbery, G.M, (1976), *The Syntax of Welsh*, Cambridge,
     Cambridge University Press.
Babby, L.H. & R.D. Brecht, (1975), 'The syntax of
     voice in Russian', *Lg 51.2*, 342-67.
Bach, E.W, (1979), 'In defence of passive',
     Linguistics and Philosophy 3, 297-341.
Bakaev, X, (1966), 'Kurdskij jazyk' in V.V.
     Vinogradov (ed.), 257-280.

BIBLIOGRAPHY

Bani, E. & J. Klokeid, (1976), 'Ergative switching in Kala Lagau Langgus' in P. Sutton (ed.), *Languages of Cape York*, Canberra, Australian Institute of Aboriginal Studies, 269-283.

Barber, E.J.W, (1975), 'Voice - beyond the passive', *BLS 1*, 16-24.

Barker, A.R.M. & A.K. Mengal, (1969), *A Course in Baluchi*, Montreal, McGill University Press.

Beedham, Ch, (1982), *The Passive Aspect in English, German and Russian*, Tübingen, Gunter Narr Verlag.

Bell, S, (1976), *Cebuano Subjects in Two Frameworks*, Cambridge, Mass., MIT Ph.D. diss., (available from IULC, Bloomington, Indiana).

     (1983) 'Advancements and Ascensions in Cebuano', in D.M. Perlmutter (ed.), 143-218.

Bennett, P.A, (1980), 'English passives: a study in syntactic change and relational grammar', *Lingua 51.1*, 101-14.

Bever, T, (1970), 'The cognitive basis for linguistic structures' in J.R. Hayes (ed.), *Cognition and the Development of Language*, New York, John Wiley and Son, 279-352.

Bjorkhagen, I, (1966), *Modern Swedish Grammar*, Stockholm, Svenska Bokforlaget Norstedts.

Blake, B, (1976), 'On ergativity and the notion of subject', *Lingua 39.4*, 281-300.

     (1977), *Case Marking in Australian Languages*, (Linguistic Series 23) Canberra, Australian Institute of Aboriginal Studies.

     (1979a), *Kalkatungu Grammar*, (Pacific Linguistic Series B. 57), Canberra, School of Pacific Studies, ANU.

     (1979b), 'Degrees of ergativity in Australia' in F. Plank (ed.), *Ergativity: Towards a Theory of Grammatical Relations*, New York, Academic Press, 291-306.

Blake, F.R, (1925), *A Grammar of the Tagalog Language*, New Haven, Yale University Press.

Bloomfield, L, (1917), *Tagalog Texts with Grammatical Analysis*, (Studies in language and literature 3. 2-4), Urbana, University of Illinois.

Bolinger, D, (1977), 'Transitivity and spatiality: the passive of prepositional verbs' in A. Makki, V. Becker Makkai & L. Hailmann (eds), *Linguistics at the Crossroads*, Lake Bluff, Illinois, Jupiter Press, 57-78.

Bock, J.K, (1982), 'Toward a Cognitive psychology of syntax: information processing contributions to sentence formulation', *Psychological Review 89.1*, 1-47.

265

BIBLIOGRAPHY

Borgert, U.H.G. & C.A. Nyhan, (1976), *A German Reference Grammar*, Sydney, Sydney University Press.

Bouton, L.F, (1973), 'Some reasons for doubting the existence of a passive transformation' in Kachru et al. 70-84.

Brame, M, (1976), *Conjectures and Refutations in Syntax and Semantics*, New York, Academic Elsvier.

Breckenridge, J, (1975), 'The post-cyclicity of es-insertion in German', *CLS 11*, 81-91.

Bredsdorff, E, (1958), *Danish: An Elementary Grammar and Reader*, Cambridge, Cambridge University Press.

Bresnan, J.W, (1978), 'A realistic transformational grammar' in M. Halle, J. Bresnan & G. Miller (eds), *Linguistic Theory and Psychological Reality*, Cambridge, Mass, MIT Press, 1-59.

_____ (ed.), (1982a), *The Mental Representation of Grammatical Relations*, Cambridge, Mass. MIT Press.

_____ (1982b), 'The passive in lexical theory' in J. Bresnan (ed.), 3-86.

Brinker, K, (1971), *Das Passiv in Heutigen Deutsch. Form und Funktion*, München, Heuber Schwann.

Brown, R, (1973), *A First Language: The Early Stages*, Cambridge, Mass., Harvard University Press.

Brown, E.K. & J.E. Miller, (1980), *Syntax: A Linguistic Introduction to Sentence Structure*, London, Hutchinson.

Burston, J.L, (1979), 'The pronominal verb construction in French', *Lingua 48.2/3*, 147-176.

Burt, M.K, (1971), *From Deep to Surface Structure*, New York, Haper and Row.

Campbell, S, (1957), *The Fundamentals of the Thai Language*, New York, Parago Book Gallery.

Catford, J.C, (1976), 'Ergativity in Caucasian languages', *Montreal Working Papers in Linguistics 6*, 37-48.

Černy, V, (1971), 'Some remarks on the syntax and morphology of the verb in Avar', *Archív Orientální 3*, 45-56.

Chafe, W.L, (1970), *Meaning and the Structure of Language*, Chicago, University Press.

_____ (1974), 'Language and consciousness', *Lg 50.1*, 111-133.

_____ (1976), 'Givenness, contrastiveness, definiteness, subjects, topics and point of view' in C. Li (ed.), 25-57.

Chaiyaratana, C, (1961), *A Comparative Study of English and Thai Syntax*, Ph.D.diss., Indiana University.

BIBLIOGRAPHY

Chandraich, B.N, (1972), 'The passive voice in
Kannada' in G.N. Reddy & P.S. Nair (eds),
*Proceedings of the Second All India Conference
of Dravidian Linguistics in Tirupati*, Dravidian
Linguistic Association of India, Trivandrum,
University of Kerala, 134-139.

Channon, R.C, (1974), 'Pseudo-reflexive verbs in
Russian' in D. Brecht & C.V. Chvany (eds),
Slavic Transformational Syntax, Ann Arbor, The
University of Michigan, 66-77.

Chappell, H, (1980), 'Is the get-passive adversative?'
Papers in Linguistics 13.3, 411-452.

Chomsky, N, (1957), *Syntactic Structures*, The Hague,
Mouton.

———— (1965), *Aspects of the Theory of Syntax*,
Cambridge, Mass. MIT Press.

———— (1973), 'Conditions on transformations' in S.
Anderson & P. Kiparsky (eds), *A Festschrift
for Morris Halle*, New York, Holt Rinehart and
Winston, 232-286.

———— (1980), 'On Binding, *LI 11.1*, 1-46.

Christmas, R.B. & J.E. Christmas, (1973), 'Clause
patterns in Kupia' in R.L. Trail (ed.), 257-343.

Chu, C.C, (1973), 'The passive construction in
Chinese and English', *JCL 1.3*, 437-470.

Chung, S, (1976a), 'On the subject of two passives
in Indonesian' in C. Li (ed.), 57-98.

———— (1976b), 'An object creating rule in Bahasa
Indonesia', *LI 7.1*, 41-87.

———— (1977), 'On the gradual nature of syntactic
change' in C. Li (ed.), 3-53.

———— (1978), *Case Marking and Grammatical Relations
in Polynesian*, Austin, University of Texas
Press.

Churchward, C.M, (1953), *Tongan Grammar*, London,
Oxford University Press.

Cinque, G, (1976), 'Appropriatness conditions for
the use of passives and impersonals in Italian'
in V. Lo Cascio (ed.), 11-53.

———— (1977), 'The movement nature of left-dislocation', *LI 8.2.* 397-412.

Clark, H. & E. Clark, (1977), *Psychology and Language.
An Introduction to Psycholinguistics*, New York,
Academic Press.

Clark, M, (1974a), 'Passive and ergative in Vietnamese' in Nguyễn Dáng Liêm (ed.), 75-81.

———— (1974b), 'Submissive verbs as adversatives in
some Asian languages' in Nguyễn Dáng Liêm (ed.),
82-91.

Clark, R.D, (1973), 'Transitivity and case in
Eastern Oceanic languages', *OL 12*, 559-605.

BIBLIOGRAPHY

Cole, P. & S.N. Sridhar, (1976), 'Clause union and relational grammar: evidence from Hebrew and Kannada', *SLS 6.1*, 216-228.

Cole, P. & J. Sadock (eds), (1977), *Syntax and Semantics 8. Grammatical Relations*, New York, Academic Press.

Cole, P., W. Harbert, G. Hermon & S.N. Sridhar, (1978), 'On the acquisition of subjecthood', *SLS 8.1*, 42-71.

Cole, P. & J.L. Jake, (1978), 'Accusative subjects in Imbabura Quechua', *SLS 8.1*, 72-96.

Comrie, B, (1975), 'The antiergative: Finland's answer to Basque', *CLS 11*, 112-121.

_____ (1976), 'The syntax of causative constructions: cross-language similarities and divergences' in M. Shibatani (ed.), 261-312.

_____ (1977a), 'In defense of spontaneous demotion' in P. Cole & J. Sadock (eds), 47-58.

_____ (1977b), 'Causative verb formation and other verb-deriving morphology' (prepared for circulation to co-workers of Centre for Applied Linguistics project: Language Typology and Syntactic Field-Work).

_____ (1978), 'Ergativity' in W.P. Lehmann (ed.), 329-394.

_____ (1982), 'Grammatical relations in Huichol' in P. Hopper & S.A. Thompson (eds), 95-116.

Constantino, E, (1970), *The Deep Structure of the Philippine Languages*, The Archives 1.2, Quezon City, University of the Philippines.

Contreras, H, (1973), 'Grammaticality vs acceptability: the Spanish case', *LI 4.1*, 83-88.

_____ (1974), *Indeterminate Subject Sentences in Spanish*, (available from IULC, Bloomington, Indiana).

Cooreman, A, (1982), 'Transitivity, ergativity, and topicality in Chamorro narrative discourse', *BLS 8*, 203-221.

Cooreman, A., B. Fox & T. Givón, (1983), 'The discourse definition of ergativity' to appear in *SL*.

Corum, D., T.C. Smith-Stark & A. Weiser (eds), (1973), *You Take the High Node and I'll Take the Low Node*, Papers from the Comparative Syntax Festival, Chicago Linguistic Society, Chicago, Illinois, University of Chicago.

Costa, R, (1975), 'A functional solution for illogical reflexives in Italian' in R.E. Grossman et al. (eds), 112-125.

BIBLIOGRAPHY

Cowan, M.M, (1969), *Tzotzil Grammar*, Summer Institute of Linguistics, Norman, University of Oklahoma.

Creider, C.A, (1979), 'On the explanation of transformations' in T. Givón (ed.), 3-22.

Culicover, P., T. Wasow & A. Akmajian (eds), (1977), *Formal Syntax*, New York, Academic Press.

Cureton, R.D, (1979), 'The exceptions to the passive in English: a pragmatic hypothesis', *SLS 9.2*, 39-55.

Curme, G.O, (1931), *Syntax*, Boston, Heath

_____ (1960), *A Grammar of the German Language*, New York, Frederick Ungar Publishing House.

Dahl, O, (1974), 'Topic-comment structure revisited' in O. Dahl (ed.), *Topic and Comment, Contextual Boundness and Focus*, Hamburg, Helmut Buske Verlag, 1-25.

Dalgish, G.M, (1976a), 'Locative NPs, locative suffixes and grammatical relations', *BLS 2*, 139-148.

_____ (1976b), 'Passivizing locatives in Olutsootso', *SLS 6.1*, 57-86.

_____ (1977), 'Personal pronouns, object markers and syntactic evidence in Dho-Luo', *SAL 8.3*, 101-120.

Daněs, F, (1964), 'A three level approach to syntax', *TLP 1*, 225-240.

Davison, A, (1980), 'Peculiar passives', *Lg 56.1*, 42-66.

_____ (1982), 'On the form and meaning of the Hindi passive', *Lingua 58.2*, 149-179.

de Guzman, V.P, (1978), *Syntactic Derivation of Tagalog Verbs*, (Oceanic Linguistics Special Publications 16), Honolulu, The University Press of Hawaii.

Van Dijk, T.A, (1977), *Text and Context*, London, Longman.

Derbyshire, D.C, (1981), 'A diachronic explanation for the origin of OVS in some Carib languages', *JL 17*, 179-392

Derbyshire, D.C, & G.K. Pullum (1981), 'Object initial languages', *International Journal of American Linguistics 47.3*, 192-214.

Dik, S.C, (1978), *Functional Grammar*, Amsterdam, North Holland.

_____ (1980), *Studies in Functional Grammar*, London, Academic Press.

_____ (1981), 'The interaction of subject and topic in Portuguese' in the collective *'Predication and Expression in Functional Grammar*, London Academic Press.

269

BIBLIOGRAPHY

Dixon, R.M.W, (1972), *The Dyirbal Language of North Queensland,* (Cambridge Studies in Linguistics), Cambridge, Cambridge University Press.
_____ (ed.), (1976), *Grammatical Categories in Australian Languages,* (Linguistic Series 22), Australian Institute of Aboriginal Studies, Canberra, Humanities Press.
_____ (1977a), *A Grammar of Yidin,* (Cambridge Studies in Linguistics), Cambridge, Cambridge University Press.
_____ (1977b), 'The syntactic development of Australian languages' in C. Li (ed.), 366-415.
_____ (1979), 'Ergativity', *Lg 55.1,* 59-138.
Dixon, R.M.W & B. Blake (eds), *Handbook of Australian Languages 1,* Canberra, The Australian National University Press.
Donaldson, Jr. W, (1970), *The Syntax of French Pronominal Verbs: A Case Grammar Description,* Ph.D diss., Indiana University, Ann Arbor, Michigan, University Microfilms.
Dryer, M, (1976), 'On explaining the syntactic properties of passive agent noun phrases in universal grammar', paper given at the 1976 meeting of the Michigan Linguistic Society.
_____ (1982a), 'Passive and inversion in Kannada', *BLS 8,* 311-321.
_____ (1982b), 'In defense of a universal passive', *LA 10.1,* 53-60.
Du'ong, T.B, (1971), *A Tagmemic Comparison of the Structure of English and Vietnamese Sentences,* The Hague, Mouton.
Duranti, A. & E. Ochs, (1979), 'Left-dislocation in Italian conversation', in T. Givón (ed.), 377-418.
Durie, M, (1983), 'Control and de-control in Achenese: levels of interpreting reality', paper read at the 1983 conference of the Australian Linguistic Society.
Duškova, L, (1971), 'On some functional and stylistic aspects of the passive in present-day English', *PhP 14.3,* 117-143.
_____ (1972), 'The passive voice in English and Czech', *PhP 15.2,* 93-118.
_____ (1973), 'Man-sätze in Czech and English', *PhP 16.1,* 5-37.
Eckman, F.R, (1974), 'Agentive and agentless passives', *Working Papers on Language Universals 14,* 59-74.
Egerod, S, (1975), 'Typology of Chinese sentence structure', paper read to the 8th International Conference on Sino-Tibetan Languages and

BIBLIOGRAPHY

Linguistics, U.C. Berkeley.

Einarsson, S, (1945), *Icelandic, Grammar, Texts, Glossary*, Baltimore, The John Hopkins Press.

Emonds, J, (1972), 'A reformulation of certain syntactic transformations' in S. Peters (ed.), *Goals of Linguistic Theory*, Englewood Cliffs, New Jersey, Prentice Hall, 21-62.

_____ (1976), *A Transformational Approach to English Syntax*, New York, Academic Press.

Erben, J, (1972), *Deutsche Grammatik*, München, Ein Abriss.

Ertel, S, (1977) 'Where do the subjects of sentences come from?' in S. Rosenberg (ed.), *Sentence Production. Developments in Research and Theory*, Hillsdale, New Jersey, Lawrence Erlbaum Associates, 141-168.

Faarlund, J.T, (1981), 'Obligatory fronting in a verb-initial language: an attempt at pragmatic syntax', *CLS 17*, 45-58.

Farkas, D., W.M. Jackobsen & K.W. Todrys (eds), (1978), *Papers from the Parasession on the Lexicon*, Chicago Linguistic Society, Chicago, Illinois, University of Chicago.

Feldman, H, (1978), 'Passivizing on datives in Greek', *LI 9.3*, 499-501.

Fiengo, R, (1974), *Semantic Conditions on Surface Structure*, unpublished Ph.D. diss., MIT.

Filbeck, D, (1973), 'The passive in Thai', *Anthropological Linguistics 15.1*, 33-41.

Fillmore, C.J, (1968), 'The case for case' in E. Bach & R.T. Harms (eds), *Universals in Linguistic Theory*, New York, Holt Rinehart and Winston, 1-88.

_____ (1971), 'Some problems in case grammar', *Working papers in Linguistics 10*, Ohio State University, 245-265.

_____ (1977), 'The case for case reopened' in P. Cole & J. Sadock (eds), 59-81.

Firbas, J, (1964), 'From comparative word-order studies', *Brno Studies in English 4*, 111-126.

_____ (1966), 'Non-thematic subjects in English', *TLP 2*, 239-256.

Foley, W.A, (1976), *Comparative Syntax in Austronesian*, Ph.D diss., University of California, Berkeley.

Foley, W.A. & R. Van Valin, (1977), 'On the viability of the notion of subject in universal grammar', *BLS 3*, 293-320.

BIBLIOGRAPHY

Frantz, D.G, (1977), 'Grammatical relations in universal grammar' paper circulated by Summer Institute of Linguistics, University of Dakota Branch.

Freidin, R, (1975a), 'The analysis of passives', *Lg 51.2*, 384-405.

_____ (1975b), 'Review of Jackendoff (1972)', *Lg 51.1*, 189-205.

Frajzyngier, Z, (1978), 'An analysis of be-passives', *Lingua 46.2/3*, 113-156.

_____ (1982), 'Indefinite agent, passive and impersonal passive', *Lingua 58.3*, 267-290.

Fraser, W.H. & J. Squair, (1962), *Heath's Practical French Grammar*, London, George, G. Harrop & Co. Ltd.

Fries, C.C, (1952), *The Structure of English*, London, Longman.

Frishberg, N, (1972), 'Navajo object markers and the great chain of being' in J. Kimball (ed.), *Syntax and Semantics 1*, New York, Seminar Press, 259-266.

Galambos, S.J, (1980), 'A clarification of the notion topic: evidence from popular spoken French' in J. Kreiman & A.E. Ojeda (eds), *Papers from the Parasession on Pronouns and Anaphora*, Chicago Linguistic Society, Chicago, Illinois, University of Chicago, 125-138.

García, E.C, (1975), *The Role of Theory in Linguistic Analysis: The Spanish Pronoun System*, Amsterdam, North Holland.

Garry, J.O, (1977a), 'Object-formation rules in several Bantu languages: questions and implications for universal grammar', *CLS 13*, 125-136.

_____ (1977b), 'Implications for universal grammar of object-creating rules in Luyia and Mashi', *SAL*, supplement 7, 85-95.

Garry, J.O. & E.L. Keenan, (1977), 'On collapsing grammatical relations in universal grammar' in P. Cole & J. Sadock (eds), 83-120.

George, L. & J. Kornfilt, (1977), 'Infinitival double passives in Turkish' *Proceedings of the Seventh Annual Meeting of the North Eastern Linguistic Society*, 65-81.

Gerdts, D.B, (1980), 'Casual to object advancement in Halkomelem', *CLS 16*, 83-101.

Givón, T, (1972), 'Review of Whiteley (1968)', *AS 31.4*, 273-277.

_____ (1979a), *On Understanding Grammar*, New York, Academic Press.

BIBLIOGRAPHY

Givón, T, (1979b), (ed.), *Syntax and Semantics 12 Discourse and Syntax*, New York, Academic Press.
───── (1981), 'Typology and functional domains', *SL 5*, 163-193.
───── (1982), 'Transitivity, topicality and the Ute impersonal passive' in P. Hopper & S.A. Thompson (eds), 143-160.
Goldin, M.G, (1968), *Spanish Case and Function*, Washington, D.C., Georgetown University Press.
Gordon, K.H, (1973), 'Clause patterns in Dhangar-Kurux' in R.L. Trail (ed.), 37-122.
Green, G.M, (1974), *Semantics and Syntactic Irregularity*, Bloomington, Indiana, Indiana University Press.
Green, J.N, (1975), 'Reflections on Spanish reflexives', *Lingua 44.3/4*, 345-391.
Greenberg, J.H, (1963), 'Some universals of grammar with particular reference to the order of meaningful elements' in J.H. Greenberg (ed.), *Universals of Language*, Cambridge, Mass.,MIT Press, 73-113.
───── et al. (eds), (1978), *Universals of Human Language*. 4 volumes [vol. 1: *Method and Theory;* vol. 2: *Phonology;* vol. 3: *Word Structure;* vol. 4: *Syntax*]. Stanford, Stanford University Press.
Grevisse, M, (1976), *Le Bon Usage*, Gembloux, Duculot.
Grimes, J.E, (1964), *Huichol Syntax*, The Hague, Mouton.
Grossman, R.E., L.J. San & T.J. Vance (eds), (1975), *Papers from the Parasession on Functionalism*, Chicago Linguistic Society, Chicago, Illinois, University of Chicago.
Groves, B.C, (1979), 'Spontaneous subject removal and es-insertion', *Glossa 13.1*, 39-50.
Gruber, J.S, (1976), *Lexical Structures in Syntax and Semantics*, Amsterdam, North Holland.
Gunase'kara, A.B, (1962), *A Comprehensive Grammar of the Sinhalese Language*, Maharagma, Saman Press.
Gustafasson, U, (1973), 'Clause patterns in Kotia-Oryia' in R.L. Trail (ed.), 191-256.
Hadlich, R.L, (1971), *A Transformational Grammar of Spanish*, Englewood Cliffs, New Jersey, Prentice Hall.
Haig, H.A, (1982), 'Passivization in Modern Western Armenian' in P. Hopper & S.A. Thompson (eds), 161-176.
Haiman, J, (1976), 'Agentless sentences' *FL 14.1*, 19-55.

BIBLIOGRAPHY

Hale, K, (1968), *Preliminary Remarks on Walbiri Grammar: II*, Mimeo, MIT.
_____ (1973), 'A note on subject-object inversion in Navajo' in B. Kachru (ed.), 301-309.
_____ (1976), 'Dja:bugay' in R.M.W. Dixon (ed.), 231-327.
Halliday, M.A.K, (1968), 'Notes on transitivity and theme in English', *JL 4*, 179-215.
_____ (1970), 'Language structure and language function' in J. Lyons (ed.), *New Horizons in Linguistics*, Harmondsworth, Penguin Books, 140-165.
Hammer, A.E, (1971), *German Grammar and Usage*, London, Edward Arnold Publishers.
Harmer, L.C. & F.J. Norton, (1957), *A Manual of Modern Spanish*, London, University Tutorial Press.
Harries, L, (1973), 'Syntactic features of Swahili sentences', *AS 32.3*, 151-161.
Harris, M.B, (1976), *The Evolution of French Syntax: A Comparative Approach*, London, Longman.
_____ (1977), 'Demonstratives, articles and third person pronouns; Changes in progress', *Zeitschrift für Romanische Philologie 93*, 249-261.
Hartung, W.D, (1966), 'Die Passivtransformation in Deutschen', *Studia Grammatica 7*, 90-114.
Hasegawa, K, (1968), 'The passive construction in English', *Lg 44.2*, 230-243.
Hashimoto, M.J, (1969), 'Observations on the passive construction', Unicorn, Princeton University 59-71.
Hatcher, A.G, (1949), 'To get/be invited', *Modern Language Notes 64*, 433-446.
Hawkinson, A.K. & L.M. Hyman, (1974), 'Hierarchies of natural topic in Shona', *SAL 5.2*, 147-170.
Heath, J, (1976), 'Antipassivization, a functional typology', *BLS 2*, 202-211.
Hershberger, R, (1964), 'Notes on Gugu-Yalandji verbs' in R.S. Pittman & H.B. Kerr (eds), *Papers on the Languages of the Australian Aborigines*, Canberra, Institute of Aboriginal Studies, 35-54.
Hertzron, R, (1975), 'The presentative movement or why the ideal word order is VSOP', in C. Li (ed.), 346-388.
Hidalgo, A.C, (1970), 'Focus in Philippine languages', *The Philippine Journal of Linguistics 1.1*, 25-32.

BIBLIOGRAPHY

Hinds, J, (1975), 'Passive, pronouns and themes and rhemes, *Glossa 9.1*, 79-106.

Hinz, J. (1944), *Grammar and Vocabulary of the Eskimo Language as Spoken by the Kushakwim and South-West Coast Eskimos of Alaska*, Bethlehem, The Society of Propogating the Gospel.

Hoard, J.E, (1979), 'On the semantic representation of oblique complements, *Lg 55.2*, 319-332.

Hollis, A.C, (1970), *The Maasai, Their Language and Folklore*, (originally published 1905), Westport, Connecticut, Negro University Press.

Hopper, P.J, (1979), 'Aspect and foregrounding in discourse' in T. Givón (ed.), 213-242.

Hopper, P.J. & S.A. Thompson, (1980), 'Transitivity in grammar and discourse', *Lg 56.2*, 251-300.

_____ (eds), (1982), *Syntax and Semantics 15, Studies in Transitivity*, New York, Academic Press.

Horn, G.M, (1977), 'An analysis of certain reflexive verbs and its implications for the organization of the lexicon', *Studia Anglica Posnaniensia 9*, 17-42.

_____ (1981), 'Motionless and traceless sources of passives', *LA 8.1*, 15-68.

Howard, I, (1968), *The So-Called Japanese Passive*, Mimeograph, Honolulu, Education Research and Development Centre, University of Hawaii.

Howard, I. & A. Niyekawa-Howard, (1975), 'Passivization' in M. Shibatani (ed.), 239-294.

Hsu, C.L, (1974), 'On the relationship between active and passive in Chinese', *JCL 2.2*, 172-179.

Hu, J.P, (1973), *Form and Meaning in Chinese* Ph.D diss., Melbourne, Monash University.

Huddleston, R.D, (1969), 'Some observations on tense and dexis in English', *Lg 45.4*, 777-806.

_____ (1971), *The Sentence in Written English*, London, Cambridge University Press.

_____ (1976), *An Introduction to English Transformational Syntax*, London, Longman.

Hudson, R.A, (1984), *Word Grammar* (ms), (to appear), Oxford, Basil Blackwell.

Hust, J.R, (1977), 'The syntax of the unpassive construction in English', *LA 3.1*, 31-63.

Hutchins, W.J, (1975), 'Subjects, themes and case grammars', *Lingua 35.2*, 101-133.

Imai, T, (1979), 'On impersonal passive in Hindi', *Indian Linguistics 40*, 85-91.

Inoue, K, (1969), *A Study of Japanese Syntax*, The Hague, Mouton.

Isaev, M.I, (1966), 'Osetinskij jazyk' in V.V. Vinogradov (ed.), 237-246.

BIBLIOGRAPHY

Jackendoff, R.S, (1972), *Semantic Interpretation in Generative Grammar*, Cambridge, Mass., MIT Press.
_____ (1977), *X̄ Syntax of Phrase Structure*, (Linguistic Inquiry Monograph 2), Cambridge, Mass., MIT Press.
Jacobs, R.A. & P.S. Rosenbaum, (1968), *English Transformational Grammar*, Waltham, Mass., MIT Press.
Jespersen, O, (1927), *A Modern English Grammar on Historical Principles*, *III*, *IV*, London, Allen and Unwin.
_____ (1933), *Essentials of English Grammar*, London, Allen and Unwin.
Johnson, D.E, (1974), *Toward a Theory of Relationally Based Grammar*, Ph.D. diss., Urbanan, University of Illinois.
_____ (1977), 'On relational constraints on grammars' in P. Cole & J. Sadock (eds), 151-178.
Jones, M.D, (1976), *A Guide to Correct Welsh*, Llandysul, Gomer Press.
Jones, M.D. & A.R. Thomas, (1977), *The Welsh Language. Studies in It's Syntax and Semantics*, Cardiff, University of Wales Press.
Jonsson, S, (1927), *A Primer of Modern Icelandic*, London, Oxford University Press.
Josephs, L, (1975), *Palauan Reference Grammar*, Honolulu, University of Hawaii Press.
Kachru, B, (ed.), (1973), *Issues in Linguistics. Papers in Honour of Henry and Renée Kahane*, Urbana, University of Illinois.
Kachru, Y., B. Kachru & T.K. Bhatia, (1976), 'The notion of subject : a note on Hindi-Urdu, Kashmiri and Punjabi' in M.K. Verma (ed.), *The Notion of Subject in South Asian Languages*, University of Wisconsin, 79-101.
Karlsson F, (1972), 'Relative clauses in Finnish' in P.M. Peranteau et al. (eds), 106-115.
Kayne, R. (1975), *French Syntax: The Transformational Cycle*, Cambridge, Mass., MIT Press.
Keenan, E.L, (1975), 'Some universals of passive in relational grammar', *CLS 11*, 340-352.
_____ (1976a), 'Towards a universal definition of subject' in C. Li (ed.), 303-333.
_____ (1976b), 'Remarkable subjects in Malagasy' in C. Li (ed.), 249-301.
_____ (1978), 'The syntax of subject-final languages' in W.P. Lehman (ed.), 267-328.
_____ (1980), 'Passive in the world's languages' to appear in T. Shopen et al. (eds), *A Field Guide to Syntactic Typology* (tentative title)

276

BIBLIOGRAPHY

Keenan, E.L, (1982), 'Parametric variation in universal grammar' in R. Dirven & G. Radden (eds), *Issues in the Theory of Universal Grammar*, Tübingen, Gunter Narr Verlag, 11-74.

Keenan Ochs, E. & B.B. Schieffelin, (1976), 'Foregrounding referents: a reconsideration of left-dislocation in discourse', *BLS 2*, 240-257.

Khai, B, (1972), *A Formal Syntax of Vietnamese*, Ph.D diss., Ann Arbor, Michigan, George Town University, University Microfilms.

Kholodovič, A.A. (ed.), (1969), *Tipologiia Kauzativnykh Konstrukcii: Morfologičeskii Kauzativ*, Leningrad, Nauka.

_____ (ed.), (1974), *Tipologiia Passivnykh Konstrukcii*, Leningrad, Nauka.

Khrakovsky, V.S, (1973), 'Passive constructions' in F. Kiefer (ed.), *Trends in Soviet Linguistics*, Dordrech, Reidel, 59-76.

Kimenyi, A, (1980), *A Relational Grammar of Kinyarwanda*, Berkeley, University of California Press.

Kirkwood, H.W, (1969), 'Aspects of word order and its communicative function in English and German', *JL 5*, 85-107.

Kirsner, R.S, (1973), 'Natural focus and agentive interpretation: on the semantics of the Dutch expletive er', *Stanford Occasional Papers in Linguistics 3*, 101-114.

_____ (1976), 'On the subject of pseudo-passives in Standard Dutch and the semantics of background agents' in C. Li (ed.), 387-415.

Kisseberth, C.W. & M.I. Abasheikh, (1977), 'The object relationship in Chi-mwi-ni, a Bantu language' in P. Cole & J. Sadock (eds), 179-218.

Klaiman, M.H, (1978), 'On the status of the subjecthood hierarchy in Hindi', *International Journal of Dravidian Linguistics 8.1*, 17-31.

_____ (1980), 'Bengali dative subjects', *Lingua 51.4*, 275-295.

_____ (1981), *Volitionality and Subject in Bengali*, (available from IULC, Bloomington, Indiana).

_____ (1982), 'Affectiveness and the voice system of Japanese: satisfaction or your money back', *BLS 8*, 398-413.

Klokeid, T.J, (1976a), *Topics in Lardil Grammar*, Ph.D. diss., MIT.

_____ (1976b), 'Lardil' in R.M.W. Dixon (ed.), 550-584.

_____ (1977), 'An outline of the framework of relational grammar' prepared for the Department of Modern Languages Colloquium, Simon Fraser University.

BIBLIOGRAPHY

Klokeid, T.J, (1978), 'Nominal inflection in Pama
Nyungan' in W. Abraham (ed.), 577-616.

Krauthamer, H, (1981), 'The prediction of passive
occurrence', *Linguistics 19*, 307-324.

Krusinga, E, (1925), *A Handbook of Present Day
English*, Groningen, P. Noordhoff.

Kullavanijaya, P, (1974), *Transitive Verbs in Thai*,
Ph.D diss., University of Hawaii, Ann Arbor,
Michigan, University Microfilms.

Kuno, S, (1971), 'The postposition of locatives in
existential sentences', *LI 2.3*, 333-78.

―――― (1973), *The Structure of the Japanese Language*.
Ph.D. diss., MIT.

―――― (1976), 'Subject, theme and the speaker's
empathy - a re-examination of relativization
phenomena' in C. Li (ed.), 417-44.

Kuno, S & E. Kaburaki, (1977), 'Empathy and syntax',
LI 8.4, 627-672.

Kuroda, S, (1965), *Generative Grammatical Studies
in the Japanese Languages*, Ph.D diss., MIT.

Laberge, S. & G. Sankoff, (1979), 'Anything you can
do' in T. Givón (ed.), 419-440.

Lafitte, P, (1962), *Grammaire Basque*, Bayonne,
France, Amis du Musée, Basque et Ikas.

Lagerwey, W, (1968), *Speak Dutch, An Aduio-Lingual
Course*, Amsterdam, Education Books.

Lakoff, G, (1970), *Irregularity in Syntax*, New York,
Holt, Rinehart and Winston.

Lakoff, R, (1971), 'Passive resistance', *CLS 7*,
149-162.

Langacker, R.W, (1976), *Non-Distinct Arguments in
Uto-Aztecan*, Berkeley, Los Angeles, University
of California Publications.

Langacker, R.W. & P.M. Munro, (1975), 'Passives and
their meaning', *Lg 51.4*, 789-830.

Lawler, J.M, (1977), 'A agrees with B in Achenese:
a problem for relational grammar' in P. Cole
and J. Sadock (eds), 219-248.

Le, T.D, (1976), 'Vietnamese passives', *CLS 12*,
438-449.

Lees, R.B, (1960), *The Grammar of English Nominalizations*, The Hague, Mouton.

―――― (1973), 'Turkish voice' in B. Kachru (ed.),
504-514.

Lehman, W.P. (ed.), (1978), *Syntactic Typology;
Studies in the Phenomenology of Language*,
Sussex, The Harvester Press.

Lekawatana, P. (1970), *Verb Phrase in Thai. A Study
in Deep-Case Relations*. Ph.D.diss., University
of Michigan, Ann Arbor, Michigan, University
Microfilms.

278

BIBLIOGRAPHY

Lepschy, A.L. & G. Lepschy, (1977), *The Italian Language Today*, London, Hutchinson.

Lewis, G.L, (1967), *Turkish Grammar*, Oxford, The Clarendon Press.

Li, C.N, (ed.), (1975), *Word Order and Word Order Change*, Austin, University of Texas Press.

_____ (ed.), (1976), *Subject and Topic*, New York, Academic Press.

_____ (ed.), (1977), *Mechanisms of Syntactic Change*, New York, Academic Press.

Li, C.N. & S.A. Thompson, (1975), 'The semantic function of word order: a case study in Mandarin' in C. Li (ed.), 163-197.

_____ (1976), 'Subejct and topic a new typology of language' in C. Li (ed.), 445-491.

Li, Y.C, (1971), *An Investigation of Case in Chinese Grammar*, South Orange, New Jersey, Seton Hall University Press.

Lightfoot, D.W, (1979), *Principles of Diachronic Syntax*, Cambridge, Cambridge University Press.

Lo Cascio, V, (1976a), 'On linguistic variables and primary object-topicalization' in V. Lo Cascio (ed.), 33-77.

_____ (ed.), (1976b), *Passive and Impersonal Sentences*, Lisse, The Peter de Ridder Press.

Lockwood, W.B, (1964), *An Introduction to Modern Faroese*, Copenhagen, Munksgard.

Luelsdorff, Ph, (1978), 'Aspects of the passive in English', *Linguistics 209*, 51-58.

Lyons, J, (1968), *Introduction to Theoretical Linguistics*, London, Cambridge University Press.

_____ (1977), *Semantics*, Cambridge, Cambridge University Press.

McCawley, J.D, (1971), 'Tense and time reference in English' in C. Fillmore & T. Langendoen (eds), (1971), *Studies in Lingusitic Semantics*, New York, Holt Rinehart and Winston, 97-113.

McCawley, N.A, (1972), 'On the treatment of Japanese passives', *CLS 8*, 259-270.

_____ (1975), 'Arguments against Keenan - Shimizu's treatment of the Japanese **passive**', *Papers in Japanese Linguistics 1*, 125-145.

_____ (1976), 'From OE/ME impersonal to personal constructions. What is a subjecless S?' in S.B. Steever et al. (eds), 192-204.

McCray, A.T, (1982), 'The left-dislocation structure in German: some overlooked sentence types', *CLS 18*, 336-347.

McNair, N. & H. McNair, (1973), 'Clause patterns in Kolami' in R.L. Trail (ed.), 123-190.

BIBLIOGRAPHY

Mackinnon, R, (1971), *Gaelic: Teach Yourself Books*, London, English University Press.

Madieva, G.I, (1967), 'Avarskij jazyk' in V.V. Vokarev et al. (eds), *Iberijsko-Kaukazskie Jazyki. Jazyki Narodov C.C.C.P.*, Moskva, Nauka, 255-272.

Mallinson, G. & B. Blake, (1980), *Language Typology. Cross-Linguistic Studies in Syntax*, Amsterdam, North Holland.

Mansion, J.E, (1962), *A Grammar of Present Day French*, London, George G. Harrap & Co.

Maratsos, M.P. & R. Abramovitch, (1975), 'How children understand full, truncated and anomalous passives', *Journal of Verbal Learning 14*, 145-157.

Martinet, A, (1962), 'Le sujet comme fonction linguistique et l'analyse syntaxique du Basque', *Bulletin de la Société de Linguistique de Paris 57*, 73-82.

Masica, C.P, (1976), *Defining a Linguistic Area, South Asia*, Chicago, University of Chicago Press.

Mathesius, V, (1975), *A Functional Analysis of Present Day English*, J. Vaček (ed.), translated by L. Duškova, Prague.

Mchombo, S.A, (1980), 'Dative and passive in Chichewa: an argument for surface grammar', *LA 6.2*, 97-113.

Mihailovic, L, (1966), 'The agent in the English passive', *English Language Teaching 21*, 123-126.

Mirikitani, L, (1972), *Kapampangan Syntax*, (Oceanic Linguistics 10), Honolulu, The University Press of Hawaii.

Mohanan, K.P, (1982), 'Grammatical relations and clause structure in Malayalam' in J. Bresnan (ed.), 504-589.

Mueller, T.H., E.N. Mager & H. Niedzielski, (1968), *Handbook of French Structure: A Systematic Review*, New York, Harcourt Bruce and World.

Mulder, J, (1976), 'Raising in Turkish', *BLS 2*, 298-307.

Mulder, J. & A. Schwartz, (1981), 'On the subject of advancements in the Philippine languages', *SL 5.2*, 227-268.

Napoli, D.J, (1976), *The Two Si's of Italian*, (available from IULC, Bloomington, Indiana).

_____ (1981), 'Subject pronouns: the pronominal system of Italian vs French', *CLS 17*, 249-276.

Naro, A.J, (1976), 'The genisis of the reflexive impersonal in Portuguese', *Lg 52.4*, 779-811.

BIBLIOGRAPHY

Naylor, P.B, (1975), 'Topic, focus and emphasis in the Tagalog verbal clause', *OL 14.1*, 12-75.

Neubaur, P, (1979), 'The score on impersonal passives: Dutch l & Polish O', paper read at the 17th International Conference on Polish English Contrastive Linguistics, Boszkowo, Poland.

Nguyễn, D.H, (ed.), (1974), *South East Asian Linguistics Studies I*, (Pacific Linguistic Series C), Canberra, ANU.

Noonan, M, (1977), 'On subjects and topics', *BLS 3*, 372-385.

_____ (1978), 'Impersonal constructions: evidence from Irish', ms Dept. of Linguistics SUNY, Buffalo, New York.

Norman, W.N, (1978), 'Advancement rules and syntactic change. The loss of instrumental voice in Mayan', *BLS 3*, 458-476.

O'Grady, W.D, (1980), 'The universal characterization of passivization', *LA 6.1*, 393-405.

Oksaar, E, (1972), 'Zum Passiv im Deutschen und Schwedischen' in G. Nickel (ed.), *Reader zur Kontrastiven Linguistik*, Frankfurt, Athenaum, 85-106.

Onions, C.T, (1904), *An Advanced English Syntax*, (revised edition (1971) by B.D.H. Miller, *Modern English Syntax*, London, Routledge and Kegan Paul).

Östman, J.O, (1981) 'The Finnish passive and relational grammar', *CLS 17*, 286-294.

Otanes, F.T. (1966), *A Contrastive Analysis of English and Tagalog Verb Complementation*, Ph.D diss., University of California.

Owen, E.T, (1914), 'The relations expressed by the passive voice', *Transactions of the Wisconsin Academy of Sciences, Arts and Letters 17*, 17-148.

Ozkaragoz, I, (1980), 'Evidence from Turkish for the unaccusative hypothesis', *BLS 6*, 411-422.

Palmer, F.R, (1974), *The English Verb*, London, Longmans.

Pandharipande, R, (1978), 'Exceptions and rule government: the case of the passive rule in Hindi', *SLS 8.1*, 153-173.

Pandharipande, R. & Y. Kachru, (1977), 'Relational grammar, ergativity and Hindi-Urdu', *Lingua 41.3/4*, 217-238.

Paterson, S, (1983), *Voice and Transitivity*, Ph.D. diss., University College, London.

Payne, T, (1982), 'Role and reference related subject properties and ergativity in Yupik Eskimo and Tagalog', *SL 6.1*, 75-106.

BIBLIOGRAPHY

Peranteau, P.M., J. Levi & G.C. Phares (eds), (1972), *The Chicago Which Hunt. Papers from the Relative Clause Festival*, Chicago Linguistic Society, Chicago, Illinois, University of Chicago.

Perlmutter, D.M. (1978a), 'Impersonal passives and the unaccusative hypothesis,' *BLS 4*, 157-189.

_____ (1978b), 'Evidence for inversion in Russian, Japanese and Kannada' to appear in D.M. Perlmutter (ed.).

_____ (1979), 'Working 1s and inversion in Italian, Japanese and Quechua', *BLS 5*, 277-324.

_____ (1980), 'Relational grammar' in E.A. Moravcsik & J.R. Wirth (eds), *Syntax & Semantics 13. Current Approaches to Syntax*, New York, Academic Press, 195-229.

_____ (ed.), (1983), *Studies in Relational Grammar 1*, Chicago, Chicago University Press.

_____ (ed.), (to appear), *Studies in Relational Grammar 2*.

Perlmutter, D.M. & P.M. Postal, (1977), 'Toward a universal characterization of passivization', *BLS 3*, 395-417, revised version in D.M. Perlmutter (ed.), 1983, 3-29.

_____ (1978), 'The 1-Advancement Exclusiveness Law' in D.M. Perlmutter (ed.), to appear

_____ (1983a), 'The Relational Succession Law' in D.M. Perlmutter (ed.), 30-80.

_____ (1983b), 'Some proposed laws of basic clause structures' ms, subsequently in D.M. Perlmutter (ed.), (1983), 81-128.

Platzack, C, (1980), 'The Swedish past participle: some arguments for a lexical redundancy rule', *Studia Linguistica* 34.1.

Postal, P.M, (1977), 'Antipassive in French', *Proceedings of the Seventh Annual Meeting of the North Eastern Linguistic Society*, 273-313.

_____ (1982), 'Some Arc-Pair Grammar descriptions' in P. Jacobson & G.K. Pullum (eds), *The Nature of Syntactic Representation*, Dordrecht, D. Reidel Publishing Company, 341-427.

Poutsma, A, (1926), *Grammar of Late Modern English*, Groningen, P Noordhof.

Prince, E.F, (1981), 'Topicalization, focus -movement and yiddish- movement: a pragmatic differentiation', *BLS 7*, 249-264.

Pullum, G.K, (1977), Word order universals and grammatical relations' in P. Cole & J. Sadock (eds), 249-277.

Pullum, G.K. & D. Wilson, (1977), 'Autonomous syntax and the analysis of auxiliaries', *Lg 53.4*, 741-788.

BIBLIOGRAPHY

Quirk, R., S. Greenbaum, G. Leech & J. Svartvik (eds), (1972), *A Grammar of Contemporary English*, London, Longman.

Radford, A, (1977), *Italian Syntax: Transformational and Relational Grammar*, Cambridge, Cambridge University Press.

───── (1981), *Transformational Syntax: A Student's Guide to Chomsky's Extended Standard Theory*, Cambridge, Cambridge University Press.

Ramos, T, (1974), *The Case System of Tagalog Verbs* (Pacific Linguistic Series B.27), Canberra, ANU.

Ranson, E.N, (1977), 'Definiteness, animacy, and NP ordering, *BLS 3*, 418-429.

Riddle, E., G. Sheintuch & Y. Ziv, (1977), 'Pseudo-passivization: on the role of pragmatics in determining rule unity', *SLS 7.1*, 147-156.

Rospond, St, (1973), *Gramatyka Historyczna Języka Polskiego*, Warszawa, PWN.

Ross, J, (1967), *Constraints on Variables in Syntax*, Ph.D. diss., MIT.

Rude, N, (1982), 'Promotion and topicality of Nez Perce objects', *BLS 8*, 463-483.

Saksena, A, (1978), 'A reanalysis of the passive in Hindi, *Lingua 46.4*, 339-353.

Schachter, P, (1976), 'The subject in Philippine languages : topic, actor, actor-topic or none of the above' in C.Li (ed.), 491-518.

───── (1977), 'Reference related and role related properties of subjects' in P. Cole & J. Sadock (eds), 279-307.

Schachter, P. & F.T. Otanes, (1972), *A Tagalog Reference Grammar*, Berkeley, California, University of California Press.

Schebeck, B, (1976), 'Thangu and Atjnjamathanha' in R.M.W. Dixon (ed.), 516-550.

Schoenthal, G, (1976), Das Passiv in der Deutschen Standardsprache, München, Max Hueber Verlag.

Schroten, H, (1972), *Concerning The Deep Structure of Spanish Reflexives*, The Hague, Mouton.

Schwartz, A, (1976), 'On the universality of subjects: the Ilocano case', in C. Li (ed.), 519-544.

Shibitani, M. (ed.), (1975), *Syntax and Semantics 5. Japanese Generative Grammar*, New York, Academic Press.

───── (ed.), (1976), *Syntax and Semantics 6. The Grammar of Causative Constructions*, New York, Academic Press.

Shimizu, M, (1975), 'Relational grammar and promotion rules in Japanese, *CLS 11*, 529-535.

BIBLIOGRAPHY

Shopen, T, (1972), *A Generative Theory of Ellipsis*, Ph.D diss.,University of California, Ann Arbor, Michigan, University Microfilms.

Shopen, T. & M. Konare, (1970), 'Sonrai causatives and passives: transformational vs lexical derivations for propositional heads', *SAL 1.2*, 211-254.

Shum, S, (1965), *A Transformational Study of Vietnamese Syntax*. Ph.D. diss., Indiana University, Ann Arbor, Michigan, University Microfilms.

Siewierska, A, (1984) 'Another theory of the passive which doesn't work', to appear in *Linguistics*.

Silverstein, M, (1976), 'Hierarchies of features and ergativity' in R.M.W. Dixon (ed.), 112-171.

Sinha, A.K, (1973), 'On stative passives and the treatment of some idioms', *CLS 9*, 615-626.

_____ (1974), 'How passives are passive', *CLS 10*, 631-642.

_____ (1978), 'Another look at the universal characterization of the passive', *CLS 14*, 445-457.

Smit, J. & R.P. Meijer, (1966), *Dutch Grammar and Reader with Exercises*, Melbourne, Melbourne University Press.

Smith-Stark, T, (1976), 'Ergativity, grammatical relations, accessibility hierarchies, Pocoman and cosmic consciousness', ms. Holyoho, Mass.

Spalatin, L, (1973), 'Some Serbo-Croatian equivalents of the English passive' in R. Filipovic et al. (eds), *The Yugoslav Serbo-Croatian English Contrastive Project Reports 8-9*, Zagreb, Institute of Linguistics, 115-131.

Speed Hodges, K. & S.U. Stucky, (1979), 'On the inadequacy of grammatical relations in Bantu', *SLS 9.2*, 91-99.

Sridhar, S.N, (1980), 'New evidence for spontaneous demotion', *International Journal of Dravidian Linguistics 8.2*, 312-322.

Starosta, S, (1973), 'Causative verbs in Formosan languages', *Working Papers in Linguistics 5.9*. Honolulu, University of Hawaii, 115-131.

_____ (1976), *Lexicase I. Prolegomena* (forthcoming).

_____ (1978), 'The one sent solution' in W. Abraham (ed.), 459-576.

Statha-Halikas, H, (1977), 'From impersonal to passive: the Italo-Celtic evidence', *CLS 13*, 578-589.

Stever, S.B., C.A. Walker & S.S. Mufwene, (eds), (1976), *Papers from the Parasession on Diachronic Syntax*, Chicago Linguistic Society, Chicago, Illinois, University of Chicago.

BIBLIOGRAPHY

Stefanini, R, (1982), 'Reflexive, impersonal and passive in Italian and Florentine, *BLS 8*, 97-107.

Stein, G, (1979), *Studies in the Function of the Passive*, Tübingen, Gunter Narr Verlag.

Stucky, S, (1976), 'Locatives as objects in Tshiluba: a function of transitivity', *SLS 6.2*, 174-202.

Subbiah, G, (1972), 'A note on agreement in Kota', in S. Agesthialingom & S.V. Shanmugam (eds), *Third Seminar on Dravidian Linguistics*, Annamalainagar, Annamalai University, 285-392.

Sullivan W.J, (1976), 'Active and passive sentences in English and Polish', *PSiCL 5*, 117-152.

Suner, M, (1982), 'Characterization of a Spanish sentence type' in J.P. Lantolf & G.B. Stone (eds), *Current Research in Romance Languages* (available from IULC, Bloomington, Indiana), 157-165.

Sussex, R, (1982), 'A note on the get-passive construction', *Australian Journal of Linguistics 2*, 83-95.

Svartengren, H, (1968), 'Become as an auxiliary for the passive voice', *Modern Sprak 42*, 272-281.

Svartvik, J, (1966), *On Voice in the English Verb*, The Hague, Mouton.

Tchekoff, C, (1973a), 'Some verbal patterns in Tongan', *The Journal of the Polynesian Society 82*, 281-292.

_____ (1973b) 'Verbal aspects in an ergative construction: an example in Tongan', *OL 12*, 607-620.

Teng, S.H, (1975), *A Semantic Study of Transitivity Relations in Chinese*, Berkeley, California, University of California Publications.

Tesnière, L, (1959), *Élements De Syntaxe Structurale*, Paris, Klincksieck.

Thomas, I.E, (1926), *Danish Conversation-Grammar*, Heidelberg, Julius Groos.

Thompson, S.A, (1973), 'Transitivity and some problems with the bei construction in Mandarin Chinese', *JCL 1.2*, 208-221.

Timberlake, A, (1975), 'The nominative object in Finnish', *Lingua 3/4*, 201-230.

_____ (1976), 'Subject properties in the North Russian passive' in C.L. (ed.), 547-570.

_____ (1977), 'Review of Ch. V. Chvany (1975), *On the Syntax of Be - Sentences in Russian'*, Cambridge, MA Slavica, *Lg 53.1*, 232-236.

_____ (1982), 'The impersonal passive in Lithuanian', *BLS 8*, 508-524.

BIBLIOGRAPHY

Titov, E.G, (1976), *The Amharic Language*, Moscow, Nauka.

Tomlin, R. & R. Rhodes, (1979), 'An introduction to information structure in Ojibwa', *CLS 15*, 307-320.

Topping, D.M, (1973), *Chamorro Reference Grammar*, Honolulu, The University of Hawaii.

Trail, R.L. (ed.), (1973), *Patterns in Clause, Sentence and Discourse in Selected Languages of India and Nepaul II. Clause*, Summer Institute of Linguistics, University of Oklahoma.

Trithart, L, (1975), 'Relational grammar and Chicewa subjectivization', *CLS 11*, 615-625.

Truitner, N, (1972), 'Passive sentences in Vietnamese', *CLS 8*, 368-378.

_____ (1979), 'Topicality: an alternative to the relational view of the Bantu passive', *SAL 10.1*, 1-30.

Tsunoda, T, (1974), *A Grammar of the Warungu Language, North Queensland*, M.A. thesis, Monash University, Melbourne.

Tucker, A.N. & M.A. Bryan, (1966), *Linguistic Analyses. The Non-Bantu Languages of North-Eastern Africa*. (Handbook of African Languages), London, Oxford University Press.

Tuyn, H, (1970), 'Semantics and the notion of transitivity in passive conversion', *Studia Neophilologica 42*, 60-71.

Valesio, P, (1971), 'The distinction of active and passive', *LI 11.3*, 407-414.

Valfells, S, (1970), 'Middle voice in Icelandic', in H. Benediktsson (ed.), *The Nordic Languages and Modern Linguistics*, Rejkjavik, Visindafelag I'slendinga, 551-572.

Van Valin Jr, R.D, (1980), 'On the distribution of passive and antipassive constructions in universal grammar', *Lingua 50.4*, 303-327.

Vasiliu, E. & S. Golopentia-Eretescu, (1972), *The Transformational Syntax of Romanian*, The Hague, Mouton.

Vinogradov, V.V. (ed.), (1966), *Indoevropeiskie Jazyki. Jazyki Narodov C.C.C.P.* Moskva, Nauka

Wagner, H, (1978), 'The typological background of the ergative construction', *Proceedings of the Royal Irish Academy, 78*, 37-75.

Warburton, I, (1975), 'The passive in English and Greek', *FL 13*, 563-578.

Warotamasikkhadit, U, (1972), *Thai Syntax: An Outline*, The Hague, Mouton.

Wasow, T, (1977), 'Transformations and the lexicon' in P. Culicover et al. (eds), 327-360.

BIBLIOGRAPHY

Whalen, S, (1978), 'The impersonal sentence in Russian and Romanian', *PSiCL 8*, 5-67.

Whiteley, W.H, (1968), *Some Problems of Transitivity in Swahili*, London, Luzac.

Whitney, A.H, (1973), *Finnish. Teach Yourself Books*, London, English University Press.

Wierzbicka, A, (1980), *The Case for Surface Case*, Ann Arbor, Karoma Publishers.

Williams, J, (1973), 'Clause patterns in Maithili' in R.L. Trail (ed.), 345-453.

Wilson, H.I, (1972), 'The phonology and syntax of the Palauan verb affixes', *Working Papers in Linguistics 4.3*, Honolulu, University of Hawaii.

Wolfenden, E, (1961), *A Re-Statement of Tagalog Grammar*, Summer Institute of Linguistics, Manila, Institute of National Language.

Wołczyńska-Sudół, A, (1976), 'Notional passive in English and in Polish', *PSiCL 5*, 153-164.

Wongbiasaj, S, (1979), 'On the passive in Thai', *SLS 9.1*, 207-216.

Woodbury, A, (1977), 'Greenlandic Eskimo, ergativity and relational grammar', in P. Cole & J. Sadock (eds), 307-336.

Zandvoort, R.W, (1969), *A Handbook of English Grammar* (ninth edition), London.

Ziv, Y. & G. Sheintuch, (1979), 'Indirect objects reconsidered', *CLS 15*, 390-403.

_____ (1981), 'Passives of obliques over direct objects', *Lingua 54.1*, 1-17.

Zubin, A, (1979), 'Discourse function of morphology. The focus system in German' in T. Givón (ed.), 469-504.

Zydatiss, W, (1974), 'Some means of rendering the English passive in German', *Linguistische Berichte 29*, 34-48.

INDEX OF LANGUAGES

Abaza 21
Abkhaz 21
Achenese 86-7
Aggrobba
Alaskan Eskimo 45
Algonkian 86
Altaic 93
Amer-Indian 23, 31, 34,
  126
Amharic 35, 162, 168-9,
  180
Amis 41
Apurinã 252
Arabic
  ·Classical 35
  Modern 100
Armenian 42
Athabascan 86
Atjnamathanha 35
Australian 162
Austronesian 35, 79, 85,
  217
Avar 20, 21, 22, 23
Aztec 185

Baluchi 126
Bantu 30, 37, 38, 45, 60,
  63, 64, 88, 217, 224
Basque 40, 43-4, 45, 46
Bengali 100, 101, 124, 126,
  137-8, 139, 198-9, 204,
  213, 224, 258
Burmese 126, 149-50

Cahuilla 35
Cakchiquel, 40, 45, 46, 227

Cambodian 126
Cebuano 41, 81
Celtic 11
Chamorro 90-1
Chicewa 30, 60, 69-71
Chiclisit 31
Chi-mwi-ni 30, 46, 55-
  6
Chinook 25
Choctan 27
Cora 35
Cupeno 35
Czech, 35, 41, 164, 173
  181, 183, 184, 185,
  226, 239-40, 245-50

Danish 108, 109, 110,
  111, 125, 254
Dhangar-Kurux 28-9, 39,
  40, 86, 126, 162,
  167-8, 170
Dho-luo 120-1
Dja:bugay 162
Dongo 162
Dravidian 35, 40, 79,
  93, 126, 162
Dyirbal 21, 25
Dutch 3, 4, 94, 96,
  101, 108, 110-12,
  117-19, 123, 125,
  129, 130, 201-2,
  204, 212, 213, 224,
  226, 248

Enga   27

288

INDEX OF LANGUAGES

English 3, 4, 12, 13, 14,
16-18, 22, 30, 39, 40,
47-52, 58, 65-8, 75-7,
79, 91, 101, 119, 126,
134-7, 139, 143-8, 159,
160, 188-93, 195-7,
214, 222-4, 227, 230-3,
235-8, 241-50, 251,
252, 253, 254, 257,
258, 260.
Eskimo 43 *see also* Alaskan
Eskimo, Greenlandic
Eskimo
Ethiopian-Semitic 162
European 127, 128, 154,
165, 180, 183, 228,
238, 255, 256

Faroese 124
Fijian 27, 30, 35, 88
Finnish 40, 42, 98-100, 102
116, 120-2, 124, 126, 129
133, 139
Finno-Ugric 93
Formosan 41, 79, 88
French 25, 95, 109, 112, 113,
115, 125, 139, 169, 170-1,
173, 206, 213, 232-4,
238-9, 245-6, 248, 250,
253

Gaelic 126
German 4, 13, 35, 95, 96-8,
101, 108, 109-12, 114-6,
123, 125, 126, 129-34,
145, 159, 163, 169-70,
173-8, 184, 194, 198,
200-4, 207, 212, 213,
224, 226, 232, 239,
247-8, 253
Germanic 162, 231-2, 236-7,
245-8, 250
Greek
Classical 30, 42
Modern 163, 166, 183, 185
Greenlandic Eskimo 20, 25,
42, 45-6
Gugu-Yalandji 42, 43
Guugu-Yimidir 162
Gujarati 126
Gurage 162

Halkomelem 30, 88, 88
Hamito-Semitic 126
Harai 162
Haya 60
Hebrew 163
Hibena 71
Hindi 101, 105-8, 125,
126, 198, 200-2,
204, 212, 213, 224,
258
Hixkaryana 220, 252
Hokan 27
Huichol 30, 35
Hungarian 23

Icelandic 102-5, 124,
129-31, 134, 169-71,
207-8
Igbo 35
Ilocano 27, 81-2
Imbabura Quechua 43
see also Quechua
Indo-Aryan 40, 126
Indo-European 23, 34,
44, 79, 91, 93, 126,
162, 163, 217, 228
Indonesian 30, 35-7,
40, 52-5, 58, 79,
85, 87, 88, 195
Irish 88
Isthmus Zapotec 27
Italian 88, 95, 100,
112, 126, 134, 139,
165-7, 170, 172-80,
181-3, 185, 211,
224, 226-7, 231-6,
238-40, 246, 249,
252-3

Japanese 30, 58-60, 127,
149, 154-8, 194-5,
211, 224
Jener 31

Kala Lagau Langgu 25
Kalkatungu 25, 26
Kannada 40, 41, 98,
100, 102, 120, 126,
211, 213, 227
Kapampangan 41, 88
Kashmiri 126

289

INDEX OF LANGUAGES

Kinyarwanda 30, 37, 39, 59, 60-4, 74, 87, 88, 208, 261
Kolami 100, 123, 126
Kota 35, 39, 40, 42, 79, 85, 86, 88
Kupia 35, 126
Kurdish 126
Kyquot 31

Lahota 20
Lahu 27
Lardil 42, 162, 166-7, 180, 195
Latin 13, 19, 20, 21, 23, 42, 96, 198
Latvian 35, 126
Lisu 27
Lithuanian 42, 88, 98, 100, 101, 126, 199, 200, 204, 212, 213
Lolo-Burmese 27

Ma 162
Maasai 100, 102
Machiguenga 30
Maithili 40, 41, 126, 227
Makah 31
Malagasy 30, 71, 89, 252
Malay 91
Malayalam 40, 42
Mayan 40
Malayo-Polynesian 15
Mandrin 21, 30, 149-50, 152, 207-8
Maori 11, 30, 68-9, 85, 91
Maragoli 30, 46, 59, 60, 62-3, 74
Mashi 30, 46, 59, 60, 62-4, 71, 73-4
Mba 162
Mojave 100, 120
Muskogean 27

Nahuatl 30
Navajo 20, 86
Nez Perce 100, 126
Ngarinjin 42, 162
Ngarluma 28-9, 39, 40, 42

Ngunga 162
Nieuan 85
Niger-Congo 93
Nilo-Saharan 93
Nitinaht 30, 31-2, 34, 39, 40, 75, 222
North-East African 162
North Russian 42, 88
Northern Paiute 180
Norwegian 224, 226, 254

Ojibwa 86, 220, 252
Olutsootso 30, 38, 71-4, 260
Ossetian 126
Oto-Manguean 27

Palauan 30, 35-7, 39, 40, 79, 85, 87, 88, 107, 217
Papago 167, 168
Pepecano 35
Persian 30
Philippine 23, 39, 41, 79-86, 88, 89, 90-91, 220
Pitta Pitta 25
Pocoman 25
Polish 9-10, 13, 26, 39, 40, 41, 113, 115, 125-6, 129-30, 145-6, 160, 169, 170-1, 174, 194, 205-6, 224-6, 228, 230, 232-3, 239-40, 245-7, 249, 250,
Polynesian 11, 23, 85
Portuguese 167, 169, 185, 231-2, 238-9, 246, 249, 254
Pukapukan 11

Quechua 30, 42, 43, 211 *see also* Imbabura Quechua
Quiche 30, 40, 45-6, 126, 227

290

INDEX OF LANGUAGES

Romance 41, 125, 162, 166,
    173, 184, 204, 236, 238,
    240, 245, 247-51
Romanian 167, 173-4, 185,
    194, 253
Russian 28-9, 40, 41, 78,
    94-5, 100, 102, 120,
    146, 162, 163, 165,
    167-8, 180-1, 183,
    199-200, 211, 213, 226,
    232

Saint Thomas Creole 181
Salish 88
Samoan 11, 23
Sanskrit 30
Seediq 41
Serbo-Croation 165, 173,
    184-5
Shona 30, 56-7, 60
Shoshoni 35, 116-7, 180
Sinhalese 126
Sino-Tibetan 23, 27, 126
Slavic 41, 125, 162, 173,
    184, 225, 231, 232,
    236, 238, 245, 248,
    251
Sonrai 35
South-East Asian 127, 128,
    149-59
Spanish, 41, 100, 112, 139,
    165, 168, 170-5, 181-3,
    185, 226, 232, 234-6,
    238-9, 246, 249, 252
Swahili 88
Swedish 30, 108, 110-13,
    119, 125-6, 130-1,
    134, 139, 160, 183-4,
    254

Tagalog 14, 20, 27, 30,
    80-6, 91, 92, 107,
    216, 217
Tamang 27
Tamil 41, 126
Tatar 162
Tanoan 31
Tera 35
Tepecano 180
Teseshat 31

Thai 21, 126, 127,
    149-52, 154-8, 194
Thsiluba 30
Tigre 162
Tigrinya 162
Tiwa 30, 39, 40, 41,
    42, 45, 75, 86, 222
Tongan 11, 21, 22, 23,
    85
Turkic 162
Turkish 14, 94, 96,
    100, 102, 119, 124
    162, 200-1, 204
    212-13
Tzeltal 126
Tzotzil 30, 40, 41,
    227

Ucluelet 31
Uigur 162
Urdui 35, 126
Ute 3, 4, 98, 100, 120,
    125, 199
Uto-Aztecan 93, 162

Vietnamese 30, 126,
    127, 149-50, 152-8

Wakashan 31
Warungu 25
Washo 27
Welsh 26, 100, 118-19,
    126, 199-200, 205
    213

Yindinʸ 20, 25
Yindjibarandi 42
Yuman 93

291

INDEX OF NAMES

Abasheikh *see* Kisseberth
Abramovitch *see* Maratsos
Alisova 76
Allan 142, 252
Allen & Frantz 31, 32-4
Amastae 180
Amrilavalli 106
Anderson, J. 5, 27
Anderson, S. 15, 20, 85, 161, 186, 215
Andrews 104
Andronov 98
Apresjan 13
Atkinson 99
Awbery 200, 205

Babby & Brecht 28, 78, 146, 215
Bach 186
Bani & Klokeid 25
Barber 162
Beedham 132, 139, 143, 160, 180, 186, 191
Bell 41, 82, 91
Bennett 7
Bever 222
Bhatia *see* Kachru
Blake, B. 21, 22, 25, 26 *see also* Mallinson
Blake, F. 80
Bloomfield 80
Bock 222
Bolinger 68, 186, 187, 191, 193
Borget & Nyhan 132

Bouton 7, 127, 141, 142
Brame 7
Brecht *see* Babby
Breckenridge 109
Bresnan 5, 141, 142, 148, 149, 186
Brinker 35
Brown 76
Brown & Miller 9
Bryan *see* Tucker
Burston 206
Burt 7

Çatford 21
Cerny 22
Chafe 219, 222, 251
Chaiyaratana 150, 151,
Channon 169
Chappell 135
Chomsky 5, 6, 7, 11, 19, 65, 67, 71, 76, 127, 140, 186
Chu 151
Chung 35, 36-7, 58-61, 68-9, 85, 91
Churchward 22
Cinque 177, 183, 224, 226, 233, 252-3
Clark & Clark 222

INDEX OF NAMES

Clark, M 128, 159
Clark, R 88
Cole, Harbert, Herman &
  Sridhar 102, 104, 124
Cole & Jake 43
Comrie 13, 76, 77, 78,
  98, 99, 101, 117, 124,
  125, 173, 199, 213
Constantino 80
Contreras 169, 177
Cooreman 85, 90-1, 92
Costa 88, 165, 172,
  173, 177, 178, 181-2,
  183
Cowan 40
Creider 251
Cureton 186, 191, 195-6
Curme 35, 132, 133, 137,
  160, 172, 207, 247

Dahl 219
Dalgish 38, 71, 120, 260
Daneš 251
Davison 186, 187, 191,
  192, 193, 258
de Guzman 80
Derbyshire 252
van Dijk 254
Dik 5, 219, 222, 224, 232
Dixon 13-15, 20, 21, 22,
  25, 56
Donaldson 169
Dryer 23, 40, 86, 211
Du'ong 150, 151
Duranti & Ochs 233, 234,
  235
Durie 87
Duškova 35, 180, 245, 248,
  254

Eckman 35
Egerod 85
Einarsson 102-4, 131, 207
Edmonds 5, 7, 141, 186
Erben 132
Ertel 228-9

Faarlund 224
Fiengo 7, 127, 160
Filbeck 150

Fillmore 5, 7, 186
Firbas 251
Foley 27, 81, 88
Foley & van Valin 20,
  23, 81, 82
Fox *see* Cooreman
Frajzyngier 100, 101,
  115, 116, 145, 182,
  197, 204
Frantz 47, 76 *see also*
  Allen
Fraser & Squair 125
Freidin 76, 127, 141,
  146, 147-8
Fries 88
Frishberg 86

Galambos 233, 234
Garcia 170, 171, 172,
  175, 181, 182, 183
Garry 71, 73
Garry & Keenan 60, 63,
  64, 80, 261
George & Kornfilt 94
Gerdts 88
Givon 3, 8, 80, 81, 84,
  88, 117, 120, 125,
  199, 217 *see also*
  Cooreman
Golopentia-Eretescu
  see Vasiliu
Gordon 28, 168, 170
Green, G. 48, 186,
  215
Green, J. 169, 175
Greenbaum *see* Quirk
Greenberg 252
Grevisse 125
Groves 109
Gruber 160, 215

Hadlich 165, 171, 174,
  177
Haiman 35, 163-4
Hale 28, 86
Halliday 27, 88, 219,
  222, 251
Hammer 132, 172
Harbert *see* Cole
Harris 121

INDEX OF NAMES

Hasegawa 7, 127, 141, 142, 151, 155
Hashimoto 151
Hatcher 135, 136
Hawkinson & Hyman 56, 88
Heath 25-6
Herman *see* Cole
Hershberger 43
Hetzron 125
Hidalgo 81
Hinds 219, 222, 251
Hinz 45
Hoard 5, 7
Hollis 102
Hopper 91
Hopper & Thompson 8, 15-9, 26, 80, 83, 85, 217
Horn 141, 142, 149, 170
Hou 150, 151
Howard 155
Howard & Niyekawa-Howard 59, 224
Huddleston 35, 127, 141, 160, 191, 206
Hudson 127, 141
Hutchins 219, 222, 251
Hyman *see* Hawkinson

Imai 105

Jake *see* Cole
Jackendoff 160, 186, 215
Jacobs & Rosenbaum 5, 7
Jespersen 9, 35, 38, 88, 137, 187
Johnson 47, 66, 67, 76
Jones 26
Jones & Thomas 118
Josephs 35-7, 87

Kaburaki *see* Kuno
Kachru, Kachru & Bhatia 106, 107
Karlsson 121
Kayne 109, 115, 125, 169
Keenan 15, 71, 76, 88, 89, 102, 124, 155, 157, 213, 252, 259 *see also* Garry

Keenan Ochs & Schieffelin 232, 234, 235
Khai 150
Kholodovič 13, 77
Khrakovsky 76, 93, 94, 112, 114, 116, 117, 215
Kimenyi 37, 60, 87, 208
Kirkwood 224
Kirsner 3, 94, 110, 125, 182, 185
Kisseberth & Abasheikh 55
Klaiman 106, 107, 124, 137, 162, 198, 211
Klokeid 31, 47, 166, 179 *see also* Bani
Kornfilt *see* George
Kruisinga 35, 88
Kullavanijaya 151
Kuno 155, 228-9
Kuno & Kaburaki 228
Kuroda 155

Laberge & Sankoff 238, 245
Lafitte 40
Lagerwey 130
Lakoff, G. 66, 67
Lakoff, R. 7, 127, 134, 141, 142
Langacker 166, 167
Langacker & Munro 5, 7, 120, 141, 142, 143, 163-4, 185
Lawler 86
Le 152, 154, 156, 158-9
Leech *see* Quirk
Lees 186
Lekawatana 150, 151, 156
Lepschy & Lepschy 134, 176, 177, 178, 179, 234
Li, C & Thompson 23, 26-7, 150, 219
Li, Y 150-1
Lightfoot 7, 127, 146, 148, 149, 159

INDEX OF NAMES

Lo Cascio 134, 172, 177, 239
Lockwood 124
Luelsdorff 144
Lyons 13, 27, 142, 162, 219

McCawley, J. 127
McCawley, N.A. 155, 157
McCray 253
McNair & McNair 123
Mager *see* Muller
Mallinson & Blake 22, 25, 82, 252
Mansion 125
Maratsos & Abramovitch 76
Martinet 21
Masica 77
Mathesius 251
Mchombo 7
Meijer *see* Smit
Mihailovic 38
Mirikitani 41
Mohanan 40
Mueller, Mager & Niedzielski 125
Mulder 14, 124
Mulder & Schwartz 81
Munro *see* Langacker

Napoli 166, 169, 174-9, 231, 246, 253
Naro 167, 254
Naylor 81
Niedzielski *see* Mueller
Niyekawa-Howard *see* Howard
Noonan 40, 88
Nyhan *see* Borgert

Ochs *see* Duranti, Keenan Ochs
O'Grady 23
Oksaar 108
Onions 88
Östman 38, 100, 116, 133
Otanes 80, 81, 82 *see also* Schachter
Owen 187
Ozkaragoz 204, 212

Palmer 187
Pandharipande 105, 201
Paterson 227
Payne 85
Perlmutter 6, 24, 119, 200, 201, 210, 211, 215
Perlmutter & Postal 6, 8, 12, 23, 43-4, 52, 47, 66, 67, 71, 76, 80, 81, 82, 89, 101, 111, 117-19, 122-3, 151, 177, 179, 180, 185, 186, 187, 197, 200-1, 204, 209-15
Platzack 130, 146, 183-4
Postal 25-6, 44, 109, 125 *see also* Perlmutter
Poutsma 9, 35, 88, 187
Prince 231, 252
Pullum 252 *see also* Derbyshire
Pullum & Wilson 127

Quirk, Greenbaum, Leech & Svartvik 88, 258

Radford 127, 141, 142, 243
Ramos 80
Ranson 223
Rhodes *see* Tomlin
Riddle, Sheintuch & Ziv 67-8, 186, 193
Rosenbaum *see* Jacobs
Rospond 246
Ross 127

Sankoff *see* Laberge
Saksena 106, 107
Schachter 20, 23, 80, 81, 82
Schachter & Otanes 81, 84
Schoenthal 35
Schrofen 169
Schwartz 81 *see also* Mulder

INDEX OF NAMES

Sheintuch *see* Riddle, Ziv
Shimizu 58, 155, 157
Shopen 76, 135, 136
Shum 150, 151
Siewierska 196
Silverstein 25
Sinha 34, 186, 258
Smit & Meijer 111, 130
Smith Stark 25
Spalatin 165
Speed Hodges & Stucky 71
Squair *see* Fraser
Sridhar 98 *see also* Cole
Starosta 5, 41, 141, 146, 186
Statha-Halikas 124
Stefanini 175, 184
Stein 132, 133, 135, 136, 137, 139, 160, 186, 189-90, 205, 206, 207, 208, 226
Stucky *see* Speed Hodges
Subbiah 35
Sullivan 129
Suñer 41
Sussex 134, 159
Svartengren 137
Svartvik 38, 137, 139, 160 *see also* Quirk

Tchekoff 21
Teng 150, 207
Tesnière 13
Thomas, A.R. *see* Jones
Thomas, I.E. 108, 110
Thompson *see* Hopper, Li. C
Timberlake 88, 124, 143, 185, 199, 212
Titov 168
Tomlin & Rhodes 252
Topping 90
Trithart 69-70, 224
Truitner 128, 150, 152-4, 159
Tsunoda 25
Tucker & Bryan 162
Tuyn 187, 191-2

Valfells 169-70

Van Valin 31 *see also* Foley
Vasiliu & Golopentia-Eretescu 167, 173

Wagner 21
Warburton 166, 167, 185
Warotamasikkhadit 150, 151
Wasow 7, 127, 146, 147, 149, 159
Whalen 199, 215
Whiteley 88
Whitney 98
Wierzbicka 195-7
Williams 40
Wilson, D. *see* Pullum
Wilson, H.I. 35
Wolfenden 80
Wołczyńska-Sudół 170, 174
Wongbiasaj 150, 151, 158, 159
Woodbury 20, 25, 42

Zandvoort 137
Ziv & Sheintuch 48-9, 51, 52, 88
Zubin 224
Zydatiss 114

INDEX OF TERMS

A 14, 19, 20 and *passim*
ablative 42
absolutive 20, 21, 22, 42,
46, 91, 92, 99, 124
abstract (nominal) 18, 91,
96
accompaniment (NP) 62-4,
88, 89
accusative (marking,
language, system) 9,
10, 21-3, 32, 42, 68,
85, 97, 99, 102, 103,
105, 121, 124, 166,
167, 175, 225
active counterpart 4,
30-5, 75, 79, 86,
94, 137, 154, 157,
256, 257, 260 *see*
also corresponding
active
actor 79-85, 90, 91
adjectival analysis 127,
145-9
adjectival conversion 149
adjectival passive 34 *see*
also stative passive
adjective 127, 130, 131,
132, 134, 139, 140,
141, 142, 145-9,
159, 160
adposition 9
advancement
1- Advancement Ex-
clusiveness Law 124,
179, 185, 209-10,
212-15

advancement to 1
47, 63, 64, 71, 77,
85, 89, 179, 180,
211-14
of 3 to 2 47-8, 53,
55 *see also* dative-
movement
of oblique to 2 47-8,
53, 55, 63, 71
sporadic 89, 209,
215
adverb 4, 39, 109, 110,
111, 114, 130-1
147, 154, 170-1
184, 199
adversative 138, 144,
150-1, 154, 159,
246
affect 15, 17, 18,
67-9, 89, 163, 187-
91, 193, 195, 208
210, 214, 215, 258
affirmation 15
agent 2 *and passim*
see passive agent
agentive passive 30,
222, 223, 225, 227,
230, 232, 234, 236,
241, 242, 243, 244,
247, 250, 254
agentless passive 30-1,
35, 38, 86, 100,
112, 111, 117, 226,
230, 237, 241, 242,
243, 244, 247, 250
see also impersona-

297

INDEX OF TERMS

lization, truncated passive.

agreement 19, 20, 21, 35-6,
42, 43, 45, 46, 60, 72,
73, 87, 88, 94, 102, 104
105, 106, 120, 146, 174,
175, 177, 178, 179, 185,
228 *see also* cross-
reference

allative 42

ambiguity 31, 134, 139, 144,
145, 149, 168, 169, 241,
242, 257

anaphoric 229, 232, 253

anticausative 27, 77-9, 164,
168-73, 256, 258, 259

antipassive 15, 25-6, 91,
259

animacy hierarchy 221, 222,
223, 228, 259 *see also*
chain of being hierarchy

animate/inanimate 14, 17, 33,
34, 86, 87, 96, 98, 100,
116, 165, 166, 168, 170,
181, 221, 223, 224, 225

applied affix 57, 60, 63,
64, 88-9, 130

argument (verbal, structure)
13, 123, 125, 199, 213
215, 257, 258, 259, 260

aspect 15, 18, 87, 99, 259
see also perfective/
imperfective

auxiliary (verb) 2, 6, 43,
44, 94, 95, 97, 104, 105,
108, 112, 113, 126-39,
143, 144, 154, 159, 176,
178, 179, 215

background 83, 182, 185, 233,
234

be-passive 126, 128-34, 137,
139-49, 154, 258

become-passive 124, 126,
128-34, 137-8, 144-5

benefactive 3, 7, 20, 24, 30,
46, 47, 48, 53, 55-60, 62,
64, 65, 74, 77, 80, 85,
88, 89, 217

beneficial 134, 138, 144,
150-1 154, 159

canonical passive 10,
28, 36, 85, 95,
112, 113, 125, 176,
181, 255

case frames 186, 262

case grammar 5, 6

case marking 3, 10,
19, 20, 41-44, 75,
104, 105, 259 *see*
also passive agent
passive subject

causal (object) 3, 30,
68, 85

cause 100, 200, 258,
259

chain-of-being
hierarchy 32, 34
see also animacy
hierarchy

chômeur 7, 24, 45, 47,
55, 83, 88, 118,
119, 122, 123

chômeur law 44-5, 47,
118

cleft(ing) 90, 91

clitic 115, 175, 176,
177, 225, 232, 253

cognitive field 228

cognizer 198, 212

come-passive 126, 134,
138, 144

common (noun) 18, 80

communicative dynami-
sim 251

complement 128, 141,
145, 146, 147, 148,
159, 160, 215,
adjectival 141, 147
clausal/sentential
127, 141, 152

complex sentence
analysis (of passives)
127, 128, 140-45,
151-60, 164, 257

concrete/concretness
18, 225

conjunction particle
formation 106, 107

constituent order 23,
24, 41, 225, 227,
235, 255 *see also*
word order

INDEX OF TERMS

context 31, 67, 169, 171,
187, 192, 193, 235,
241, 250, 251, 252
contrast 205, 221, 224,
228, 229, 231, 236
see also focus
controller 14, 64
conversational implicature
134, 135, 138, 249,
257, 258
coordination 148, 206
copula 42, 142-3, 148
core categories 20, 53
54, 56, 72, 120
coreference/coreferential
90, 121, 123, 128,
152, 153, 159, 164,
185, 187, 205-8, 235,
253, 254
corresponding active 4,
28, 31, 34, 41, 76,
94, 119, 128, 139,
155, 158, 196, 227,
256, 257, 258, 260
see also active
counterpart
corresponding passive
10, 18, 36, 41, 65,
69, 105, 190, 248,
249 *see also*
passive counterpart
count (noun) 18
crossreference 33, 44,
45, 46, 70, 71, 72,
120, 121 *see also*
agreement pronoun

dative-movement 48, 53-9,
62, 65, 88,
dative 13, 25, 42, 58,
102, 103, 104, 105,
198, 211 *see also*
indirect object,
recipient
deep structure *see*
underlying structure
definite/indefinite 17,
37, 82, 83, 84, 85,
105, 116-17, 119,
173, 174, 175, 176,
182, 191, 222, 223,

231, 236, 238-51,
259
deictic 108, 253
deletion 22, 39, 87,
122 *see also*
demotion
demotion 6, 7, 47, 58,
59, 76, 77, 88,
89, 95, 107, 114,
117-124, 127, 136,
158, 213, 217
det 108, 110
detransitivization 44,
217, 259
direct object 2 and
passim, see also
P, patient
in RG 12-13
in TG 11-12
morpho-syntactic
characterization 9
vs P 14-15, 19-20
direct passive 149-54,
157, 158
disjuncture 221, 232
discourse 8, 15, 83,
221, 229, 230, 234,
236, 237
distribution of infor-
mation 220, 222,
223, 224, 225, 227,
250 *see also*
information struc-
ture
ditransitive 46, 51,
56, 57, 59, 64, 65,
123, 133, 146, 217,
259
dominance 5, 11, 12
dooy-passive 151
dummy 4, 93, 101,
108-12, 117, 118,
119, 123, 180, 213
248
dynamic 4, 140, 144,
183

egocentric bias 221,
236
ellipsis 229

299

INDEX OF TERMS

embedded clause 109, 110,
  141, 158
emphasis 221, 229
Equi-NP-deletion 91, 104,
  106, 107, 141, 153
er 108, 110, 111, 248
ergative (marking,
  language, system,
  verb) 20-2, 27, 42,
  44, 85-6, 91, 92,
  105
es 108, 109, 114, 213,
  248
exceptions (to passiviza-
  tion) 186-216
existential (verb, re-
  lation) 91, 142-3,
  191
experiencer 27, 91,
  198, 212

familiarity (of speaker)
  228
Final-1-Law 111
final position 221, 226,
  252 *see also* focus,
  new, word order
first person plural
  (indefinite subject)
  115, 238, 239, 242,
  243, 245, 247, 248, 250
floor 233
focal position 221, 226,
  232, 236, 247, 248
focus 3, 23, 185, 219,
  220, 221, 222, 226,
  232, 236, 247, 251,
  252
  of contrast 231, 232
focus-system 79, 81-5, 86
  88, 90, 91, 92
focusing 107, 221, 225,
  250
foreground 83, 185
fronting 222, 236
functional domain 217
functional grammar 5

generic 191, 241
gerund 213

get-passive 126, 134-8,
  143-4, 159, 258
given 3, 23, 183,
  218-20, 222,
  223-31, 233, 234,
  236, 247, 250,
  251, 252
go-passive 126, 128,
  134, 137, 138, 144
goal 82, 83, 84, 90,
  91, 92, 215
grammatical relations
  6, 24, 87, 91, 137,
  225, 256, 258

higher verb 142
human/non human 15, 96,
  100-1, 113, 114-17
  180-2, 185, 199-200,
  204, 221, 222, 234,
  235, 238, 245, 248

il 109, 115, 125, 248

ill-formedness 210
imperative 12, 81, 124,
  132, 160
imperfective 35, 36,
  87, 129, 130, 183
impersonal active *see*
  indefinite active
impersonal passive 1,
  2, 12, 87-8, 93-125,
  145, 159, 164, 167,
  173-80, 182, 185
  187, 197-205, 213,
  215, 255, 256, 259
  of intransitive verbs
  101, 105, 115,
  118-20, 185, 198-200
impersonalization 2,
  217, 218, 241, 246,
  248-51, 254
inanimate *see* animate
indefinite *see* definite
indefinite active
  clauses 112-17,
  164-73, 182, 174-5
  215, 238-51

300

INDEX OF TERMS

indirect object 7, 27, 49, 50, 83, 230 *see also* dative, recipient advancement 48
indirect passive 149, 154-9, 257, 258
infinitive 147, 247, 254
information structure 218, 219, 222
initial position 219, 220, 221, 222, 224, 225, 227, 231, 233, 249, 251, 252 *see also* given, topic, word order
intonation 232
intransitivity 9, 33, 44-5, 65 and *passim*, *see also* transitivity, unaccusative, unergative
Instrumental/instrument 3, 7, 25, 30, 33, 35, 41-2, 46-7, 62, 63, 64, 71, 74, 77, 85, 88, 89, 165, 200
inversion 209-11, 215

kinesis/kinetic 15, 44

left-dislocation 90, 231-7, 252-3, 254
lexical functional grammar 5
lexical rule 7, 76, 141
lexicon 7, 82
literary flavour 229, 245, 254
locative 3, 7, 24, 25, 30, 38, 42, 47, 68-74, 77, 80-1, 84-5, 88, 89, 260

main verb 126-8, 141-4, 151-3, 155
man-construction 95, 112, 114-17, 173, 238, 245, 247, 250, 254
manner (NP) 3, 25, 46, 62-4, 88, 89

manner adverbial analysis 186
marked/unmarked 81, 82, 218, 219, 220, 221, 222, 224, 225, 226, 227, 232, 235, 247, 250, 251
mass (noun) 18
matrix (clause, verb) 66, 110, 114, 128, 159, 257
meaning preserving requirement 140
middle (verb, voice) 13, 68, 103, 163, 169
modal 30, 131, 132, 138, 183, 257-8
mode 15
mono-transitive 64, 147 *see also* transitive
mood 16, 45, 99, 259

negative (clause, marker) 26, 157, 212, 257
new 3, 23, 183, 218, 219, 220, 221, 222, 223-6, 231, 232, 233, 234, 236, 247, 250, 251, 252
nominative 9, 10, 20, 32, 41, 94-5, 99, 102, 105, 120, 121, 166-7, 175, 225, 253
nominalization 48, 51
non-distinctiveness 163-4
non-human *see* human
notional passive 169

object 10 and *passim see also* direct object, indirect object, P, patient cognate 37, 87, 207-8 individual/non-individual 15, 16, 18, 83

301

INDEX OF TERMS

prepositional 49, 50,
    230, 253
oblique (marking, position,
    relation) 6, 7, 24, 25,
    37, 49, 50, 67, 68, 92,
    120, 127, 209, 227
    advancement 63, 66
on-construction 95, 112,
    114-15, 117, 173, 238,
    245, 247, 250
one 238, 242-5, 247, 249
    250, 254
One Advancement Exclusive-
    ness Law *see* advancement

P 14, 19, 20 and *passim*
    in Chi-mwi-ni 56
    in English 48-9
    in Indonesian 53
    in Kinyarwanda 60
participant 7, 13-15, 17,
    18, 22, 45, 86, 116,
    160, 196, 200 *see also*
    argument
participle 122
    impersonal 113, 240,
    245, 246, 247
    passive 42, 99
    past 2, 94, 97, 104,
    112, 127, 134, 137,
    139, 140, 142, 145-9,
    159, 160, 178, 179,
    185
particle movement 67
particle spelling 66
partitive 26
passive 1 and *passim*
    distribution of 23, 27
    in RG 7
    in TG 5, 6
    lack of 23, 27
    obligatory 36, 86, 170
passive/active relation-
    ship 5-7, 76-6, 140-1,
    127
passive agent 1 and *passim*
    in impersonal passive 94,
    96-7, 100-1, 104, 105,
    107, 116, 117, 124,
    198-201, 204

in reflexive passive
    164-5, 167-8, 170,
    174, 180-2, 185
    lack of 30, 35, 78,
    94, 100, 107, 138,
    174, 185 *see also*
    agentless passive
    marking of 32, 33,
    35, 40-5, 53, 69,
    72, 94, 95, 97-8,
    104, 105, 138
    obligatory 35-9,
    82-3, 85, 86, 87,
    256, 259
    pronominal 34, 37,
    70, 205, 206, 224,
    236
    reflexive 70, 79,
    205-6
    restrictions on 32-3
    37, 86, 96, 100
    180-2, 185, 198-200,
    204, 205, 222, 223,
    224, 236 259
passive characteriza-
    tion of 2-3, 5, 6,
    7, 28, 75-6, 79,
    84, 137
passive counterpart 8,
    32, 97, 186, 196,
    215 *see also*
    corresponding
    passive
passive frequency of
    83, 91, 218, 230,
    236, 250, 259
passive function of
    217, 230, 233, 256,
    258
passive motivation
    222, 223, 227
passive subject 29-30,
    38, 46, 75, 77
    in reflexive passive
    165-6, 168
    restrictions on 31-3,
    37, 38, 48, 165-6,
    205-8, 222, 223,
    236

INDEX OF TERMS

semantic role of 29-30,
45-6, 48, 53, 56, 58,
59, 62, 63, 64, 69,
70, 71, 77, 89, 92, 183,
184, 255
in impersonal passive 3,
4, 93-117, 173-80, 255
passive and topicalization
3, 41, 84, 123, 125,
182-3, 217, 222-37,
247, 248, 249
passive transformation
6, 76, 83, 114, 140-1
passivization 8, 10, 11,
15 and *passim*
double 58, 60, 178,
185
patient 3, 14, 20, 23,
27, 32, 41, 46, 55-60,
63, 74, 80-5, 88, 89,
90, 91, 125, 183, 212,
222-4 226, 227, 228,
232, 234-6, 247, 248,
250 *see also* direct
object, P
people 238, 241, 242,
245, 249-50
perfective 35, 36, 87,
105, 106, 128, 129,
130, 131, 132, 142,
163
periphrastic passive 1,
2, 29, 108, 112,
126-61, 182, 183,
184, 218, 229, 241,
246, 247, 248, 249,
251, 254, 255
personal passive 1, 2,
28-92, 93, 100, 103-6,
109, 113, 119, 145,
159, 164-73, 182,
187-97, 217, 218, 227,
255, 256, 259, 260,
261
perspective 227-8
pitch 219, 221
point of departure 219, 228
point of view 221, 227-8
possessive (NP) 207
possessor (NP) 155

postposing 41, 111,
121, 178
postposition 21, 58,
105
pragmatics 186-7, 193,
195-7
pragmatic function 3,
23, 219, 247, 259
predicate 66, 142-3,
164, 200, 201, 204,
211, 212, 214, 215,
259
predication 219, 232,
234, 253
predicative adjective
construction 127,
130-1, 137, 139
preposing 41, 111, 121,
122
preposition(al)
(marking, phrase,
verb) 21, 32, 39,
44, 47-51, 56, 57,
60, 62-3, 65-72,
80, 87, 88, 89, 94,
97, 98, 140, 142,
193
prepositional passive
192 *see also*
pseudo-passive
presentative structures
101, 125
Pro 175-6
progressive 128, 140
promotion 6, 7, 12, 47,
48, 55, 62, 63, 69,
76-7, 84, 89, 100,
102, 107, 114,
117-24, 127, 136,
158, 217 *see also*
advancement
pronoun 20, 99, 100,
257
anaphoric 232
copy 179
coreferential 90-1
crossreferencing 86,
87, 120
possessive 205, 207
reciprocal 205-6

303

INDEX OF TERMS

reflexive 54,55, 79,
170, 205
relative 26
resumptive 231
subject 116-7, 175,
205, 234, 235, 239
pronominalization 60, 63,
70, 72-3, 166-7
proper (noun) 18, 80
propositional content 3,
30, 257
prosodic characteristics
218, 221, 222, 224,
232, 234
pseudo-passive 65, 186,
192, 214, 258
punctuality 15, 17, 18,
83

quantifier 30, 191, 257,
258

raising 66, 73, 104, 141,
146
recipient 3, 20, 30, 32,
46-8, 53, 55-7, 60-5,
74, 77, 85, 88, 89,
103, 159, 184, 217
see also dative,
indirect object
reciprocal 25, 163,
205-6
reference vs role
domination 23
referential/non-referential
17, 83, 228
reflexive (construction,
marker) 25, 54, 55,
163-7, 170, 172, 179,
184-5, 240, 245, 247,
249, 258, 259
illogical 169
pseudo 169
quasi 169
reflexive passive 1, 2, 29,
145, 162-85, 241, 245,
246, 248, 250
reflexivization 60-1, 63,
81, 82, 83, 104, 105,
107, 125

register 229, 231,
244, 246, 250
Relational Anihilation
Law 44-5
relational grammar 5,
6, 12, 24-5, 41,
44, 47-8, 83, 85,
89, 111, 117-24,
179, 209-15, 219
relativization 1, 15,
26, 49-51, 54-5,
60-1, 63, 73-4,
91, 121-2
repair mechanism 229
result 187-8, 190-5,
214, 215
rule government 186-7,
215

S 14, 19, 20 and
passim
S- passive 30, 109,
112, 183-4, 254
second person singular
(indefinite subject)
238, 239, 242, 244,
245, 248-50, 254
selectional restrictions
200
semantic hierarchy 221
semantic representation
140
semantic role 3, 79-80,
81, 82, 90, 139,
184, 255, 259
si/se 175-80, 240
someone 238, 241, 242,
245, 250, 254
source (NP) 3, 30, 68,
85, 215
speaker identification
228-9 *see also*
egocentric bias
specified/unspecified/
specificity 78, 83,
115, 116, 165, 173,
179, 245, 254, 259
speech 221, 230, 231,
236, 237, 244-52

304

INDEX OF TERMS

state vs action 1, 4,
  15-6, 127, 130, 131,
  134, 140-5, 148,
  183-4, 256
stative passive 34, 127,
  136-7, 139, 148-9,
  159, 160, 256, 258
Stratal Uniqueness Law
  89, 118, 122-3
stress 205, 206, 232,
  252
  contrastive 115
  increased 225
  tonic 3, 219, 221,
  232
strict subcategorization
  186
stylistic factors 129,
  133, 134, 184, 248
Subject 1, and *passim see
  also* passive subject
  functional role 227-8
  in RG 6, 7, 12-13
  in TG 11-12
  in Philippine-type
  languages 79-82, 89, 90
  indefinite active 95,
  112-117, 119, 173, 175,
  176, 177, 182, 238-51,
  254
  morpho-syntactic
  characterization 9
  topic and 185, 217, 222,
  224, 227, 228, 229, 236
  vs S/A 14-15, 19-20
subject auxiliary inversion
  115
subject object inversion
  141
subjectivization 84, 224,
  228, 229, 235
suprasegmental features
  218, 248
syncretisim 225
synonymy 7, 30, 141,
  157, 257
synthetic passive, 1, 29,
  142, 145

telic 17, 18
temporal (NP) 3

tense 87, 99, 259
terms 6, 73, 74
thematic relations 186,
  215
theme 149, 160-1, 215,
  222, 251
third person plural
  (indefinite subject)
  115, 238, 239, 241,
  245, 248-50
topic 3, 23, 34, 43,
  81, 83, 84, 88,
  117, 123, 125, 182,
  185, 217, 219-2,
  224, 226-9, 231-5
  discourse 252, 253
  hanging 253-4
  position 182, 183,
  224, 225, 235, 247,
  251
  prominence 23, 27
  shifting 233
topicality
  discourse 222, 237
  hierarchy 222
  inherent 222, 224,
  235, 236, 237
topicalization 1, 2,
  49, 51, 56, 57, 63,
  74, 88, 107 123,
  182-3, 217, 218,
  222-3, 225, 227-37,
  248-51
tough movement 48, 50,
  51, 52, 73
traditional grammar
  12, 35
transformation grammar
  5, 6, 24, 25, 65-6,
  140-1, 219
transitivity 2 and
  passim
  Bolinger's conception
  68
  Dalgish's conception
  73
  Dixon's conception
  13-14
  Hopper & Thompson's
  conception 15-19,
  83-5

305

INDEX OF TERMS

ergativity and 20-2
in RG 12
in TG 11
morpho-syntactic
characterization 9-10
passive and 8-15, 44-74
260-2
truncated passive 130, 256,
257 *see also* agentless
passive

unaccusative (verb, clause,
hypothesis) 91, 209,
212-15
underlying structure 12,
14, 66, 74, 140-1,
155, 158
unergative (verb, clause)
212, 214-16
universals 2, 15, 19-23,
262
uno 95, 112, 114-15, 117,
173, 238, 246, 247,
249
unspecified object deletion
25, 259

valency 13, 262
vantage point 227-8
verb second (language)
224
verbal morphology in
passive 3, 29, 39, 40,
42-5, 53, 69, 72, 78,
87, 94-5, 97-100, 104,
105, 113, 255, 259
lack of distinctive, 35,
37, 40, 87-8, 112
voice 80, 83, 89, 163
volition 2, 15, 16, 17,
187-9, 191, 193, 195,
198-9, 201, 204, 208,
210, 214, 215, 224
word order 5, 9, 10, 11,
12, 24, 25, 91, 221,
222, 230
in passive 3, 32-3, 35,
37, 40-1, 91, 102, 105,
172, 184, 259

written language 229,
230, 244, 246, 250,
252

Y- movement 231